HOW TO PROVIDE EXCELLENT SERVICE
IN ANY ORGANIZATION

WAYNE PUBLIC LIBRARY, NJ

3 2352 05158956 6

658.812 DIS $17.95

Disend, Jeffrey E.

How to provide excellent
service in any or

WAYNE PUBLIC LIBRARY
MAIN LIBRARY
475 Valley Road
Wayne, NJ 07470

Books May Be Returned At Any
Branch Of The Library

APR 21 1992

HOW TO PROVIDE EXCELLENT SERVICE ▫ IN ▫ ANY ORGANIZATION

A BLUEPRINT FOR MAKING ALL THE THEORIES WORK

JEFFREY E. DISEND

APR 21 1992

CHILTON BOOK COMPANY   Radnor, Pennsylvania

Copyright © 1991 by Jeffrey E. Disend
All Rights Reserved
Published in Radnor, Pennsylvania 19089, by Chilton Book Company

No part of this book may be reproduced, transmitted, or stored
in any form or by any means, electronic or mechanical,
without prior written permission from the publisher

Library of Congress Catalog Card Number 90-55318
ISBN: 0-8019-8007-0

Designed by Adrianne Onderdonk Dudden
Manufactured in the United States of America

1 2 3 4 5 6 7 8 9 0   9 8 7 6 5 4 3 2 1 0

CONTENTS

PART SIX
IMPROVING SERVICE IN NONPROFITS

PART SEVEN
PROVIDING SERVICE DURING AND AFTER A REORGANIZATION

APPENDIX A

APPENDIX B

FOREWORD

This book is not just about giving good customer service, it's about survival in the 90s. It's no secret that the world is going about rapid and dramatic change: technology is exploding, competition is closing in from every direction, customers are becoming more sophisticated, our management styles are under major transformation. But what seems to have eluded so many organizations is the simple secret that giving excellent customer service is the key to success. As a vice-president of 3M states it, "Customer service is no longer *a* competitive edge, it's *the* competitive edge."

All the evidence is in, the jury has given its verdict: if you want to succeed, you *must* give top drawer customer service. All the top companies focus on service; pick the leader in any field you wish to name, and the odds are that they give outstanding customer service. Yet, for some reason, it has not become the burning issue it needs to be. Most organizations are still internally focused rather than customer focused (for a great explanation of that, read the book), boards rarely have a member who has a high customer contact position, companies and governmental bodies rarely give a lot of thought to (and pay the least to) the people they employ in front-line positions, and, as probably any customer can tell you, there is still almost no training for customer contact people, let alone any academic courses in high school or college. (During the last few years, I have worked with thousands of people in customer service seminars, and haven't met more than a handful of people who have had any training whatsoever in the customer contact profession.) Would we expect our accountants, engineers, or computer programmers to work without preparation for their career?

Why has this come about? Why are we so concerned about manufacturing, design, marketing, accounting, research, product development, inventory management, advertising, office layouts and time clocks, but give so little emphasis to serving our customers? Perhaps because no one has really taught us how. Here is a book that can change all that. Here is a blueprint, a management plan, a "How to . . ." manual that can get people in your organization tuned in to the issue of the 90s. Jeff Disend's book has it all, and is a *must read* for everyone in your organization, particularly all managers and supervisors, because customer service is everyone's job. Among hundreds of other ideas, it will tell you what kinds of people to hire for customer contact work, what kind of and how much training they should have, how to get everyone committed, how to motivate and reward your people, how to evaluate your customer service, and how to assess your own organization.

If you are like most working people, you already have plenty to do. But may I suggest, you have no greater priority than reading this book, and *acting* on it.

Larry Venable
Speaker, Trainer, Management Consultant

ACKNOWLEDGMENTS

It's impossible to thank everyone who influenced and helped with the creation of this book. Many friends, associates, clients, and seminar participants contributed indirectly or unknowingly by passing on anecdotes, suggesting ideas, and sharing personal experiences.

I'm especially grateful for the ideas, comments, and suggestions from Bill Baker, Terry Carnes, Richard and Susan Coffing, and Barbara Jones. Their sharp eyes and sharper minds helped me shape, define, and redefine my ideas.

Thanks also to Brenda Bradley and Ann Alexander, our dedicated, professional, hardworking staff. Special thanks to Brenda for relentlessly making numerous phone calls and sending letters and faxes in pursuit of information, ideas, research, articles, and verification of sources and data.

And finally, I owe a huge debt of gratitude to my partner (and spouse), M. Kay duPont, for her honest feedback and expert proofreading. More than that, it was Kay's encouragement, diligence, hard work, and sacrifices for our business that allowed me the time and freedom to work on the book. She put up with my temporary marriage to the book instead of to her; my late nights, weekends, and holidays living with the book; things that didn't get done at home or at the office; nd my occasional irritability after long hours of writing.

INTRODUCTION

Customer service is one of the hottest business topics today. Everybody's talking about it. There are hundreds of books, videotapes, films, and seminars about customer service. Yet very few organizations actually *do* anything about it. The result is that service hasn't improved much in many organizations and is actually worse in some. Why? Because most executives and managers don't know how to go about improving service in their organizations.

A practical approach to service

Managers and executives say to me, "I know we can improve. I'm a big Tom Peters fan and I've read Karl Albrecht and Ron Zemke's *Service America!* What I need now is someone to show me how to make it work in *my* organization." Unfortunately, most efforts at improving service are ineffective because they're superficial, simplistic, piecemeal, and directed at the wrong people in organizations.

All of us in business of any kind, and all of us as consumers, should be indebted to people like Tom Peters, Zemke and Albrecht, Robert Desatnick, Michael LeBoeuf, Jan Carlzon, and others for sounding the alarm, calling our attention to the importance of quality service.

In this book, we'll look at why most efforts to improve service *don't* work, and we'll examine what kinds of efforts and approaches *do* work. My purpose is to build on the groundwork that's been laid by others by offering new ideas, approaches, and practical solutions.

Another message I frequently receive from managers and executives goes something like this: "Yes, I want to improve service in this organization, but I want it to be easy, fast, inexpensive, and not take too much of *my* time. What can you do for the people I manage? And can you do it by next month?"

My answer is *no*. Making organizations service-oriented involves more than sending people to seminars. It means changing the way all the employees in your organization think about themselves and their customers. It must be an organization-wide process from the top down and from the bottom up. It must be ongoing. And it takes time. Anything else is a waste of your people's time and your organization's money.

In Part One, we'll look at why service is so important to any organization, and we'll begin to examine what constitutes excellent service. We'll also compare the beliefs and practices of traditional and service-oriented organizations.

Before we can achieve good service, we must understand the causes of poor service. The reasons for poor service are as diverse as the organizations themselves, yet there are some causes that are common to many organizations. We'll examine these causes in Part Two.

Part Three is a blueprint—a road map—for improving service, and Part Four offers specific things you can do to improve service in *your* organization. It also provides an Action Plan to help you get started actually putting your ideas to work.

Part Five contains examples of excellent and poor service practices in a variety of organizations. Part Six looks at how the ideas presented throughout the book apply to government, nonprofits, and regulated industries, and Part Seven specifically addresses providing service during and after mergers, acquisitions, and takeovers.

Throughout the book, I'll use the term "organization" to refer to companies, associations, government agencies, and other enterprises. I suggest thinking of the term "organization" on several levels. Of course, it refers to an overall organization, such as IBM or Delta Airlines; but in this book it also refers to the specific division, regional office, department, or unit you work in, even if you're the only person in that work unit. And, regardless of the size of your work unit, "your organization" means you personally—your ideas, beliefs, decisions, and behaviors.

I also address you, the reader, as "you" throughout the book, but it is an ever-changing "you," due to the broad scope of the material and its applicability to many different parts of an organization. "You" may at various times refer to customer-contact people, to managers, to executive officers, and even to the company itself (for example, "what you do better than your competitors.") For the most part the basic concepts are universally true and useful, regardless of the specific "you" being addressed at any given point.

How to get the most value from this book

Some organizations have made huge strides to improve service. Others have taken only baby steps. Some want to move further and faster to improve service than others do. Some organizations, and their managers, are open to the idea of improving service; others resist it. Within your own organization, your responsibility for improving service may be different from someone else's. For example, you may be looking for ideas in an area another person or division has already addressed.

Because of these differences, I've struggled with two questions as I've decided what information to present and how to present it. First, how do I provide practical ideas that will be universally useful to organizations that are already quite service-oriented, to those that have a long way to go, and to all those in between? Second, how do I give you solid, practical ideas you can implement right away when there are so many differences in organizations that can affect the kinds of ideas that can be implemented?

I discovered that there are no easy answers to these questions, but here's what I decided. For the first question, I suggest you think of this book as you would a cookbook. Most cookbooks provide detailed, step-by-step instructions for novices and inexperienced cooks. Experienced cooks and cooks who've already tried a recipe often don't need the basics or as much detail. They may ignore parts of a recipe, skip certain steps, substitute ingredients, and add more of some flavoring and less of another. In short, they adapt the recipes to fit their needs, tastes, and abilities. Even though they don't use all the information, the recipe contains all the details. Thus, I have used the cookbook approach in presenting the ideas and suggestions in this book.

The second question was harder to answer. I decided that I could only go so far in providing you with specific ideas for improving service in organizations. The next level of implementation depends on your organization's unique culture, history, structure, management style, formal and informal communication channels, reputation, service orientation, and so on.

Below are some suggestions I believe will help you get the most out of this book:

☐ This is not a textbook. It's fine to skim, or even skip over, parts that don't apply to your organization or sections that reflect what you're already doing. You can always go back to them later if they become applicable or if you are seeking a slightly different approach.

☐ As you read, continuously think about how the ideas and examples apply to *your* organization. For example, in Part Two ask yourself, "Do we have any of these problems? If so, to what degree? If so, what can we do to correct them? If not, what can we do to prevent them?" In Part Four ask yourself, "Which of these things are we already doing? How can we adapt these ideas to fit our situation and our needs?" If you and your organization have primarily *internal* customers, look for ways to adapt the ideas and solutions offered here to your situation.

☐ Don't just read this book, *use* it: highlight, underline, and write notes in the margins about things that relate to your organization.

☐ Just reading about improving service won't change it. So as you read, make notes. When you find ideas you can use and think of things you can *do*, jot them down on the Action Pages at the back of the book, (so you can find them easily and flip quickly to make notes). By the time you're finished with the book, you'll have all your notes in one place and you'll have a list of specific things to do to improve service in your organization.

☐ Take action. Don't be afraid to try out the ideas you read about. Many managers tell me, "You've given me so many good ideas, but there's so much to do that I don't know where to start." Others say, "I'm afraid if I don't do things in the right order, none of it will work." My advice is simply to start where you are and do what you can. Don't be so intimidated by the notion that you have to do everything all at once that you do nothing.

Also, keep in mind that you can't really screw up. Almost anything you do is likely to produce some change for the better, and there's very little you can do that can't be stopped, revised, improved, or changed in some way if it doesn't work. But you won't know what works until you try.

The truth is there are no absolutes, no right or wrong answers. Rather, improving service is an ongoing process of trying some things, seeing how they work, changing them as needed, and then trying other things. The service leaders constantly tinker with their systems to fine-tune them.

PART ONE

THE IMPORTANCE OF SERVICE

- ☐ SOME SERVICE SITUATIONS

- ☐ WHY IS SERVICE SO IMPORTANT?

- ☐ WHAT SERVICE-ORIENTED ORGANIZATIONS DO DIFFERENTLY FROM OTHER ORGANIZATIONS

SOME SERVICE SITUATIONS

The following sarcastic "letter" was given to me by a participant in a customer service seminar:

Dear Sir:

It seems you have some questions about our Customer Service Policy. Well, let me fill you in.

The items you received meet the same high standards afforded all our customers. We think you're being extremely unreasonable and petty for returning your order and then demanding a full refund just because it was damaged. From what you told my manager, it wasn't what you ordered anyway. So what's your beef?

For the record, we want you to know that we always ship whatever comes off the production line, whether it meets specifications or not. And we are reasonably confident that our packaging contains the proper materials a good deal of the time. So a few pieces got broken. Accidents happen! Besides, it wasn't our fault. Our dispatcher says the freight company damaged your shipment—again. So don't blame us for their shoddy work. I'd like to see *your* production area some time. I'll bet you have lots of problems too!

Incidentally, you've really ticked off our scheduling and production people with your arbitrary remarks about late delivery. After all, your last order was shipped only 3 months late. You shouldn't complain—that's a lot better than some of our customers get. What do you expect, perfection?

In the future, if you'll give us larger orders or higher dollar volume, we'll really bust our tails for you. As it is now, we've got bigger and more important customers to take care of before you. If you increase your orders, we'll try to guarantee a maximum late delivery of 2 months. That's a 30-day improvement over your current orders.

As a customer, you certainly have the privilege to ask us to check future orders closer for accuracy and shipping dates. However, if you continue to be so picky about getting what you order and getting it on time, you'll force us to study our procedures and then reorganize just to serve you better. During all that chaos you'll create, everything will slow down. Shipments will be so late and you'll be in such a bind that you'll gladly accept any old junk we want to get rid of.

As for credit on your last order, you should know by now that we have a very strict policy on returned goods. Since we didn't authorize you to return this stuff, you've caused us a lot of extra work and hassle handling your order and getting your refund approved. And, since our policy is to never give money back, we can't send you a check as you demanded. Instead, we'll give you a credit on your next order, as long as it's placed within the next 30 days.

By the way, don't make any more idle threats about canceling your order and taking your business elsewhere. We've heard that tune before, and, frankly, we're not impressed. Besides, since we're already in production, the only way we could stop now is if you pay a 90 percent cancellation charge. Otherwise, you own it.

In summary, if you work with us, we'll work with you.

Warmest personal regards,
Customer Service Department

Sometimes office humor is closer to the truth than slick, company-produced publications. You may have seen letters like this one—they're usually tenth-generation copies, on cheap paper, covered with black specks from all of the copies, and full of misspellings and graphic language. They're usually passed from person to person with a wink and a smile. I've only cleaned up the foul language and corrected the spelling on this one. Through its biting sarcasm, this letter reflects the attitude of many employees toward customers and describes the state of service in many organizations today.

The example below, told to me by a client, illustrates a major problem in many organizations today: employees don't see the difference between "doing their jobs" and satisfying customers. The client, Barry Merrell, is the operations manager for a restaurant chain. Here is his story about what happened in one of the chain's restaurants:

The restaurant usually opens for lunch at 11:30. It was a bitterly cold and windy January day, about 11:15, and the front door was still locked. I was on the phone in the back of the restaurant, talking to the manager at one of our other restaurants. From where I was sitting, I could see the entire dining room. All the employees were busy setting tables, getting ready to open for lunch. I could also see the front door. One employee was vacuuming the carpet near the front door.

At about 11:20, I noticed four or five people standing outside the door. Their shoulders were hunched against the cold and they were stomping their feet and blowing into their hands. It wasn't hard to tell that these people were *cold*. One person tapped on the glass and got the attention of the employee vacuuming the floor. I watched as the customer pointed to his watch and mimed, "What time do you open?" The employee signaled "11:30." I almost had a fit! I covered the mouthpiece on the phone and yelled to the server, "Open the door!" The employee yelled back, "We don't open until 11:30, and we're not set up yet."

I put my call on hold, walked to the front of the restaurant, unlocked the door, and said to the shivering customers, "Please come in. We're not quite ready for business yet, but it's a lot warmer in here than out there." I seated them at a table near the door and said, "I hope you don't mind the noise of the vacuum cleaner. Can I get you a hot cup of coffee while you wait?"

Here's another familiar situation:

I was in a nationally known bookstore in a shopping mall looking for a book. As I turned into the reference book section, I saw an employee in the aisle restocking that section with books from a cart. The cart was right in front of the reference book section. I sort of danced around her and the cart while trying to read the book titles, attempting to locate the book I needed. I know the employee saw me (we made eye contact), and it must have been apparent that I was looking for something—not just browsing to kill time or hoping to accidentally find an interesting book to read. She never asked if she could help me find something, and she never moved herself or the cart out of the way so I could see the books. Her job, as she saw it, was to stock those books from that cart. It didn't matter that there was a customer in the way.

How about this one:

A neighbor of ours moved from one part of town to another. His new residence was also in a different county. He called the State Department of Motor Vehicles to get information about getting a new driver's license. It took 3 days for him to get through because the lines were always busy. When he finally reached someone and explained why he was calling, he was asked for his driver's license number and put on hold. Several minutes later a different person came on the line. He explained again that all he wanted was information on how to get a driver's license for his new address. She told him that the process was handled by a different department and he'd have to hang up and call the other department's number. No, she couldn't transfer him.

Why were the customers in these situations treated the way they were? What determined how the employees reacted in each situation? If you were the customers in these situations, how would you want to be treated? Most important, how would you want the *people in your organization* to handle similar situations?

It's no secret: Service in America stinks. These examples of unfortunate situations are indicative of the service in many organizations today. Of course, there are some pockets of acceptable—and even exceptional—service. But too many interactions with companies, retailers, government agencies, restaurants, and other firms are unsatisfactory. Only a small percentage of businesses, associations, government agencies, and educational institutions are truly service-oriented. Most operate under what I call a *traditional* approach to service. And the result of traditional service practices is service like that in Barry's restaurant or in the bookstore.

What many organizations call customer service is simplistic, insulting, and ineffective. Think about it: Does it really make sense to think you can make an organization as service-oriented as, say, Disney, Marriott, or Federal Express by sending customer service reps to a 1-day program on how to answer the telephone and handle irate customers—when the organization's products are not consistently high-quality, deliveries are slow, managers have poor human relations skills, employees are dissatisfied and unmotivated, and executives make decisions based solely on the bottom line? Of course not, yet that's what happens in thousands of organizations. And they wonder why their service levels aren't improving, why customers keep complaining, and why they're losing market share!

And most available customer service training programs don't work because they teach the wrong things—to the wrong people. If they really worked, you and I—as customers—would encounter fewer problems with products that don't work, fewer organizations that act like they're doing us a favor to help us, fewer employees who don't seem to care because "they just work here," fewer cases of slow service, and so on.

So why all the fuss? Why all the concern about service? Why not just make the best product possible (or offer the best service), price it right, and let people come and get it?

Because that way of doing business isn't enough anymore. Organizations must increasingly distinguish themselves from competitors, especially when products or services are similar. Service has become *the* competitive edge in most industries, and most organizations can't afford *not* to improve the quality of their service.

Below are examples of two organizations—a large corporation and a small business—that did distinguish themselves because of their service.

About two years ago, my kitchen faucet started dripping. It's one of the single-lever types that mixes the hot and cold water together. Now, I'm not what you'd call a super handyman. I can handle *minor* repairs, and I thought I knew enough about plumbing to fix a dripping faucet. In this case, I couldn't even get the old faucet out so I could take it to the hardware store and say, "I need a new one of these." I knew the faucet was made by Moen, so I called a couple of dealers for help. I suspected there was something I wasn't doing right to get the faucet apart. Part of the problem was trying to describe the faucet and the problem over the phone. The conversations went something like this:

JEFF: I have the silver cap off the top and there's a brass thing, like a post sticking up about an inch.

DEALER: Is it threaded?

JEFF: I don't know. Let me look. No, it's smooth. It's wider at the base than at the top, if that helps.

DEALER: That must be model 1273-J. Does it have hole in the top?

JEFF: I don't see a hole. All I can see is this postlike thing sticking up. My problem is, I can't get the cartridge out.

DEALER: Can you see the retainer clip in the base?

JEFF: What retainer clip?"

You get the idea: it was as if we were speaking different languages. After several calls, one dealer referred me to the local sales representative for Moen. After listening to the problem, he said he didn't think he could help me. He gave me an 800 number and said I should talk to Lynn Garrett at Moen's corporate office in Ohio. I called and explained the problem to him. Lynn knew exactly what I was talking about. He described over the phone precisely what I should do to get the unit apart and what I needed to buy (Kit 1225). He also suggested buying another kit with some other parts to provide a good seal around the base once I replaced the cartridge.

I hung up and followed Lynn's instructions for getting the cartridge out. I still couldn't do it. I called back, feeling even more frustrated (and incompetent) than before. Lynn was on another call, so I spoke to someone else. Between the two of them they spent about 15 minutes with me on the phone—on their nickel. They were understanding, knowledgeable, and empathetic. They were patient and never made me feel stupid. Consider how easy it would be for them to get fed up with people, since their job is to sit there all day and talk to klutzes like me from all over the country who are having problems with their kitchen or bathroom plumbing and who don't know a monkey wrench from a soldering gun.

Here's a different situation, involving a small business that is service-oriented:

One day I picked up my shirts from the cleaners. When I got home, I noticed one shirt had an inch-long tear on the back, just under the label, and another had pulled apart at the shoulder seam. These damages may not have been the cleaner's fault, but I took them back in and said, "These shirts didn't look like this when they came in." The manager apologized and agreed to repair the shirts. He had his seamstress repair both shirts at no charge to me. I was satisfied. When I came in to pick them up, he apologized again and gave me a $15 credit on cleaning "for the inconvenience and trouble he caused me." In my eyes, repairing the shirts was enough. In his view, it wasn't.

WHY IS SERVICE SO IMPORTANT?

There are at least five reasons why the level of service is so important to organizations; these are discussed in the next few pages.

Customer expectations are higher than ever before

The consumer-advocacy trend that began in the late 1950s has gained strength, thanks to people like Ralph Nader and the establishment of consumer protection agencies at both the state and federal levels. As a result, our standards are higher today. We expect products that work, and we expect service organizations to deliver what they promise. We also expect more than ever before.

Think about cars, for example. Twenty years ago, only the very rich could afford air-conditioning. Heaters were an option, radios a luxury. Now, virtually every car comes with a heater (by law in many states), and "factory air" is commonplace. Today, buying only a plain, monophonic, AM radio in a new car is almost laughable. Instead, we have stereophonic (or quadraphonic) AM/FM radios, cassette decks, and compact disc players in cars. We have power steering, power brakes, electric windows, reclining seats, and more. We've come to expect more in our cars and in everything else.

The interesting thing is that you can never go back. Once you've had a car with air-conditioning, you'll never want to be without it again. This aspect of human nature means that to provide slightly better service and to continually satisfy customer needs, products and services must continually improve. To stay the same—to maintain the status quo—is to perish. Imagine if one car company had decided 20 years ago that it was not going to change, because it was happy with all the features and accessories it offered and was not going to alter anything or add anything new just because its competitors were. Such a company would have lasted only a few years, if it was lucky. Even the venerable Volkswagen Beetle, which boasted that it always stayed the same, actually went through changes over the years. It might have *looked* the same, but the precision engineering for which Volkswagen is still known was improved every year.

The service industry is growing

There are more businesses providing more services today than ever before. Service businesses currently employ over 60 percent of the work force. And services now contribute 56 percent of the gross national product. As we move further away from an agriculture- and industry-based economy, there are more and more service and informational businesses starting up. When "service" is your only business, service quality and how it is delivered become critical.

Competition keeps increasing

There's more competition in every industry than ever before. Survival depends on getting and keeping a competitive edge, and product differences alone are rarely enough. Providing exceptional service by consistently exceeding customer expectations provides a difference that gives a competitive advantage.

Distinguishing your company, your products, or your services from your competition is more important than ever before. It also gets harder the more competition you have. When there are only a few companies that offer what you do, it's easier for customers to recognize you and remember you. When there are dozens, or hundreds, it's a different story. That's when the little things really make a difference.

For example, a clean suit is a clean suit. A drugstore is a drugstore. A bank is a bank. Banks all do essentially the same thing and offer the same services. Almost every bank has checking accounts, savings accounts, money market accounts, and safe deposit boxes. They all have vaults, make loans, and have night deposit boxes.

Most drugstores are also alike. They carry mostly the same over-the-counter and prescription medicines. If you want Bayer aspirin, or Johnson & Johnson Band-Aids, or Eli Lilly insulin, or Parke-Davis penicillin, you can find what you want at practically any drugstore.

Studies show that one of the major factors in selecting a cleaner or a drugstore is location. People tend to patronize stores close to where they live or work—stores they can get to easily. In many neighborhoods, there are often several drugstores to chose from. When products and services are exactly (or nearly) the same, little things make a big difference. Service can be that difference.

The importance of even small differences is familiar to athletes. In sports, fractions of a second can be the difference between victory and defeat. In jumping events, fractions of an inch can make the difference between a gold medal and no medal. Many businesses haven't yet recognized the importance of this concept of slight differences.

Service-oriented organizations know that just to *survive*, and then to grow, they have to do more to distinguish themselves from the competition. New products, new features, and consistenly high quality are all important. Without these, good service won't matter. Good service alone won't help if the products and services an organization offers are shoddy. But just offering new products, new features, and high quality isn't enough, either. Successful, service-oriented organizations realize that service is more than icing on the cake. It is *the* competitive edge.

One of America's most service-oriented organizations says it best:

> In spite of the enormous range of products, services, customers, employees, facilities, systems, and situations that exist in today's business world, survival depends on making people happy. The ability to deliver superior service is perhaps the most significant measure of a company's prospects for the future. [From a Disney brochure for a seminar called "The Disney Approach to Quality Service"]

Quality service means repeat business

It's relatively easy to get people to buy from you once, but long-term success depends on repeat business. Expanding the number of customers and their frequency of purchase is vital. Companies must continually attract new customers, and they must also keep their existing customers. Providing exceptional service by meeting—and exceeding—customer expectations helps ensure that customers come back.

Quality service is profitable

In the late 1970s, McKinsey & Company studied 43 of America's best-run companies, most of which are also recognized as being very service-oriented. The results of the study were later chronicled by Tom Peters and Bob Waterman in a well-known book called *In Search of Excellence*. Peters and Waterman reported that net income for the excellent companies increased 10.4 percent from 1978 to 1983 while the rest of the economy averaged a 2.7 percent loss.

Research done by the Strategic Planning Institute in Cambridge, Massachusetts, shows that companies with high levels of customer service charge an average of 10 percent more and grow twice as fast as do poor service providers. Such companies also grow in market share by an average of 6 percent annually, while poor service providers generally *lose* 2 percent annually.

Fortune's list of most-admired companies in 1989 included many service leaders, such as 3M, Wal-Mart, Boeing, and Herman Miller. The 10 most-admired returned an average of 22.5 percent to investors over a 10-year period. The organizations on *Fortune*'s list of the 10 least-admired companies returned only 0.6 percent.

In almost every industry, organizations recognized as exceptional service providers have healthy bottom lines. For example:

☐ Nordstrom is a Seattle-based, service-minded department-store chain. Nordstrom's sales rose 47.5 percent from 1986 to 1989, and its earnings over that time increased 85 percent in an industry that's had a 9.4 percent *decrease* in profits. The chain's sales per square foot figure is more than twice the retail industry average.

☐ An investment of $1,000 in Wal-Mart in 1970 when it made its first public offering would be worth over $250,000 today.

☐ Scandinavian Airlines System (SAS) lost $17 million the year before Jan Carlzon took the reins. The following year the company posted an $80 million profit as a result of shifting its focus toward customers.

☐ From 1984 to 1988, Walt Disney Company's earnings increased from $97.8 million to $522 million.

☐ University National Bank in Palo Alto, California, offers many services and special touches that other banks don't, and its return-on-assets ratio is 75 percent higher than the average for other banks in California.

People are often willing to pay more when they believe that products and services are high quality and are delivered properly.

Colin Bessonette, travel editor for the *Atlanta Journal and Constitution*, did a story several years ago about the Cunard Sea Goddess cruises. He described the furnishings, destinations, food, and entertainment on these ships. The cruises cost $2,900 to 9,000 per person, depending on time of year, destination, and length of cruise. That's a lot of money to most folks. Was it worth it? Bessonette explains that the crew puts out a guest register at the end of the cruise for guests to register their comments. What do Sea Goddess passengers (customers) say?

"Great."

"This was our second time on Sea Goddess, and it won't be the last."

"The staff is wonderful. . . . We love it."

"We intend to travel with you again."

"The staff is so friendly."

Bessonette notes: "Page after page, the theme is the same: pleasure, thanks, credit to the staff; no criticism, no problems, no flaws. And no complaints about the cost."

In every industry, people are willing to pay more for higher quality and better service, if organizations will only give them the choice. In Part Two, we'll see why many organizations don't provide excellent service. But first, let's look at some characteristics of organizations that provide exceptional service and some characteristics of organizations that don't.

WHAT SERVICE-ORIENTED ORGANIZATIONS DO DIFFERENTLY FROM OTHER ORGANIZATIONS

In one way, customer service is like computer science, robotics, and financial planning: Twenty-five years ago, these subjects did not consist of organized bodies of information, and there were few rules, few established practices or industry standards, and no body of experience to tell what worked and what didn't. In the area of customer service, pioneers such as Disney, Bill Marriott, Sr., Ray Kroc (McDonald's), J. C. Penney, Thomas Watson (IBM), and John W. Nordstrom didn't really *know* if their ideas would work—or why. But that's not true today. Thanks to these leaders and many more like them, we know a lot more about what constitutes good service.

In 1980, Citibank compiled the results of a study conducted with 18 highly service-oriented companies. Citibank conducted detailed, structured interviews with 90 managers in these companies to learn how they think and what they do to create and maintain excellent service. The 18 companies studied are listed below according to industry:

Industry	*Companies*
Airlines	American, United
Appliances	Whirlpool
Business equipment	IBM
Entertainment/leisure	Walt Disney World
Financial services	Citicorp
Food	McDonald's
Hotels	Western International (Westin)
Insurance	John Hancock, Hartford
Rental cars	Avis, Hertz, National
Retail merchandise	Sears, Spiegel
Utilities	Commonwealth Edison, Consolidated Edison (New York), Telephone/AT&T

Throughout this book I'll refer to this study as "the Citibank study" and to these companies collectively as "the Citibank companies."

The Citibank study showed that, regardless of their size or the industry they're in, service-oriented firms have many things in common. They have similar policies and practices for delivering service; they think about service in the same ways; and their people talk about service in the same way, often using the same words. The message is: There's no mystery about what it takes to be a service leader. And the things they do will work in any company. They will also work for associations, government agencies, nonprofit organizations, schools, and other organizations too. Specifically the Citibank companies do the following:

1 Promote from within

2 Continually monitor service levels via service audits

3 Make sure senior management is actively, visibly committed to service excellence

4 Regularly recognize and reward outstanding service by employees

5 Invest heavily in formal, ongoing training

6 Practice teamwork and open communications

7 Measure service performance against explicit standards

8 Actively seek customer feedback on service and use it in decision making

9 Use employee attitude surveys to continuously assess the organization's internal health

10 Have a strong sense of employee accountability ("Each of us is the company.")

In the early 1980s, the American Business Conference (ABC) hired McKinsey & Company to study midsize, high-growth companies—companies with minimum annual sales (at that time) between $25 million and $1 billion *and* annual sales or earnings growth of at least 15 percent for the previous 5 years. The 101 companies initially studied actually averaged an 18 percent sales increase, a 20 percent increase in earnings, and a 38 percent increase in market value for the period 1978 to 1983. Some of the companies McKinsey & Company studied are listed below:

Automatic Data Processing (data processing)

Charter Medical Corporation (health care)

Cox Communications (newspapers)

Drexel Burnham Lambert (financial services)

Dunkin' Donuts (food)

Herman Miller (office furniture)

Kinder-Care Learning Centers (child care)

La Quinta Motor Inns (lodging)

Levitz Furniture (furniture)

Shop & Go (convenience stores)

Donald K. Clifford Jr. and Richard E. Cavanagh published the results of that American Business Conference study in *The Winning Performance* in 1985. The common characteristics Clifford and Cavanagh found in the medium-sized companies they studied were as follows:

1 Market-driven innovation is the best competitive edge. It creates value for the customer.

2 The value the customer receives is more important than the mere cost of the product or service.

3 It's best to expand only into related products or markets and to expand by edging out with small, sure steps, not giant leaps.

4 Bureaucracy is the greatest threat to success. These companies avoid traditional management functions and make employees into entrepreneurs.

5 The bottom line is much more than profit. These companies are as interested in making a difference as in making a fortune.

6 Leaders are obsessed with and excited about the business.

7 Leaders have the ability to transform their obsession into lasting energy and values for the organization.

In the mid-1980s, Milind M. Lele and his associates studied 15 companies that he described as "winners"—companies known for exceptional customer satisfaction and long-term financial performance. Lele did surveys, interviewed executives, and studied their systems, policies, and procedures. The companies he studied are listed below according to industry:

Industry	*Companies*
Aerospace	Boeing
Airline	Swissair
Automobile	Mercedes-Benz of North America
	Jaguar
	Subaru

Industry	*Companies*
Computer/office equipment	IBM
Farm equipment	Deere & Company
Film/office equipment	Kodak
Food distribution	Kraft Foodservice
Home laundry equipment	Maytag
Insurance	Northwestern Mutual Life Insurance
Office equipment	Xerox
Overnight delivery	Federal Express
Real estate services	Century 21
Recreation	Six Flags

The results of the study were published in 1987 in *The Customer Is Key*. Lele identified six characteristics shared by these service leaders:

1 They set "impossibly high" standards for themselves.
2 They are obsessive about knowing, even better than customers themselves, what customers want.
3 They create and manage customers' expectations.
4 They design their products and services to maximize customer satisfaction.
5 They put their money where their mouth is.
6 They make customer satisfaction everybody's business.

In 1988, Development Dimensions International studied the specific skills people must use to produce effective customer satisfaction. The study surveyed over 2,000 people in *Fortune* 500 companies and compiled a list of 9 skills and 17 competencies from an extensive review of over 100 books and articles on service practices. The approaches the study identified as being essential for producing customer satisfaction are as follows:

1 Make the customer feel important.
2 Listen and respond to customers' feelings.
3 Ask for and offer suggestions.
4 Acknowledge customers.
5 Clarify details about each specific situation.
6 Meet (or exceed) customers' needs.
7 Make sure the customer is satisfied.
8 Appear trained and prepared.
9 Follow through.

From these studies, customer service literature, and firsthand experience with numerous organizations, I noticed several common elements in customer-focused organizations: They have a well-defined mission and a culture that focuses attention on the customer. They also hire, train, manage, and reward people differently than do organizations that are less service-oriented.

TWO VIEWS of CUSTOMER SERVICE

The Traditional Approach To Service	The Customer-Focused Approach to Service
The product is the key. Service is only icing on the cake.	The product alone won't cut it. Too many others offer similar products. Service is critical to survival. It is the competitive edge.
"Service" means different things to different people in the organization. There's no common understanding of what good service is.	Everyone shares a common vision of "service" and knows what constitutes exceptional service.
Good service is the absence of dissatisfied customers.	Service means providing more than customers expect. It's also turning unhappy customers into satisfied customers.
Customer service primarily involves how you interact with customers in person or on the phone, smiling, being nice, and resolving customer problems or complaints.	Service involves every aspect of the business: the products and services offered, quality, pricing, packaging, delivery, and follow-up. It also includes all the behind-the-scenes activities in finance, data processing, purchasing, warehousing, and personnel that affect how the organization produces and delivers its products and services.
Customer service is primarily the responsibility of the Customer Service Department or other designated people. Often heard as, "I have my own work to do. Taking care of customers is somebody else's job."	Satisfying customers is the #1 priority of every employee, from the CEO down. It's too important to be delegated to a few people or departments. Everyone believes, "I'm it! I'm personally responsible for the quality and service our customers get."
Customer service is a program. It's something you do or something you send people to for a few days.	Customer service isn't a program or even a set of skills. It's not something to send people to or a concept to get excited about for a few weeks. It's an attitude, an obsession, a way of life, an ongoing process.
The organization comes first. The most important people are (in order) executives, managers, supervisors, front line employees, stockholders, and customers.	The customer comes first. The most important people are customers.
People in the organization talk about service. Much of it is lip service. The prevailing attitude is, "Give them as little as we can for the money."	The organization lives and breathes service. People don't just talk about it, they practice it. The prevailing attitude is, "What else can we do for them?"
Customer service is for customers--people or organizations outside the company.	Every employee and department has both internal and external customers. Everyone lives by the belief, "If you're not serving the customer, you'd better be serving someone who is."
What happens happens. We just do our thing. We don't have much control over what our customers do.	Every aspect of the customers' experience must be managed. When these "moments of truth" are unmanaged, service deteriorates.

The Traditional Approach to Service	The Customer-Focused Approach to Service
Service performance is not considered in performance evaluations or promotions, except for front line, customer-contact people. Customer satisfaction indicators have little or no bearing on pay or promotions.	Service, as measured by customer satisfaction, is an important part of performance evaluations, base pay, bonus pay, and promotions for everyone in the organization.
Exceptional service is rarely noticed, recognized, or rewarded. There may be a once-a-year event where the focus is on the front line. Few people know about exceptional service by individuals or work units.	Exceptional service by individuals and teams is continuously recognized and rewarded, including those who have little direct customer contact. The deeds of service heroes are well known to everyone.
The role of supervisors and managers is to plan, organize, delegate, control, and evaluate the work of their subordinates.	The role of supervisors and managers is to support and empower the front line--to provide them the resources, information, freedom, training, encouragement, and coaching they need to best meet the customers' needs.
Policies, procedures, paperwork, facilities, and communications are largely designed for the convenience of the organization. There's often an attitude of "what's best for me" that leads to protecting turf, backbiting, politics, and we/they. It's heard as, "That's not in this department. You'll have to call so-and-so." These practices often result in inconvenience or confusion for customers.	Everything the organization does is focused on the customer. Policies, procedures, paperwork, facilities all say to the customer, "This is all designed to meet your needs." Since everyone shares a common goal, there's more teamwork, cooperation, and interdepartmental projects.
They strive for big breakthroughs and hot new products and features. They look for ways to make quantum leaps in products or services offered. They want to make 100% improvements in a few areas.	They strive for continuous improvements. They look for ways to make incremental improvements. They seek to improve many things by 1%.
There's a short-term orientation that concentrates on the bottom line, profits, and costs. Decisions are based more on costs, payback, and budget than on satisfying customers. Management wants to see immediate, tangible results. The organization incurs costs for handling customers.	There's a long-term orientation that concentrates on satisfying customers, meeting their needs, and exceeding their expectations. While not ignoring the here-and-now, they're more concerned about building and keeping customer satisfaction for the future. Management believes that putting customers first is profitable and they make investments in customer satisfaction. There are few cost-versus-customer decisions.
Customer complaints represent failure and are to be avoided; discouraged. Customer complaints and problems are an irritant, something to be "handled." The emphasis is often on "taking care of it" at the time, placating customers, and not making bad situations worse. Often the same problems and complaints recur because the organization does nothing to correct them.	Customer complaints are welcomed, even encouraged. They are an opportunity to learn from customers, uncover weak areas, and correct these. The emphasis is on resolving problems to the customer's satisfaction to keep the customer. The organization often overreacts to resolve problems and maintain customer good will.

The Traditional Approach To Service	The Customer-Focused Approach to Service
They know enough about their business and know what their customers want (or at least what they're going to give them). Executives rarely work the front lines or call on customers. Hourly workers (as in manufacturing) rarely meet their customers or see how their products are used. Ideas for improvements come largely from marketing, research, engineering.	They can never know enough about their business. They're always trying to find out what their customers want: What problems are they having? How can our product or service be more useful to them? Executives work on the front line and "shop" the company. Hourly workers regularly go out to meet with customers, see how customers use their products, learn about other customer needs. Ideas for improvements come largely from listening to customers.
Customers automatically recognize what makes their products and services better than their competitors.	They must insure that every employee knows what makes them better. They realize it's their responsibility to clearly and continually communicate these differences to customers.
They see no connection between employee satisfaction and customer satisfaction. They rarely survey either customers or employees. They might do a survey every few years, but they share the results only with senior managers and department heads.	They recognize the connection between employee satisfaction and customer satisfaction and measure both constantly. They use formal and informal means to find out from customers and employees how they're doing, and we openly publish results, especially to the front line.
Employees are cogs in the organization's machinery. They must be told what to do, then monitored, watched and controlled. Most employees want to do as little as possible and will rip off the organization every chance they get. Rules, policies, and practices are needed to protect the company from employees. Most employees can't be trusted to make important decisions without checking with management.	Employees are superstars whose talent is waiting to be unleashed. They can do anything and everything--set standards, check quality, manage budgets, train. Employees can be trusted if they feel important and responsible. The people closest to the customer--the front line--can and should have the freedom to make decisions on the spot about how to satisfy customers. Their decisions are supported by management. Rules and practices that demean people or hinder their ability to serve the customer are eliminated.
People who have direct customer contact at the front lines are the lowest paid, least skilled, and least motivated employees. They get the least training and have the highest turnover.	The people at the front line <u>are</u> the company. The organization defines the experience, skills, and temperament required for customer contact positions. They hire people who are empathetic, caring, and intelligent. They train them diligently and reward them well for performance.
Customer service training emphasizes skills, techniques, how-tos ("If the customer says or does this, you say or do that"). It's often called "smile training" or "charm school."	The emphasis in all training is on developing confidence and self-esteem first. People also learn to see customers and the organization from a different perspective. Social skills is a hiring issue, not a training issue. Job-specific knowledge and skills build competence and confidence.
Once people are trained, they're trained.	Training is continuous and ongoing for all employees, including executives. People need to keep up with changes in their industry, products, competition. They also need to continue to grow and develop.

In customer-focused organizations, the roles of frontline employees and their managers are different. Also, the bottom lines show more profit.

As I studied what successful, service-oriented organizations do, I began to get a picture of a different kind of organization, one that's different from the more traditional organizations of the past that believed if they just made a good product, advertised it, and priced it right, people would buy it. I began to compare the qualities and characteristics of highly successful, service-oriented organizations to more traditional organizations. This comparison led to "Two Views of Customer Service." A detailed look at the characteristics of traditional and customer-focused organizations follows in Part Two.

PART TWO

WHY SERVICE IS SO BAD IN MANY ORGANIZATIONS

☐ MISDIRECTED FOCUS

☐ TRADITIONAL ATTITUDES TOWARD SERVICE

☐ MISGUIDED OR NARROW APPROACH TO SERVICE TRAINING

☐ OUTDATED ATTITUDES ABOUT EMPLOYEES

☐ MANAGEMENT'S CONTRIBUTIONS TO POOR SERVICE

Before we can begin to improve service in organizations, we have to understand the reasons service is so bad. Without understanding and addressing the causes, there's little hope for improvement. We will merely continue to treat symptoms.

There are many causes for poor service. Each of the causes can exist to a greater or lesser degree in any organization. Of course, not all of these reasons apply to every organization. But many do. The more of these factors at work in an organization, and the stronger their severity, the worse the service will be. The sad (and often dangerous) part is that most organizations don't know—or won't admit—that these problems exist.

Before we look at specific causes of bad service, let's consider what "service" means to various organizations, for there's no common understanding among or within organizations about what service is. Service is a broad concept, like motivation, communication, management, leadership, and quality. All of these concepts are so broad that, even though people may understand what they mean, everyone may define a given concept differently. Ask 10 people to define just one of these terms and you'll get 10 different definitions. This lack of a standard definition can cause a lot of confusion.

Service can mean different things to different organizations. For example, in some organizations, service means fixing products that don't work. A good example of organizations using this definition is car dealers, which have separate "sales" and "service" departments. Another example is organizations who employ high-tech repair people and refer to them as "customer service" or "field service" representatives.

In other organizations, customer service refers to the process of handling problems or complaints and to the person or department that does the handling. When customers don't get what they ordered, get something late, receive the wrong size or color, are charged too much, or are angry for some reason, "customer service" handles the situation.

In some organizations, customer service is a euphemism for the sales or order-entry functions. Customer service representatives in banks, telemarketing companies, and some other organizations are the people who answer the phone, handle walk-in customers, or go out to call on customers.

And in some organizations, customer service means a training program or motivational program certain employees go through. In some organizations, customer service refers to the organization's responsiveness, technical knowledge or expertise, or to a professional and helpful manner by employees. In other organizations, service refers to convenience, frills, and other "extras." In still others, good service means being nice, friendly, and courteous.

The Zenger-Miller Company, a management consulting and training company, conducted a study on the quality of service in over 200 organizations.

The Zenger-Miller report highlights part of the difficulty in defining service. According to the report, most organizations describe service quality at two extremes:

> The narrowest definition is accuracy and efficiency in completing a transaction. That is, does the order-entry clerk get the order right and efficiently, or does the retail clerk make a high number of sales transactions with few returns or complaints? People (or organizations) with narrow definitions of service quality are often baffled when they get "out-serviced" by competitors with large-scope definitions of service quality.
>
> At the other end of the spectrum are definitions that are focused on the customer, the product, or the transaction. Two examples . . . are: "Meet the customer's expectations," and "The only difference between stores is how they treat customers."

What else does service mean? In some businesses and industries, service refers to the *manner* in which products are delivered or things are done. We say of restaurants, "The food was good, but the service was terrible." Or we say, "Their products are great and they have the best price in town, but their service stinks."

Sometimes service means actually serving or delivering something, as waiters and waitresses (commonly called servers), domestics, or cafeteria workers do. In some businesses, service (or services) refers to all the programs, alternatives, choices, and capabilities offered to customers. And, to make matters even more confusing, "service" is frequently used within the same organization to mean several of the definitions discussed here.

Although many organizations have formal statements about service, they're generally part of an overall mission or purpose statement. They're also usually quite general and include such sentiments as "The customer is king," or "Satisfaction guaranteed," or "Your money back if you're not satisfied."

Confusion about what service means also arises from references to the "service industry" or the "service sector." It's hard to avoid hearing or reading these days that we're becoming a "service economy." *Megatrends, Service America!, Thriving on Chaos,* and other works tell us that the "service sector" is the fastest growing sector of our economy.

The *service sector* generally refers to enterprises that do not produce tangible outputs, and the term is frequently used to distinguish those enterprises from manufacturing (or agricultural) concerns. The service sector includes:

Accounting and other financial services

Amusement and recreation businesses, including food service

Business services

Engineering and architectural services

Hotels, motels, and other lodging places

Medical and dental practices, laboratories, and clinics

Personal service

Repair services

Tour and travel agencies and operators

Vocational and correspondence schools

In talking about service today, the primary focus is on organizations such as restaurants, hotels, airlines, hospitals, banks, museums, accountants, utilities, colleges, and others that provide mostly intangible "services." However, even in a "service" economy there will always be tangible, manufactured *products*. Imagine accountants performing their services without calculators or computers. Imagine a cleaning service without vacuum cleaners, mops, and cleansers. Imagine an attorney without law books, office furniture, or word processors. Imagine a cruise line without ships, deck furniture, or liquor. (Imagine a doctor without a BMW or Mercedes!)

There isn't a service I can think of that doesn't rely on some products, even if only paper and pens. So if we're creating more service businesses, they're going to be needing more products *and* services to deliver *their* services. There will always be retail stores. They may not look like they do today or transact business in the same way, but they will exist.

So let's not get carried away with the idea that intangible services is all we need to be concerned about. There are still plenty of companies that make and deliver products: furniture, cars, clothing, food, toys and games, computers, sporting equipment, office supplies and equipment, tools, carpeting, tractors, recreational vehicles, and so on. There is a service component in *every* organization in *every* industry. No matter what the organization makes, does, or provides, there is a dimension that addresses *how* it makes, does, or provides what it does. There's something more than the "product" itself, and that something includes quality, delivery time, meeting customer needs, billing, the organization's reputation, and similar factors.

Now that we have a broad understanding of what service means, we'll look at some of the causes of poor service in organizations today.

MISDIRECTED FOCUS

Organizations are inwardly focused, not customer-focused

In many organizations, policies, procedures, paperwork, facilities, and communications are designed largely for the convenience of the organization. Of course, this varies by organization, but the focus is largely internal. This internal focus shows up in many ways. For example, in many cases the physical layout of stores, offices, waiting rooms, warehouses, and other facilities are designed to make things easier for *employees*, even if it means making things more difficult or confusing for customers.

Here are some typical examples of organizations that have internally focused practices that don't put the customer's interests first:

☐ Banks that are only open from 9:00 A.M. to 4:00 P.M. on weekdays. This schedule is more for the convenience of employees than customers, since most customers must be at their own jobs during these hours. Many can't (or don't want to) leave work during lunch to do banking. Automatic tellers have helped this problem for routine transactions but not for other banking services. Why not open early in the morning for customers on their way to work or stay open in the evenings until 6:00 or 7:00?

☐ Hotel switchboards that keep a caller on hold and require two calls to reach a hotel guest. Too often, the switchboard rings the guest's room and just lets the phone ring 15, 20, up to 30 times. Many times the switchboard operator never comes back on the line at all, so in some cases callers have to place a second long-distance call to leave a message for the guest.

☐ Car dealers that are closed on Sunday. Surely this scheduling is for the convenience of employees, not customers. Most customers work during the week and have more time to look for cars on weekends. How many customers could dealers have at 2:00 on a Tuesday? Why not open at noon instead of 10:00 A.M. on weekdays, stay open until 9:00 P.M. (most do), and use the extra hours saved during the week to open on Sunday afternoons when most customers can shop?

☐ Auto service centers that are open only from 8:00 A.M. to 6:00 P.M. on weekdays and that have no loaner cars or customer drop-off service. These hours are no doubt convenient for employees, but they are inconvenient for many customers who must arrange for rides, take two cars, and leave work early to get to the garage before it closes.

☐ Doctors and dentists who don't see patients in the evenings or weekends. What if you get sick on the weekend? Or have a toothache? Even for routine work like cleanings or fillings, many people can't go during the week. Why not have office hours in the evenings and on Saturdays?

☐ Most automated telephone-answering systems. Many require callers to listen to a long list of department names and telephone extensions in order to determine who can best solve their problems or answer their questions. This may be more convenient for the organization, but it's time-consuming and irritating to customers, especially when callers don't know which extensions they need or else really need to talk to a *person* but the sytem won't let them.

☐ Offices and retail stores where executives and managers park closest to the door, other employees park a little farther away, and customers must park farthest away of all.

☐ Airlines that deny first-class upgrades to frequent flyers but allow off-duty employees to fly in those seats.

☐ Organizations that require *customers* to go out of their way to correct problems the organization caused. Have you ever picked up a take-out order at a restaurant, come home or to the office, and found that the restaurant gave you the wrong items? Or put in only three sandwiches when you paid for four? Or maybe you've bought something from a store across town, brought it home, and found that it didn't work, was broken, or had some other problem. In most situations like these, your only recourse is to go back to the place of business yourself. The merchant made a mistake, but the *customer* is inconvenienced in trying to resolve it.

In inwardly focused organizations, people tend to be preoccupied with their specific job tasks, rules, forms, problems, and reports. People at the front line tend to place more emphasis on following the rules than on meeting the needs of customers. Employees in these organizations have lost sight of—or never had sight of—the big picture: that the organization is there to meet customer needs and that its methods, rules, policies, and practices are supposed to *support* that goal, not get in the way.

A large audiovisual supply company has organized its customers by geographic areas. Each territory has an account representative who sells and services organizations in that district. A customer was having difficulty getting information, quick response time, and deliveries from his account rep. Several times when he needed certain supplies, no one responded, and he had to go to the supply company's office to get them. On one visit, he happened to meet a different sales rep who was knowledgeable and helpful. When the next snafu occurred, the customer asked that this account rep be assigned to him. The company said no. He took his business elsewhere.

When organizations are focused on internal issues instead of concentrating on satisfying customers, it often leads to a "what's best for me" mentality, turf protecting, internal politics, "us against them" behavior between departments, excessive rules, and bureaucracy. Sometimes inward focus shows up when departments within an organization are at cross-purposes:

Several years ago, I was working with a company in the wine business. One day I heard a salesman as he came back from an appointment. He was very excited because he'd finally landed a big account he'd been working on for weeks. A grocery store chain had finally agreed to put in end-aisle displays in all 45 stores. This would mean high visibility for his products, good in-store locations, lots of point-of-sale advertising, and increased sales. He ran into the promotions department at his own company and announced his triumph. The response from one of the marketing people was a disgusted, "Oh, damn! Now I've got to build 45 displays." The focus in this company was internal, not external.

Sometimes the internal focus even results in telling customers, "If you won't do it our way, we don't want your business."

A client told me about a letter he'd received from a bank offering him a bank credit card with a preapproved credit line of $5,000. He was interested. He called to get some more details and to tell the bank they spelled his name incorrectly. He was told they could only correct the spelling if he requested the change in writing. He thought that was odd and explained that the bank presumably wanted his business because *they* had contacted him. He was told that in writing was the only way he could make the change. There are probably sound, practical reasons for requesting changes in writing, but the inflexible rule came across to this potential customer as insensitive and inconvenient.

Internal focus is also evident in the way organizations handle customer inquiries and complaints. The United States Office of Consumer Affairs (USOCA) commissioned several studies in the late 1970s dealing with consumer-complaint-handling practices in business and government agencies. The research was conducted and reported by Technical Assistance Research Programs Institute (TARP). The studies were repeated in the early 1980s to determine the degree to which consumer complaints or the complaint-handling practices had changed.

One of their findings revealed that some companies and government agencies require customer complaints to be in writing. The four reasons organizations gave most often for requiring written instead of telephone or in-person complaints are (1) it provides for a more detailed and accurate record of the facts; (2) it screens out frivolous complaints; (3) it limits the number of complaints; and (4) some agencies are required by law or regulations to have written complaints (in case there is litigation later).

All of these reasons are typical for internally focused organizations. The major concern seems to be the work load, convenience, and protection of the organization, not the swift resolution or prevention of customer problems. In fact, TARP found that none of these reasons has much validity. In a service-oriented, customer-focused organization, the emphasis is on resolving the customer's immediate problem as soon as possible and eliminating the causes of the dissatisfaction. Requiring written complaints as the only means of complaining does not accomplish these.

For me, the epitome of inward focus versus customer focus is telephone music—the music you hear when you're put on hold. It's better than silence, but it's still internally focused. It communicates, "We know our customers will be on hold a lot, sometimes for a long time. Rather than correct that situation, we'll let them listen to music (or a commercial for our products or services)." It's easier, and no doubt cheaper, to play music than to install additional lines and to hire and train additional operators. But is it? How many customers don't wait, but instead call a competitor? How many call someone else next time, because they didn't like waiting?

The more the focus of an organization is internal, the more service suffers.

Organizations are product-driven or technology-driven, not customer-driven

In many organizations, the focus is on technology, not customer satisfaction. Rick Tucci, senior vice president of the Forum Corporation, a leading training, consulting, and research company, describes what can happen when organizations emphasize products and technology. Tucci describes a manufacturer of electrical components that was engineering-driven instead of customer-driven. The company built its reputation on the quality of its products, which were known as the best in the industry. For example, one of the company's leading products was a switch that was so well made that the company advertised it as being "built for eternity." But most of the *companies* using the switches didn't last that long. The switches were also higher-priced than most competitive switches.

Foreign competitors recognized the situation, created a less costly—though less perfect—product, and began to outsell the company. Customers were satisfied with the foreign products that did the job and cost less. In its drive to create an exceptional product, the company had forgotten about its customers.

To deal with declining sales, the company retrained and redirected its sales force to "be more customer-specific." Sales representatives were taught how to penetrate client companies and uncover customer needs, rather than just "taking orders." Still, sales and market share continued to erode.

As Tucci explains it,

> The sales force was being directed by senior management to serve the customer—"Find out what the customer wants and the company will figure out a way to deliver it." At the same time, however, the sales force was still being told by the marketing group to sell specific products: "We have a great new gizmo; go out and make ten sales calls." The marketing group, in turn, was being told by the engineers that they had made another product and, once again, had made it better than anyone else in the world: "If we can build it, you can sell it." Unfortunately, there was no one out there to buy that product. The company was still being ruled by the engineering force that had historically played the biggest part in its success.

In this situation, it would be better to invert the whole process by having the salespeople out in the field asking their customers what problems they were having and what they needed, feeding that information back through marketing to test the response to new products, and *then* have engineering build them. Too many organizations are so driven by their engineering or design capabilities—or other technology—that they forget about customers.

TRADITIONAL ATTITUDES TOWARD SERVICE

Service is departmentalized

Because organizations are integrated systems, exceptional service doesn't occur in a vacuum. Service must include every aspect of the business: the products or services offered, as well as their quality, pricing, packaging, delivery, and so on.

Service is more than knowing telephone etiquette, smiling, being courteous, and handling customer complaints. It's also more than just meeting obvious or stated customer needs. And it's more than an absence of problems or complaints. It's even more than a fast response to problems or complaints when they do arise. It's finding ways to determine what customers want and then consistently meeting, or exceeding, those expectations.

Many traditional organizations believe that the quality of service is primarily the responsibility of those who deliver it at the front line. The prevailing belief is, "I have my own work to do. Taking care of customers is somebody else's job." This is like making the shipping-room workers responsible for the design and quality of the products.

Sometimes this attitude is heard as, "We don't handle that in this department. You'll have to call so-and-so." When customers are referred from department to department or from person to person, a company forces customers to learn its organizational structure and communication system to get their needs met.

In traditional companies, most people who are not on the front line have no direct customer contact. People who are not in contact with customers tend to focus inward and concentrate on their own projects or goals. Their vision is shortsighted: they often have no idea how their company's products or services are used by their customers, by their customer's customers, or by the end users. They don't see the big picture. They are not connected in any meaningful way to their customers. They don't see that they "work for" their customers; they believe that they work for their bosses or for their company.

To call a client I dialed the same number I've been dialing for months, wishing to reach the personnel department; however, the woman who answered said, "Legal Department." I said,

"Oh, I thought I was calling Personnel. I'm trying to reach John Doe. Is this 555-5228?" "Yes. Call 555-5000 [the main number] and they'll give you his number."

Why not transfer me to John, look up the number in the company directory, or at least transfer me to the switchboard instead of having me make another call?

Ron Zemke and Karl Albrecht, authors of *Service America!*, say:

> Elitist attitudes and factional interests die hard in most organizations. Sometimes accounting people act as if they think the organization exists so they can keep books on it. Some engineering people act as if the organization exists to support their intellectual hobbies. Some physicians act as if the hospital exists to cater to their overfed egos. It takes a very strong management to get the people in the various camps to see themselves as supporting the people and processes that deliver the quality of experience the customer considers important.

In effect, there are artificial barriers that define each person's or department's responsibilities. People are often reluctant to cross these barriers for fear of stepping on someone's toes. As a result, satisfying customers, meeting customer needs, and handling customer problems are seen as something only certain people or departments should do.

Organizations see service as an extra

In many traditional organizations, service is seen as an extra, a marketing ploy, something soft. As a result, systems and procedures for delivering service are frequently not planned or managed. They're not part of the overall strategic plans of the organization because they're not seen as necessary or important. If they exist at all, they just grow on their own.

The budget, number of employees, equipment, supplies, and other resources for service-related positions also send a message to the employees about how the organization feels about customers and service. In many organizations, the message is: "Production (or sales) is what really matters. Service is just icing on the cake."

Another indication that organizations see service only as something that is nice to do is where corporate positions dealing with service are placed in the corporate hierarchy. Are service-focused people managers, directors, or vice presidents? Are they on the executive committee? Do they report directly to the president? In traditional organizations, people responsible for quality, service, and customer satisfaction rarely report directly to the president. They're often managers reporting no higher than to a director or vice president. This lack of status for service positions sends a message about how important (*un*important) service is to an organization. Not surprisingly, in a service-oriented organization the people responsible for service are frequently high-level managers with both the responsibility and the authority to change the organization's policies and practices to serve customers better.

Organizations have unrealistic or nonexistent service standards

In traditional organizations, if service standards exist at all, they are often set at the top and are then passed down the organization through various levels of management. They're sometimes set without knowledge of, or regard for, the realities of the job as performed at the front line. Employees are expected to abide by the standards without thinking. If the standards are outdated, unclear, or unrealistic, so is employee performance—and service.

If the focus, practices, beliefs, and policies necessary to be service-oriented are not well thought out, articulated, and reinforced, what evolves is a haphazard, inconsistent approach to service. If no standards are set, or if they are not enforced, employees set their own. And the standards they set may be different from those the organization expects.

Even worse, the standards people unconsciously set for themselves usually lean toward ease and convenience, even if service or productivity suffer. This tendency contributes to the situation discussed earlier where employees do things for their own convenience, even if it means inconvenience for customers.

When employees set their own standards by default, it's impossible to achieve consistent service. One result is that customers don't know what to expect. They might get good service one day or at one location and poor service the next day at another location.

In the organizations surveyed by Zenger-Miller, service values are frequently stated in company slogans but are not put into practical application. Only a handful of the companies surveyed say that employees know and understand the organization's service quality standards. Of those employees who do understand the standards, most believe there are major discrepancies between the standards and actual expected and acceptable behavior.

Service-oriented organizations have specific, rigorous standards that every employee understands. Nothing is left to chance. A customer of such an organization gets the same level of service anywhere, anytime.

Organizations believe that good service means having no dissatisfied customers

In many organizations, customer service means keeping customers happy and handling complainers. Traditional organizations believe that customers primarily want smiling, pleasant, cheerful, helpful people to deal with them. Such organizations use the number of customer complaints as the primary barometer of service levels. They believe that "if no one's complaining, we must be doing a good job." However, as we'll see later, research by TARP and other groups shows that most dissatisfied customers *don't* complain—they just go away.

Service gets only lip service in many organizations

Many organizations *say* they're customer-oriented, and people in those organizations *talk about* service. But much of it is just talk—just lip service.

Stanley Marcus, the venerable retailing genius of Neiman-Marcus, said the following in an interview by *Inc.* magazine:

> Oh, sure, the public companies pay lip service to the idea of satisfying the customer, but most of that is pious nonsense. They'd like to have customers happy and satisfied, but not if it's going to cost them three cents worth of earnings in the current quarter. Given the choice between customer service and that three cents, customer service goes right down the drain.

If you look at the way many organizations spend their time and money, their actions contradict their words. For example, the Zenger-Miller study reports that "even people who, in group interviews, speak with emotional charge in their voices about the importance of service quality, report otherwise on surveys that [customer service] ranks moderate to low in the priority of action items."

Many organizations *tell* customers they're service-oriented, but their *actions* seem to say, "Let's give customers as little as we can for the money." It often comes across as, "This is our product. Here's our service. Take it or leave it."

Here's the way that attitude looks in practice:

My wife and I were flying back from the West Coast on Eastern Airlines. It was a breakfast flight. Our travel agent had a standing order to arrange for low-calorie meals. For this flight, both of our reservations were made through the same travel agent, at the same time. Our confirmation sheets showed the special meal requests. We had preassigned seats next to each other. Kay got a low-calorie meal, but I didn't. The flight attendant told us, "We only had one request for a special meal on our list." That communicates to me that they don't care about special orders or they're not capable of handling them.

To put this in perspective, let me describe the regular breakfast I was served. It was a cheese omelet on a slice of ham, a piece of sausage, a crumb cake, a bowl of fresh fruit, and a container of orange juice. The low-cal meal was a box of Special K, a half-pint carton of milk, and the same fruit that was on the other tray. These three items left the tray looking empty in comparison. Nothing on the low-cal tray had to be prepared or cooked—it was all prepackaged. It gave the impression of, "You want a special meal? Here! Eat this! A box of cereal and some milk and we're done with it. You special meal people are a pain in the neck!'' It silently communicated, "We don't want to go out of our way to meet your needs. If you want something special, you'll get the minimum we can give you."

Slogans and campaigns can also fall into the category of lip service. T. C. Gilchrest, president of the National Safety Council, spoke to Council members about slogans at the 1987 national conference: " 'Safety first' has long been the battle cry in the war against workplace accidents, but is this approach realistic? To the CEO of a corporation, 'Safety first' is a slogan with no real meaning. What does 'Safety first' mean to the bottom line? . . . We need to stop selling slogans and start pushing the hard facts of what happens when you neglect safety. Until then, this nation's safety efforts will not improve."

The same is true for service. "Service first," "The customer is king," "We serve you better," and similar themes are often empty slogans with no real meaning for CEOs, or for employees. Organizations must also stop selling service slogans and start pushing the hard facts of what happens when customers are neglected. Until then, service efforts in this country won't improve.

MISGUIDED OR NARROW APPROACH TO SERVICE TRAINING

Service programs are for frontline employees only

Numerous studies have shown that the way employees deal with customers can make or break a business. Few will argue this point. Unfortunately, too many organizations try to improve service *only* at the front line; that is, only with those employees who deal directly with customers.

The Zenger-Miller report noted some common characteristics in programs designed to improve service quality. The people most likely to get any training in service quality are people with customer-contact jobs. Management's participation is limited to deciding that there will be a program. Most programs are less than 8 hours long, have no follow-up or management support, and are not integrated with performance management systems or anything else.

We did our own survey of over 100 public seminars, in-house seminars, packaged programs (including films and video programs), newsletters, booklets,

CHART 1   TARGET AUDIENCES

67%	Customer-contact people, including customer service reps, account reps, telephone operators, and over-the-counter people in offices, retail, government, and service establishments
22%	Managers of the above *in addition to* those listed above
5%	Executives, managers, business owners, and trainers
4%	Sales reps
2%	Field service reps

and bulletins devoted to customer service. Chart 1 summarizes target audiences for the materials we studied, based on each provider's written description of the suggested intended audience.

It's easy to see from these results that most organizations—and most vendors supplying organizations with training programs, seminars, and other materials—are aiming most of their customer service efforts only at the front line, with token, "oh by the way" inclusion of customer service managers. Very few programs or materials are aimed solely at middle or upper management. And we discovered very few approaches to improving service that took an organization-wide, top-down, long-term, systematic approach.

Only a few programs even mention other people in the organization, such as those involved in manufacturing, engineering, accounting, and so on. It seems that program creators—and users—believe that providing excellent service is only important for those in customer-contact positions.

Organizations offer training programs *instead of* making other needed changes

I talk to people in countless organizations of all sizes, in all industries. Many tell me they, too, realize the importance of employee interaction with customers. Many are looking for programs on "interaction skills." One human resources manager of a state agency in Texas told me his top management "sees the need for doing something about service and they want programs for those who deal with the general public on how to treat people more like people." This attitude is typical of organizations that want to address a service problem. This state agency, and many other organizations, are attempting to deal with only the visible tip of the iceberg. Many organizations either don't recognize—or don't want to tackle—the bigger, more complex, less obvious issues that affect service.

If *employees* are not treated "more like people," offering them a few courses on interaction skills (or anything else) isn't going to make them treat the public much better than they did before—or much better than the employees themselves are treated. Managers would do better by asking if the people in direct contact with customers have the skills, knowledge, and personality best suited for customer contact. Do the systems, procedures, and policies of the *rest* of the organization support the front line in delivering quality products and speedy service *all the time*?

The problem is often compounded when people are "forced" to go to training and they see nothing being done to change systems, procedures, people, or anything else. Employees say to themselves, "Oh, they think *I'm* the problem. So they're going to send me to these classes. Meanwhile, I still can't get the materials I need, and we still can't get shipments to our customers on time."

For example, participant material from a training program by a nationally known training company tells trainees: "Serving customers well means dealing with them courteously and helping them resolve problems with your company as quickly and easily as possible. If you deal with customers directly, brighten their day with a friendly smile, a pleasant telephone greeting, a cheerful willingness to help." Encountering smiling, cheerful, willing employees is certainly more pleasant than dealing with frowning, grumpy people who won't go out of their way for anyone. But that's not enough! If the rest of the organization can't consistently deliver quality products or services on time, all the smiles and cheerfulness in the world won't make up for it. If your car isn't ready when promised (and you need it immediately for a trip), it doesn't really matter how friendly the service manager is. If your flight is delayed because of crew problems, mechanical problems, or catering problems, it doesn't really matter how cheerful the ticket agent or cabin attendants are. If the last three shipments your company got from a supplier were late, damaged, or contained the wrong items, it really doesn't matter how nice and courteous the salesperson is. Training frontline employees to be friendly, helpful, courteous, and pleasant is important, and it's hard to do business for long without such employees. But just promoting these surface characteristics for the front line is not enough.

Service programs focus on external customers

In many organizations, the customer service focus is on handling people or situations outside the organization. Very few organizations address the issues or relationships between *internal* service quality and customer satisfaction. People in traditional organizations frequently don't realize they even *have* internal customers. While many organizations have done little to learn the expectations of their external customers, they've done even less to learn who their *internal* customers are and what they want.

CHART 2   LENGTH OF SEMINAR PROGRAMS

	1/2 Day	1 Day	2 Days	3 Days	4 Days	Total Programs
Public seminars	5	13	8	3	1	30
In-house programs or seminars	1	2	2	2	2	9

This discussion about internal customers is not to be confused with the earlier discussion of internal focus. The point here is that people in an organization must recognize that their common purpose is to satisfy external customers. Individual employees, departments, and work units are dependent on each other to do this, and they are, in essence, internal customers of one another. Most of the customer service programs we examined don't address the importance of people, departments, and entire organizations working together to serve customers. Even fewer address the fact that personnel, purchasing, accounting, and other departments with little end-user customer contact do have their own internal customers.

Service training is often nonexistent, insufficient, superficial, outdated, misdirected, or misleading

Dinah Nemeroff, author of the Citibank study mentioned in Part One, suggested that many of the companies studied could benefit from "a thorough reassessment of their on-going training programs." And these companies are among the best in both product and service quality! If her observations led to this recommendation for *these* companies, imagine what training must be like in other companies.

The 1989 Direct Marketing Association annual conference placed service at the top of its agenda. There were four roundtable discussion groups that proposed to address "Cutting-Edge Customer Service." However, despite the title of the discussions, the only topics addressed were returns, billing and payment, order-taking and order delivery, and inquiry and complaint handling. Such a limited view of customer service will not do much to help an organization become service-oriented and customer-focused. As another example of such a limited approach, the vice president for administration for a major national health care company says that the company's customer service programs concentrate on four areas: telephone skills, handling complaints, giving customers good treatment, and selling.

Our study of customer service training showed that most seminars last 1 day or less (see Chart 2). Only about 25 percent of the in-house programs have a leader's guide which includes discussion questions and role plays.

Our study also showed that 37 of 39 film and video programs that listed running times were less than 30 minutes long. The other two ran 1 to 2 hours. The average length for all such programs was 24 minutes. Even with a lively discussion following the tape or film, it's hard to imagine the programs lasting more than 2 hours.

The majority of training programs appear to focus on providing techniques rather than on changing the perspective, beliefs, or attitudes of frontline people (see Chart 3).

I can't comment on the specific content or the quality of every program we surveyed. My associates and I have examined some of the programs, attended some of the seminars, and previewed certain films and packaged programs. I assume that, like most training programs on sales, time management, stress, or any other topic, some programs are better than others. That's not my point. The point is that even if these programs are good, they're only a small part of an overall approach to improving service. Unfortunately, too many organizations depend on videos, films, seminars, newsletters, posters, and the like instead of taking a broader, more comprehensive approach. It's the "Let's train the troops at the front line" approach. And in some organizations, it's a "We're OK, let's fix *them*" approach.

Several studies besides ours have looked at the types of programs aimed at improving the quality of service in organizations. Most programs fall into one of four categories:

1 Sales skills
2 Motivational or PMA (Positive Mental Attitude) programs
3 Telephone or courtesy skills, including listening skills
4 Problem-solving skills

Sales skills.   Even in best-selling programs and books on customer service, a major theme is sales skills. These programs generally involve teaching sales skills to customer-contact employees to improve their ability to sell additional related items or to cross-sell items from other divisions or product lines. The focus of these programs is largely on increased business from existing customers. Most books and programs don't concentrate on improving customer perception or satisfaction with products or services over the long term. As a result, most employees take a one-time-only approach to selling.

Results from sales skills programs for customer service people vary. For example, in organizations that are not traditionally sales-oriented, such as banks or utility companies, the whole idea of selling is often hard to get across. It's inconsistent with the long-held, conservative belief that "The customers will come to us." When sales skills *are* taught, getting people to use them is difficult. One study found that without incentives, people rarely

CHART 3   TOPICS OR FOCUS OF PROGRAMS
(as described in the promotional materials or in the program materials; 80 programs represented)

Topic or Focus	No. of Programs That Address the Topic	Percentage
Frontline topics listed:		
Handling angry or upset customers, complaints, and tough customers	42	52.5
Telephone skills, techniques, and courtesy	21	26.2
Importance of employee attitudes, keeping a positive frame of mind, keeping your head when dealing with customers, "you are the company" to customers, self-esteem, and confidence	20	25.0
Showing empathy and caring, developing rapport, making good first impressions	20	25.0
Importance of service, satisfying customers, meeting their needs and expectations	18	22.5
Courtesy, smiling, using customers' names, eye contact	14	17.5
Generic communications skills, people skills, customer interaction skills	13	16.2
Listening	12	15.0
Problem solving	11	13.7
Motivation, "Do better," what *not* to do	9	11.2
Teamwork	8	10.0
Identifying and dealing with different personalities	7	8.7
Selling, cross-selling	6	7.5
Understanding the customer's point of view	6	7.5
Internal and external customers, everyone has a customer	5	6.2
Nonverbal and nonvisual communications	4	5.0
Negotiating, getting agreements	3	3.7
Appearance and grooming	3	3.7
How to avoid offending customers, killer phrases to avoid	3	3.7
"What to do when . . ."	3	3.7
Handling stress and pressure	3	3.7
Writing skills	2	2.5
Asking questions, probing to get information	2	2.5
Handling time pressures, time management	2	2.5
Understanding customer buying habits and patterns	2	2.5

CHART 3   TOPICS OR FOCUS OF PROGRAMS, *continued*
(as described in the promotional materials or in the program materials; 80 programs represented)

Topic or Focus	No. of Programs That Address the Topic	Percentage
Management topics listed:		
Service management, strategies, mission; service delivery systems	12	52.1
Motivation, how to motivate employees (to provide better service)	12	52.1
Establishing service policies and standards	8	34.7
Hiring practices	7	30.1
Training	5	31.7
Monitoring and measuring service	5	21.7
Learning what customers want	3	13.0
Handling upset/difficult customers	3	13.0
Marketing/selling (the importance of) service within your own organization	3	13.0
Importance of a positive work environment	2	8.6
Changing the culture of your organization	2	8.6
Understanding customer behavior, perceptions	2	8.6
Improving field service levels	1	4.3
Surveying competitors' service programs, practices	1	4.3
Problem solving and problem prevention	1	4.3
Managing incoming customer calls	1	4.3
Self-management/career management	1	4.3
Importance of effective management/leadership	1	4.3
Avoiding pitfalls in customer service programs	1	4.3

Note: Percentages total more than 100 percent because many programs cover several topics.

take the initiative to cross-sell. However, with incentives, making sales sometimes takes precedence over meeting customer needs or other job responsibilities.

Motivational or PMA programs. These programs are frequently aimed at frontline employees. They are not intended to provide knowledge or skills, but rather to change attitudes. One person called them "shot in the arm" programs intended to pump up employees' attitudes toward their company, jobs, and customers. They're often run by outside consultants and typically consist of a series of 2- to 4-hour sessions.

Results show that any good feelings gained in these programs quickly disappear. In fact, these kinds of programs often have the opposite effect—they foster cynicism, because many employees perceive these programs as hypocritical and phony. People quickly sense that they're being "motivated" to do better but aren't being given the skills or other resources they need to improve service. Employees often perceive these programs as "Do as I say, not as I do." Employees tend to become wary of programs that contain more fluff than stuff.

Telephone and courtesy skills.   These programs emphasize telephone skills such as listening, asking questions, handling complaints, and being courteous. Another focus is interaction, or social, skills. Programs with this focus teach people to smile, to be courteous, and to be nice to customers. Such programs are often called "smile training" or "charm school." These programs are intended to improve the efficiency of customer-contact employees and to train them to present a warm, positive, friendly image to customers.

As with motivational programs, employees quickly see the difference between the way they're taught to treat customers and the way they're treated themselves. When positive, courteous, caring, helpful employees perceive managers as being unsupportive, rude, insensitive, or indifferent, the employees get confused, angry, and resentful.

Problem-solving skills.   These programs deal with ways to handle upset customers. They're usually aimed at customer-contact employees. They cover things such as identifying and dealing with different personality types and resolving small problems before they become bigger problems. Zenger-Miller's observation is that these programs are designed to handle *problem customers* rather than *customer's problems*.

Most of these programs only give employees the skills to deal with customers and the immediate problems they present. They rarely give people the tools or authority to get to the causes of problems or to prevent similar problems in the future.

The disturbing thing is that these four common kinds of programs reflect the way organizations view their customer service training. If we assume that consulting companies, training houses, and audiovisual producers develop and sell what their customers (corporations, associations, hospitals, and others) will buy, and if we also assume that these organizations (their customers) buy training programs and materials to solve service problems or improve service performance, we can make some inferences about the way organizations view service based on the kinds of programs and materials they buy. If organizations place considerable value on service training for senior managers, we'd see many programs for senior managers. We didn't. If organizations believe pep-rally-type programs are needed, we should see many of these being offered. We did.

A typical example of what we found concerns courses offered by the American Management Association (AMA). The AMA catalog describes a course called "Fundamentals of Customer Service" as a program for customer service reps with less than 2 years of experience. The topics include listening and communicating (asking questions, getting your point across in writing or on the phone, and so on); keeping information flowing; relaying trends or problems; problem solving; complaint resolution; and time management.

Another AMA course, aimed at new managers, is called "Managing Your Customer Service Operation." According to the catalog, this course "views customer service as an essential part of the marketing and selling efforts of successful companies." The topics listed include interviewing and hiring; writing training manuals; motivating with incentives; communicating (improving writing skills, creating forms for logging and summarizing information, and so on); training reps on telephone techniques; establishing standards; solving problems; and handling complaints. Although this course appears to take a broader approach than many, the focus is still on a "customer service department," not on service being the responsibility of *everyone*. And judging from the topics listed, it appears that AMA's client companies still see the major roles of customer service departments as sales and complaint resolution.

Another example of what we found concerns the Dartnell Corporation, a major producer of training films, tapes, and books. In 1988 Dartnell introduced a subscription newsletter called *Customers*. Their sample issue, sent to prospective customers (potential subscribers), was titled "Courtesy—A Must In Customer Contact." The issue contains articles on politeness, handling problems, handling angry customers, and proper telephone techniques.

I believe that the focus of this newsletter communicates that how-to's, fix-it's, and techniques are the answer to improving customer service. I also believe this approach is inadequate and misleading, but it's apparently what Dartnell's corporate customers want. It's indicative of how organizations view service and the training that's needed to improve it.

In many organizations, training is simply nonexistent. In *From Losers to Winners: How to Manage Problem Employees and What to Do If You Can't*, V. Clayton Sherman says that most companies force people to learn the ropes by trial and error. He makes the obvious point that people need to know the rules in order to play the game. Too few companies spend the time to teach the rules. We've all heard (or experienced) situations in which a newly hired employee was given a day—or even an hour—of "training," handed a manual or an order book, patted on the back, and told to "Go get 'em!"

In many other organizations, training is inadequate. Employees are trained in a few areas, but the training is far from complete. This is like taking someone who's never seen a tennis match and has no understanding of the game, giving a one-day lesson on how to put a topspin on the ball and how to return the opponent's 10 trickiest shots, and then sending that person to play in the U.S. Open. The tennis class doesn't include anything about the rules of the game, the strategies, or the basics of how to play. It starts with tricks and techniques and playing *defensive* tennis. And it assumes that every opponent will have the same 10 tricky shots. In tennis, it's far better to teach the fundamentals of the game, because basic knowledge and skills *are* what's needed to handle anything any opponent launches. The fundamentals are also needed to play *offensive* tennis. In organizations, the same holds true. It's better to first give people a solid foundation in the basics and give them the knowledge and skills they need; then, when they've mastered the basics, give them the extras—the finesse.

Illustrative of the problem is what happened at Rich's, a chain of 20 department stores in the Southeast. Rich's president, Winfrey N. Smith, indicated that the 18 hours of training employees were currently getting was probably not enough. He announced that store employees were going to receive an additional 4½ hours of training on such things as how to use cash registers and other store systems, and how to sell merchandise. Smith observed, "As silly as it may seem, we are currently showing new employees a map of our stores rather than walking them through the stores."

Rich's is certainly not alone in this kind of training predicament. Many organizations, in practically every industry, offer training that consists mostly of "head work." Trainees learn information, but they never have a chance to practice using the knowledge or the skills they learn. Instead, they practice on real customers in real situations.

Even role plays in a training-room environment are often not enough to teach people how to handle real-world situations. Being able to recite the rules or write the steps of a procedure is one thing. Doing it well under pressure is often another, and this ability comes only with practice.

Unfortunately, the traditional approach is, "All they need to know is what we tell them." Information is shared with employees on a need-to-know basis. And someone else always determines what they need to know. This leads to practices such as withholding information about company revenues, market share, profits, and competitive activity from employees.

Some training programs are also misleading. The leader's guide for a training film on customer service released in 1988 suggests that trainers tell their customer-contact people that "the fundamental point remains: being the best in customer service means being friendly, helpful, and courteous. . . ." This same leader's guide says, "Indirectly, the customer is our boss."

This is another case of producers of training programs misleading trainees in their clients' companies. Traditional organizations still see that the customer is only *indirectly* the boss—implying that the direct boss is someone inside the company and higher up in the organization. Service-oriented organizations recognize that the customer *is* the boss. Not indirectly, but *directly*. And such organizations are structured to best serve their customers.

The key to making organizations more service-oriented is changing what people at every level believe, think about, and do. And 1-, 2-, or 3-day workshops don't change behavior or attitudes for more than a few days or weeks. A different approach is needed. Training is necessary, but it's not the only solution.

Changing attitudes, practices, systems, and values cannot be done overnight. Programs that try to do this too quickly cause resentment and lose credibility. Such programs usually address surface issues only. The most effective approach must be implemented over several months, not days or weeks, because that's how long it takes.

Another training approach in traditional organizations is to cover every situation employees might encounter when dealing with customers. I call this "what to do if . . ." training. It's knee-jerk-reaction training. It goes like this: "If the customer says or does this, you do that." Many programs include specifics about

- ☐ What to do when several customers demand your attention at the same time
- ☐ What to do when an angry customer attacks you
- ☐ How to respond to a customer who has several legitimate complaints
- ☐ How to establish rapport with customers quickly
- ☐ The 10 most powerful words you can use with customers
- ☐ The 10 words or phrases to avoid using with customers
- ☐ What to do if this particular situation or that particular situation arises

Teaching "what to do if . . ." is futile because you can never cover every situation employees will encounter. And yet the focus of many training programs is on such surface-level, situation-specific topics. They teach in-the-moment responses rather than addressing the attitudes and beliefs that must underlie all responses. Using this approach is like teaching doctors to treat only symptoms of illness without attempting to deal with underlying causes.

Training that emphasizes responses to specific situations or that places major emphasis on rules and procedures often results in canned approaches to dealing with customers and their problems. Programs like these also continue to reinforce outdated, ineffective beliefs in organizations. They attempt to maintain the status quo and seek only to change the outward, superficial actions of the front line. They don't acknowledge the role of the rest of the organization in providing good service.

It's unlikely that any training program could ever hope to cover every situation employees might encounter—even if a program lasted a week. Since training programs for frontline employees often last only a few hours, it's no wonder this approach is rarely effective. When employees aren't given an understanding of what the organization values, what good service is, and what the guidelines are for handling customers, they get frustrated, anxious, and stressed when they face situations that weren't covered in their service training.

If employees act out of their own initiative and are then berated by their supervisors, it compounds the problem. They're less likely to try to help the customer again, and their self-esteem is often damaged. Eventually, to keep from getting punished, they stop trying to do anything or they get fed up and leave. Either way, the organization and its customers suffer.

I believe there's a time and a place for much of the training we found in our survey (assuming it's good). But it must be in context—it must be *part* of a broader approach and not offered instead of it. And it must be given at the right time, with the right participants, proper management support, the right content, and guarantees of follow-up on the job. In fact, the best approach includes a combination of in-class and on-the-job activities.

Another aspect of the training dilemma is that traditional, internally focused companies often demonstrate the belief that once people are trained, they're trained. This is particularly true as people move up the ranks. The attitude of some long-term managers and executives is, "I don't need any more training. I wouldn't have made it this far unless I was pretty smart. Besides, I've been around a long time. I've seen all that stuff before. What more can you teach me?"

A similar note was sounded by A. William Wiggenhorn, corporate vice president and director of education and training for Motorola. He believes that more emphasis must be placed on the training effort and that "most companies have a plan to upgrade their equipment, but few have comparable plans to upgrade their people."

Organizations handle their training in different ways. Some organizations have the resources in-house to develop and conduct training. Others don't. The problem is that many organizations *think* they have the resources and capability to improve service through training but actually don't. Many training managers see it as a sign of incompetence if they admit that they can't develop everything in-house. Too often, training departments are either ineffective or out of touch with the pulse of the business. They get in the way, or they get caught up in their own smugness with "we can do it all" attitudes. As a result, they often develop training programs when other actions are called for. When training *is* called for, instead of seeking qualified outside assistance, they develop programs that have inadequate or incomplete content and are poorly presented.

Another problem with many in-house and purchased programs is that they frequently miss key elements. For example, studies have shown that only 7 percent of our communications is transmitted by our words. Up to 85 percent is communicated nonverbally—93 percent if you include tone of voice. Yet most training concentrates on the words, on saying the right things. Even well-chosen words don't help if the intention, appearance, stance and posture, distance, tone of voice, rate of speech, inflection, eye contact, and other factors aren't appropriate.

Most people aren't aware of how important these other factors are in communicating with customers (or coworkers, bosses, spouses, children, and so on). Unless they've seen themselves on videotape or have had a trained observer give them feedback, most people don't know how *their own* nonverbal behavior could be hurting them. This is particularly true of frontline employees. They often have neither self-awareness nor the ability to communicate effectively, yet they need these skills most because they're the ones who have the most contact with customers.

Overall, then, instead of emphasizing *what* to say or getting people all pumped up and enthusiastic in training programs, more emphasis should be placed on knowing *how* to communicate and on having the knowledge and confidence to help customers regardless of the specific situation that presents itself.

OUTDATED ATTITUDES ABOUT EMPLOYEES

Customer-contact people are often unsuited to their positions

Most organizations don't realize how critical their frontline people are. They don't realize that rude, slow, inept acts by the frontline can negate years of goodwill and millions of advertising dollars.

Research and practical experience reveal that constant customer contact requires a certain temperament. It also requires verbal and nonverbal communication skills, problem-solving skills, and the ability to make decisions on the spot. Since frontline people are often the lowest-paid, least-motivated, and least-trained people in the organization, often they do not have the right skills or personality characteristics to be effective.

The problem is compounded by the fact that customer-contact positions are often both entry-level and exit-level positions. They are obvious entry-level positions. Less obvious is the tendency in some organizations to move people who don't "fit in" or aren't making it in other areas into these positions. They're often people who are one step away from leaving, either by quitting or being fired.

Organizations are becoming more complex: Jobs are becoming more specialized, technology is more complicated, companies increasingly operate in a world marketplace, and many increasingly provide services rather than products. In this environment, it's critical to have people with the right qualifications.

Sadly, many organizations don't know what makes a good secretary, product manager, salesperson, waiter, cashier, or customer service representative, so they don't know what to look for when hiring them. Nor have organizations determined the education, work experience, life experience, or other characteristics most likely to predict success in each job. Instead, they make subjective, "gut level" guesses about what qualifications employees need.

Even if organizations have identified the qualifications needed, they often hire people without the background or experience they'd prefer, just to fill a vacancy. And, too often, organizations set pay ranges that often prohibit hiring people with the background or experience needed. On the other hand, *service-oriented* organizations typically hire employees for what they can do today *and* what they can contribute over the long run.

Knowing what to look for when hiring is becoming more complicated. And finding service-oriented people who will fit the bill isn't easy either. In *Service America!*, Zemke and Albrecht observe that being a naturally service-oriented person requires

> a familiarity with the idea of an intangible having economic value, and adeptness in conceptualizing *intangible* outcomes. It requires a tolerance for ambiguity, an ease in dealing with lack of direct control over every key process, and a finely tuned appreciation of the notion that the organization is equally dependent on soft (or people-related) skills and hard (or production-related skills). Last but not least, it requires a tolerance for—perhaps even an enjoyment of—sudden and sometimes dramatic change. The only constant in service is change.

Some people just won't "fit in" in every organization; they won't be happy or productive. Some of these people are already in place in organizations—some because they were mis-hired, others because their skills, experience, and temperament were suited to the organization in the past. In either case, having the wrong people in certain job positions hurts both the employee and the organization, especially when these employees have frequent customer contact.

Organizations don't see any connection between employee satisfaction and customer satisfaction

Traditional organizations rarely survey either customers or employees to learn how they feel about things, what they want, or how they're being treated. Rarely are customers or employees asked for their ideas or suggestions. If traditional organizations *do* conduct surveys, they generally share results only with senior managers or department heads.

Service-oriented companies recognize the connection between employee satisfaction and customer satisfaction and measure both regularly. They use both formal and informal means to find out from customers and employees how they're doing. They openly publish the results, especially to the front line.

Why is employee satisfaction so important to customer satisfaction? Dinah Nemeroff said it best in the Citibank study introduced in Part One: "Customer relations mirror employee relations." If you treat your employees with care and respect, your employees will treat your customers the same way. If employees are given no authority and are rule-bound, underpaid, and unmotivated, customers tend to get cold, indifferent, "I just work here" service.

Service is likely to suffer if the organization's culture allows supervisors to yell at employees, use a sarcastic or demeaning tone, or reprimand employees in front of other employees or customers, or if supervisors never give employees the benefit of the doubt in disagreements. Also, if employees don't have the tools, equipment, or information they need, or if they don't have a clean and safe work environment, service is likely to suffer. If you've ever experienced cold, indifferent, "I just work here" or It's not my job" service, chances are that's the way employees are treated by their own organization. Here's an example:

It was Saturday, July 5. Kay and I stopped in a discount self-serve shoe store. Usually on a 3-day holiday weekend on a hot, sunny summer day there aren't a lot of customers in shoe stores. They're out playing. That was true on this day—there were no customers in the store. With our business and travel schedules, we often have to shop when we can, and this seemed like a good time to shop for some casual shoes Kay needed.

The door of this store faced the main aisle. About halfway down the aisle there was a rolling cart parked sideways. There were two employees, a woman and a man, at the cart doing inventory—checking shoe sizes, styles, and prices and marking inventory sheets. The female employee was nicely dressed in a modest, summery dress. She had her back to the door so she couldn't see if any customers came in. The front door was open and there was no bell or buzzer. She also couldn't hear if any customers came in because the radio on the cart was blasting. The male employee was dressed in faded denim cutoffs and a sleeveless muscle shirt, and he was barefoot—in a shoe store! He looked up when we came in, but then he ignored us. The shoe size we wanted was in the main aisle, on the other side of the cart, but we couldn't get to it because the cart was positioned so no one could get through.

We decided to see what these two employees were going to do. We walked down the next aisle, one aisle over from where they were working. We walked halfway down the aisle so we were standing near the two employees, separated only by the gondola between the aisles. We spent about 5 minutes looking at shoes and trying several on. Kay found several styles she liked and in a louder than normal voice said things like, "I really like that. I wonder if they have it in the next size." We walked up and down this aisle looking at shoes and trying them on. We were never more than 3 or 4 feet away from where these employees were working. We could very plainly hear their conversation (which was about everything *but* shoes or customers), so we knew they could hear us. They just couldn't see us.

In the 15 minutes we were in that aisle these two employees never said one word to us. Keep in mind that there were no other customers in the store. On a slow day, when there's time to interact with customers, they were busy interacting with each other and their inventory sheets. For all they know, we could have been their biggest sale that day—or the only sale. As it turned out, we left without buying anything. We also agreed not to go back again. What did the indifference of those two employees cost that company?

I later went back to the store and talked to several employees about how they feel they're treated. You guessed it: The company headquarters is in another city, and they rarely see their district supervisor. The people I spoke with said they were only working there until they could find something better. They felt that their jobs were boring and they were underpaid. They also said they didn't see any reason to do anything special for customers because they got paid the same either way. The female employee we saw doing the July inventory later told me she was angry she had to work on a holiday. She thought the store should have been closed and had suggested that to her supervisor. She was told that it was a stupid idea and that she'd "better be there." The supervisor told her he was going to call at 10:00 to be sure she was. Oh, yes, the store went out of business 6 months later.

Perhaps people in your own organization sometimes provide indifferent, "I just work here" service. Most organizations don't even know what kind of service they're providing. They don't know how their customers perceive the service they're providing. If they do know, they rarely suspect that their internal employee satisfaction has anything to do with external customer satisfaction. They don't realize that how an organization treats employees affects how employees treat customers.

I recall two companies I've worked with that were exceptionally cold, secretive, austere places to work. It was no surprise that their senior managers were cold, manipulative, secretive, and aloof and that their influence reached every employee.

A typical incident occurred one day when a group of managers was coming back from lunch. The managers were still talking and chuckling about some amusing topic they'd been discussing. As they reached the top of the steps that came up from the cafeteria, the vice president for administration happened to be walking by. He scowled at them and very seriously said, "This is a place of business. There'll be no laughing here!" Would you want to work in a place like that?

This same vice president liked to come in around 7:00 A.M., although normal working hours at this company are 8:30–4:30. His window faced the parking lot where his employees parked, so he could see when people came and went. And he did! Employees, even managers who reported to him, told me they always felt like they were being watched and being treated like little children.

This company had one of its three warehouses adjacent to the corporate offices. Of course, the warehouse had a union—a sure sign the employees felt they needed protection from management. This company finally had such difficulties with the union that it had to close the facility to escape the union's demands.

In the other similarly cold company, the vice president for human resources was a former labor negotiator who treated people (in a nonunion company) as if they were all thugs trying to "get" something. Employees at this company told me, "I wouldn't turn my back on him for a minute." That company is now out of business.

I learned of a similar situation from one of our employees, Ann Alexander. She once worked as a cashier in a supermarket chain store, and she describes some incidents that reveal what it was like working there:

Once when there were no customers at my check-out line for a few minutes, one of the bookkeepers looked down at me from the store office and said in a demeaning and contemptuous tone of voice, "You'd best be cleaning that register while you're just standing there." She wasn't even my boss!

Another time, an item didn't have a price on it. The customer told me the price, but I had to send someone to check it. That was the company's policy. The customer got upset that I didn't take her word for it. I apologized and explained to her that I was supposed to have someone check the price. It took so long to get the price check that the manager finally came over to see what the holdup was. After the woman left, he took me into the office and cussed me out. Everyone in the store could hear him. He wouldn't even listen to my explanation of what happened, even though I was just doing what I'd been taught.

And there was one regular customer who paid by check. On two occasions, I got the manager's approval for his checks. The next time that customer came in, I accepted the check. It turns out all his checks were bad. When the manager got in trouble for approving the first two checks, he came after me. It was terrible. He was standing there in the middle of the floor near the check-out lines, with customers all around, yelling at me for accepting that man's checks.

I waited until all the customers in my line were gone and then went to the time clock to check out—for good. My time card was already in my hand when the manager came over. He said, "If you leave now, don't bother coming back. Or you can bring your mother in tomorrow and the three of us can discuss this." My mother! I couldn't believe he had the nerve to tell me that. After acting like a child, he tried to treat me like one! I just punched out and left.

Service-oriented organizations have a very different view of their employees and they treat them differently. Bill Marriott Jr. sums it up like this: "We have

Wayne Public Library
WAYNE PUBLIC LIBRARY
14 JAN 02 07:59pm
CHECKOUT

22352005053987

Delivering knock your socks off
32352052177331   Due: 04 FEB 02 *

Sustaining knock your socks off
32352051746565   Due: 04 FEB 02 *

How to provide excellent service
32352051589486   Due: 04 FEB 02 *

Phone renewal: 694-4272 Ext. 5210
Thank you!

to be friendly with our people. Then they'll be friendly with our customers." This kind of thinking reinforces the idea that an orientation toward service, like so many other beliefs and practices in organizations, flows from top to bottom and then from inside to outside.

There is other evidence that the way employees perceive their own organizations affects the service they provide. One study by Benajmin Schneider and David Bowen highlights how strongly customer relations mirror employee relations. Schneider and Bowen surveyed both customers and employees at 28 banks and concluded that there is significant correlation between the way customers view service and the way employees view the internal organizational climate. When employees view the organization's human resource policies favorably, customers have a favorable perception of the quality of service they get. A positive work climate means positive customer service.

Along these lines, the Zenger-Miller report made the following observation:

> A courteous and helpful front-line employee does make for greater customer satisfaction. This employee must also, however, take responsibility for resolving issues and assuring action. If the organization as a whole is not prepared to be responsive, then the employee will have to deliver service *in spite* of the company, creating employee stress and frustration. For courtesy skills to have maximum impact, employees need to experience positive, task-oriented behavior from others inside the organization that mirrors the behaviors they show to external customers.

In many cases, employees deliver substandard service because they believe it is acceptable. That's what they see around them, so they come to belive it's the norm. Psychologically, their stress and frustration is then much lower because they're in alignment with what they think the company wants.

Other research, by The Forum Corporation, shows that turnover is inversely correlated with employee perceptions of service quality. That is, companies where employees perceive service to be poor have the highest turnover. The Forum Corporation's research shows that length of time with the company, job function, and amount of customer contact have little influence on this correlation. Apparently, then, poor service is perceived as poor service by most employees, regardless of what they do, where they work, or how long they've been with the company. We know that high turnover is usually a reliable indicator that all's not well in an organization. High turnover in organizations that are poor service providers often indicates that employees know when their organization provides poor service and they don't want to be a part of it. It also indicates that companies that don't take care of their customers also don't take care of their employees.

Employees are underutilized

One of the biggest differences between traditional, internally focused organizations and customer-focused organizations is how they see their employees—their beliefs about what employees are capable of and how they should be treated. Beliefs often operate at a subconscious level. Most traditional managers aren't even aware of the way they perceive employees. They often deny the beliefs described below.

In traditional organizations, employees are seen as cogs in the organization's machinery, incapable of setting their own goals, standards, or schedules. Managers believe that most employees want to do as little as possible and will rip off the organization every chance they get. As a result, managers believe that employees must be told what to do and then monitored, watched, and controlled. Rules, policies, and practices are put in place to protect the company from the employees. And employees certainly are not trusted to make important decisions on the front lines without checking with management.

Actually, just the opposite is true of most employees. In a survey of U.S. workers, the U.S. Chamber of Commerce and the Gallup Organization found that 72 percent of the surveyed employees spend at least some time thinking about ways to improve their organizations. In fact, 44 percent said they spend "a lot of time" thinking about improvement—yet only 29 percent of those surveyed see any real possibility of their ideas coming to fruition in their organizations. People who are doing the jobs and working with customers *are* thinking about how to do things better, yet their organizations don't seem to pay much attention.

Do people really have that many good ideas? Rubbermaid Inc. got over 12,500 ideas from employees in just one division in one year. Squibb Corporation gets over 27,000 suggestions from employees each year through its computerized suggestion terminals. Toyota gets an average of 50 ideas a year per employee, Canon gets 70 per worker, and Panasonic gets 100.

According to Robert Lewis, founder of Network Builders International, most organizations don't know what resources are available to them: "It's amazing how much hidden talent goes to waste in organizations. People have information, skills, experience at solving certain problems, and no one knows they have it. Even people who've known them 15–20 years don't know they have it." Lewis is a pioneer in the area of uncovering hidden resources in organizations and has developed methods for determining what resources are critical to an organization and then identifying the people who have them.

Lewis describes a common situation in which someone in an organization spends a lot of time and money researching a new computer system, or trying to solve a problem, only to find out later that someone else—maybe in another division or location—has already done that research or solved that problem. "Knowing how to find people who have talents, knowledge, and experience in certain areas can save companies time and money," says Lewis.

So what's the cause of the problem? Jan Carlzon, head of Scandinavian Airlines System, says that "most frontline employees have been following regulations for so long that few have the courage to try something unusual. Instead of making a decision that a superior might dislike, they will delegate responsibility back up—in the most extreme cases, all the way to the board of directors. (This happens more often than most corporate executives would care to admit.)"

Of course, just telling people to be more creative and less dependent on supervisors, and to take more responsibility, doesn't mean such changes will happen overnight. Author and organizational consultant Peter Block believes there are several factors at play. Block says there are strong influences from male-dominated, patriarchal institutions—such as schools, churches, the military, and many traditional companies—that have helped make people dependent on hierarchical authority.

Block also believes that organizations are set up to maintain a degree of control over others. The budgeting, planning, and performance appraisal systems (as well as other systems) are set up to exercise that control. And Block believes that many people go to work for large organizations so the organization will take care of them. The unwritten contract between many employees and their employers is: "I'll go to work for you and give you the best years of my life. In return, I want you to take care of me, protect me, provide meaningful work for me, and keep me safe." The result is that many employees have come to believe their destiny is in someone else's hands, usually someone above them.

The need to keep employees dependent on supervisors is so strong, it even shows up in books on customer service. William Martin's book, *Quality Customer Service*, was designed to be used as a self-study training tool for improving service in the hospitality industry. In it, there are several case studies in which readers decide how they'd handle particular situations. At the bottom of the page for one case study, framed by a box, is this recommendation:

WHEN YOU FIND YOURSELF CONFRONTED WITH A DIFFICULT SITUATION YOU DON'T KNOW HOW TO HANDLE, INVOLVE YOUR SUPERVISOR.

CERTAIN PROBLEMS MAY REQUIRE YOUR SUPERVISOR TO HANDLE THEM. IF SO, FIND OUT WHAT THESE PROBLEMS ARE, AND OBSERVE HOW THEY ARE HANDLED.

Rather than teaching people how to handle difficult situations or giving people the authority and responsibility—and the skills, support, and confidence—for handling difficult situations, this author (and presumably the hotels and restaurants that buy this book) assumes that only supervisors can and should handle difficult situations. This approach does very little to train employees how to handle situations (and I wonder how the supervisors learned).

Don Munson, executive vice president for Division Operations at Lennox Industries, says that in order to get people committed to being customer-focused, "People must understand they're valuable. You must give them the opportunity to make contributions. That means letting people know you've hired them for their minds, not just their backs."

MANAGEMENT'S CONTRIBUTIONS TO POOR SERVICE

Managers may actually be the cause of service problems

W. Edwards Deming is the quality guru responsible for much of Japan's economic recovery following World War II. More recently, he was a major factor in the turnaround at Ford Motor Company and its "Quality is Job 1" approach. Deming believes that managers, not workers, are responsible for 80 percent of the defects in a product or service. Deming says the workers aren't bad; rather, the system is bad.

In many cases, management doesn't know, or denies, that it contributes to the problem. In a study of 651 managers in 10 organizations, Caleb S. Atwood found that

- [ ] 45 percent did not understand that people repeat behavior that is rewarded
- [ ] 61 percent did not believe it was appropriate to brag about employees or their accomplishments
- [ ] 47 percent did not believe that employees should suggest solutions to problems or grievances (indicating a reluctance to involve and communicate with employees)
- [ ] 41 percent did not understand—or believe—that improving quality reduces operating costs

Atwood was a founding vice president of the American Productivity Center and is currently president of E.R.I.Q. Inc., a Houston-based firm that specializes in measuring management expertise.

Not surprisingly, all 10 companies found that they were far less effective than they thought in communicating their policies, procedures, and centrally held beliefs to their managers. Perhaps most interesting is the degree of confidence managers expressed in the correctness of their survey answers (their confidence rating averaged slightly over four on a five-point scale). Atwood explains that confidence is an important issue because it determines how likely managers are to use their knowledge effectively. In this study, Atwood found that managers were just as confident about their "wrong" (ineffective, demoralizing, or counterproductive) answers as they were about their correct ones. This means that while managers may not know what they're doing and may not understand their companies' policies, procedures, and beliefs, they are certain that they do.

Since management influences every aspect of an organization, management's role in service is critical. There are a number of reasons that management unknowingly condones existing problems, creates problems, or interferes with efforts to improve service:

1 Organizations are overly dependent on managers to identify and solve problems, to provide answers, and to be creative.
2 Managers cling to outdated beliefs and practices and take a narrow, blinders-on approach to service.
3 Managers use a decision-making mode that pits cost against customer.
4 Organizations, and managers, have a short-term orientation to the business.
5 Managers are too far removed from customers.
6 Managers are not committed to service quality.
7 Managers pay too little attention to hiring and training.
8 Managers actually subvert attempts to change.

Let's look at these reasons in more detail.

1. Organizations are overly dependent on managers to identify and solve problems, to provide answers, and to be creative.   In our Western culture, we tend to think managers are all-knowing, all-powerful. As a result, our organizations depend on managers for answers and underutilize the talents and knowledge of other employees. This isn't the case in Pacific Rim cultures. For example, in 1979, Konosuke Matsushita, the executive advisor of Matsushita Electric Industrial Company (Panasonic), made some comments in an off-the-cuff conversation with a group of American businesspeople about global competition. His remarks illustrate this point:

> We are going to win and the industrial West is going to lose out. There is nothing you can do about it, because the reasons for your failure are within yourselves.
>
> Your firms are built on the Taylor model; even worse, so are your heads. With your bosses doing the thinking while the workers wield the screwdrivers, you're convinced, deep down, that this is the right way to run a business. For you, the essence of management is getting the ideas out of the heads of bosses and into the hands of labor.

We are beyond the Taylor model. Business, we know, is now so complex and difficult, the survival of the firms so hazardous in an environment increasingly unpredictable, competitive, and fraught with danger, that their continued existence depends on the day-to-day mobilization of every ounce of intelligence.

For us, the core of management is precisely this art of mobilizing and pulling together the intellectual resources of all employees in the service of the firm. Because we have measured better than you the scope of the new technological and economic challenges, we know that the intelligence of a handful of technocrats, however billiant and smart they may be, is no longer enough to achieve a real chance of success.

Only by drawing on the combined brain power of all its employees can a firm face up to the turbulence and constraints of today's environment.

Matsushita may be right. In 1979, the U.S. trade deficit with Japan was $10.5 billion; in 1989, $45 billion.

Others have also commented on U.S. managers' narrow, blinders-on approach to their organizations and their refusal to look at things differently. Frederick Herzberg, writing about job enrichment, observes that years of tradition have led managers to believe that the content of existing jobs is sacrosanct and that the only alternatives available are the ways in which people are stimulated to do those jobs. He urges managers to approach jobs with the conviction that jobs *can* be changed.

2. Many managers cling to outdated beliefs and practices and take a narrow, blinders-on approach to service.   Although I'll talk more about beliefs in Part Four, let's now consider the importance of management's collective beliefs and practices regarding service, customers, what employees are capable of, what management's role is, how managers interact with employees, and how managers reward or punish employees.

In the Citibank study, executives themselves acknowledged that their "instincts" or "gut feel" or "long years in the business" may not accurately reflect today's diverse customer reactions. But that's sometimes hard to swallow for many managers.

D. Quinn Mills, a Harvard Business School professor and author of several books on business and management topics, talks about how hard it is for managers to accept that they're part of the problem: "It's hard for us to admit that we [as management] are the problem, but when foreign managers are in the same plants with the same people and the productivity and morale are at an all-time high, we've got to conclude it was us, not them"

Lewis Schiffman, a health promotion consultant and president of Atlanta Health Systems, tells of a manufacturing and design company that implemented wellness programs for its employees. The seminars were done well and employee participation was good, but after 3 months employees realized that learning how to eat the right foods, exercise, and handle stress better wasn't what they needed. They recognized their main source of stress to be their senior manager. The employees realized that they needed a manager who was consistent, who would recognize and use their talents, and who would respond to their needs. Schiffman concluded that "managers often miss the signals of employee burnout and low morale. Such managers often manage by responding to crisis, not by design. They often see themselves in an adversarial position with their employees and believe 'you can't get good help anymore.' "

3. Managers use a decision-making mode that pits cost against customer.   Cost-versus-customer decisions are often evident in situations like this one:

A customer came into a department store to buy a remote TV antenna. He explained that he was taking the TV to his vacation cabin that had no cable, so he needed an antenna that connected directly to the back of the TV set. The employee showed him the box containing the antenna and assured him the antenna would do the trick. When the man got to his cabin, he found that the antenna couldn't be attached to the TV. It was useless. He was furious.

When he got back from vacation, he went to the store. The supervisor he spoke to apologized for the inconvenience, gladly exchanged the antenna for the correct one, and gave him his $46 back.

Traditional organizations only look at monthly, quarterly, or annual results. Because they only look at the bottom line, they don't understand an act such as replacing the antenna *and* returning the customer's $46. They see the extra money only as a cost, and the accounting department would wring that supervisor's neck for such an action.

We've already seen that many organizations believe that good service means fewer customer complaints. This same misguided thinking is also applied to employees. Traditional organizations often reward employees for *not* making mistakes—and punish them for ideas that don't work out or projects that fail. The result is an environment in which employees do only what's expected and what keeps them out of trouble. In these organizations, going out of the way for a customer, bending the rules, taking risks, or spending extra time on a customer request or project is not rewarded and may be punished.

4. Organizations, and managers, have a short-term orientation to the business.   In November 1986, the president of Massachusetts Institute of Technology, Paul E. Gray, appointed a 16-member panel to determine why U.S. productivity is declining and to make recommendations for improving it. The commission spent 2 years studying all aspects of eight industries. They visited over 200 companies and conducted over 500 interviews in the United States, Europe, and Japan. Their report, *Made in America: Regaining the Productive Edge*, concludes that American business is weakened by short time horizons and a growing concentration on short-term profits. The report points to "excessive concern over immediate profit, even to the sacrifice of longer-term opportunities" and calls attention to the "preoccupation of financial institutions and corporate managers with short-term performance indicators like quarterly earnings."

Concern over short-term orientation is also voiced by people like Ronald L. Vaughn, the Max Hollingworth Professor of American Enterprise at the University of Tampa and president of Strategic Testing and Research. Vaughn is a leading expert and author on quality. In an article on service by Thomas Oliver in *The Atlanta Journal and Constitution,* Vaughn is quoted:

> Part of the problem with service is that it is not a priority of management, and part of that is tied to their short-term orientation. If you are evaluated on quarterly or yearly profits, that's what you will pay attention to. Add to the short-term orientation the fact that many middle managers plan to change companies several times in their careers, there's little incentive to act in the long-range interests of the business.

Traditional organizations don't understand making a long-term investment in customer satisfaction, repeat business, and positive word-of-mouth advertising.

A few weeks after the TV antenna incident, the same customer decided to buy a microwave oven and a VCR he'd been thinking about. Instead of going to a local discount store, which he'd planned to do, he went back to the department store because of the way he was treated. He spent over $700 that would have been spent elsewhere. That's a pretty good return on a $46 investment.

---

5. Managers are too far removed from customers.   The Marketing Science Institute sponsored research on what constitutes quality service. The report, prepared by A. Parasuraman and several associates, identified several "gaps" between the service customers expect and what they actually get. Parasuraman's research indicates one reason for these gaps is that service executives may not understand what customers perceive as quality service. And even if they *do* know, executives may not attach enough importance to these factors.

Each promotion has taken senior managers further from daily contact with customers. In fact, Georgia State University marketing professor Kenneth Bernhardt says that many company executives insulate themselves from their customers: "They don't shop. They fly in corporate jets and ride in limos. Their hotel rooms are reserved for them by someone else, and someone checks in for them. And at the highest levels, their assistants shop for their Christmas presents."

Bernhardt has personal experience with how this can affect service. He was moving to Boston to become a visiting professor at the Harvard Business School and had several problems with the moving company. Bernhardt tried to resolve them through normal channels and, when that failed, called the president of Allied Van Lines. The president's secretary asked if he was a customer. Bernhardt said he was. The secretary said, "Oh, the president doesn't talk to customers."

Zemke and Albrecht sound a similar note in *Service America!*:

> It's very easy to believe in the importance of service to the customer and the impact of the culture, and yet not believe that *your* role in the game "counts." If you are the president of the company, it is easy to tell yourself, "But I am at the helm. I hardly ever see a customer anymore. I only see bankers, managers, and stockholders."

Many senior managers grew up in the school that taught them that their responsibility as managers is to look after the well-being of the company, not the well-being of the customers. Dr. Grady Bruce, professor of marketing at California State University at Fullerton, and Eric Johnson, a partner in Johnson-Layton Company, say senior managers don't have a customer perspective because they're often specialists in other areas:

> They just don't have insight into what's going on at the customer's level. Instead, they are professional managers, highly skilled in retailing, marketing, sales, or finance, backgrounds not normally required for a retail or service chain to grow and prosper in these highly competitive and changing times. They are expected to look after the company's well-being, a task which is often contradictory to the day-to-day desires of the customer.

6. Managers are not committed to service quality.   Parasuraman's research revealed that another reason for "gaps" in service is "the absence of total management commitment to service quality." He reports on an earlier study on product quality by David Garvin that notes: "[T]he seriousness that management attached to quality problems [varies]. It's one thing to say you believe in defect-free products, but quite another to take time from a busy schedule to act on that behalf and stay informed." Parasuraman and his associates believe that the same holds true for service businesses.

Part of the problem is management's lack of responsibility for changing its approach to customers. Here's a particularly poignant example that appeared on the CBS program "60 Minutes" in June 1988:

The story was about the effects of post-traumatic stress disorder (PTSD), a psychological illness that haunts thousands of Vietnam veterans. It is essentially delayed stress. The symptoms include extreme anxiety, horrible nightmares, flashbacks to the war, profound depression, acts of violence, and suicide. Many PTSD sufferers are homeless and unemployed, and are drug abusers.

Most veterans who experience the symptoms of PTSD don't know what's wrong with them. Neither do many of those who try to help them. Steven Michad, a veteran and a therapist, explained on the show about Vet Centers—storefront meeting places throughout the country intended to spread the word about PTSD to veterans and offer them help. Congress created the Vet Centers to supplement the Veteran Administration's paltry efforts to deal with the problems of the Vietnam veterans. Vet Center staffers wanted to provide help out on the streets, where the people who needed it were. According to Michad, the Vet Center program was "jammed down the VA's throat."

Commentator Dan Rather noted that Congress then moved to expand the program but at the same time announced a plan to close down the centers. The net effect of these conflicting actions was to force the Vet Centers off the streets and into the VA mental hygiene clinics. As a result, some veterans with PTSD were treated in psychiatric wards. The VA admitted that this plan wouldn't save any money or provide any better care than vets were getting in the storefront centers.

The problem is that many of the verterans don't trust the VA or its hospitals. They see them as places where people go to die or to be controlled by drugs. The vets *do* trust the Vet Center program and its counselors. Michad says, "They don't see it as a VA program."

Then the VA began closing centers even earlier than the mandated date. Dr. Arthur Blank, who works for the VA as director of the Vet Centers, confirmed that the Vet Centers are necessary and they do a good job. He also said that closing them early was "policy matter" he couldn't comment on. When asked what he was doing to try to keep the centers open, Blank replied that it wasn't his job to try to influence Congress to change the legislation, even if he disagreed with it; his job is only to provide services to veterans.

In this case, the VA's "customers" are taxpayers—veterans who risked their lives in combat. But senior managers didn't think it was their responsibility to look into, or even try to change, a policy that hurts these "customers"!

---

7. Managers pay too little attention to hiring and training.   Management sometimes tacitly condones placing improperly trained people who may lack the experience, skills, or temperament for customer contact into customer-contact positions. Managers either openly or covertly encourage hiring practices that will cost the company the least. They condone hiring the least-expensive workers available instead of searching for people with the skills, knowledge, and abilities the organization needs—even if the organization has to pay more for such people. This is typical traditional, short-term, cost-versus-customer thinking.

In other cases, management's lack of initiative in *demanding* that hiring practices and training be improved also contributes to the problem. Ignorance of the problem and inactivity do nothing to correct the problem and, by virtue of doing nothing, maintain the status quo.

8. Managers actually subvert attempts to change. In *The Improvement Process*, H. James Harrington, IBM's top quality assurance manager and chairman of the American Society for Quality Control, reports that even when companies attempt to implement procedures to improve quality, production, or service, managers are often the cause of failure:

> "The improvement process doesn't always work. A study of the causes of failure listed:
> - [ ] Management misused the process
> - [ ] Management didn't participate in the process
> - [ ] Management felt that employees, not management, were the problem
> - [ ] Management was unwilling to make a long-term commitment to the process
> - [ ] Management didn't make the process part of its ongoing business activities"

Because management is often so much a part of the problem, it's difficult for most companies to diagnose and treat themselves. Unfortunately, many managers don't realize or admit that *their* beliefs and practices may be contributing to the level of service their organization delivers. This makes for an interesting situation: Managers recognize the need for some changes in the organization and try to correct these by themselves, which is like surgeons operating on themselves, or attorneys defending themselves, or psychiatrists counseling themselves. In medicine, law, psychiatry, and other areas, professionals frequently seek outside help and rely on specialists. In organizations, managers usually don't. They try to do it all themselves.

Communication is inadequate

Inadequate communication is a problem with several dimensions. Let's first look at communication to and from customers. Then we'll look at communication within organizations—to and from the front line.

Communication with customers. Those who manage internally focused organizations typically believe they already know enough about their business. They think they know what their customers want—or at least what they're going to give them. This is often true of production- or manufacturing-driven companies.

Years ago, the wine industry in this country typified the production-driven mentality: wineries made wine from what they had available. For decades, much of the wine made in the United States was red because most of the grapes planted in this country were red. Different varieties of red grapes were grown for sacramental wine, grape juice and jelly, and for bootleg wine during prohibition. Much of the wine was jug wine—inexpensive, nonvintage, sweet, high in alcohol, and low-quality—made from blends of undistinguished grapes.

As wine companies became more consumer-oriented, they started asking what customers *wanted*. This new focus on customers resulted in a major shift in production. Today, white wine outsells red. Many consumers today also want drier wines, varietal wines, and vintage-dated wines. So wineries plant or purchase grape varieties in response to customer preferences, rather than producing according to what's plentiful or cheap.

In most organizations, the majority of employees have little direct customer contact. In many companies, those in management rarely work on the front lines or call on customers. Production people rarely meet their customers or see how their internal or external customers use their products. Other than workers who produce consumer products (cars, refrigerators, soft drinks, etc.), machine operators or assemblers rarely see where their finished pieces of work go, how others in the operation use the pieces, or what problems others may be having with them. It's even rarer for employees to see how other businesses use what they make or provide. The larger the organization, the more this is the case. As a result, many employees don't know who their customers or end users are; they don't have a sense of working for the customer. They end up working for personal or departmental objectives that can conflict with organizational goals. It's no wonder employees think they work for their bosses and not for the customer!

In traditional organizations, ideas for improvement come largely from marketing, research, engineering, or other departments. Such organizations frequently play what Len Caust calls the "sausage game." Caust, the former information services manager for Lever Brothers, described the sausage game to Laurence Shames in *The Big Time: The Harvard Business School's Most Successful Class and How It Shaped America*:

> So here's what the sausage game is. You win yourself a market with a nice all-meat sausage, the best sausage you can make. People eat that sausage and they say "hmmm-hmm." So now you've established the product.
>
> Now you can afford to start slipping in some sawdust. Add the sawdust by small enough increments and no one'll ever notice. They'll still say "hmm-hmm," because people are creatures of habit.
>
> Of course, five or six increments down the road, you'll end up with a product that bears little or no resemblance to what you started with, but you'll get away with

it, for a while at least. Your market share will hold, your margin will increase, and everybody will think you're smart. I've seen it happen.

The same thing happens with service. Many companies start out providing quality products and exceptional service—all the extras. As time goes by, it becomes easier to coast.They gradually stop doing one thing, then another, then another. They stop doing many of the things that got them to the top in the first place. Just like with sausage, people don't notice the slipping service at first. Eventually, the company's service and reputation bear little resemblance to what it started out with. In the meantime, if one or more of the company's competitors have been gradually *improving* service by *adding* new products, features, or services, the gap widens twice as fast.

Service-oriented companies and their managers take a different approach to their customers. They believe they can never know enough about their business. They are relentless in trying to find out what their customers want, what problems they're having, how their products or services can be more useful to them. Executives work on the front line and "shop" the company. Employees at all levels regularly go out to meet their external customers. They see how customers use their products. They learn about problems their customers may be having and about problems they may be creating for their customers. They realize that customers are the best source of ideas on how to improve their business, products, and service. Ideas for new products and improvements in products and services come largely from listening to customers.

Employees and managers in service-oriented organizations also know firsthand how their own organization works: how each department fits into the big picture of satisfying customers; where forms, components, and products go; who does what; what problems other departments are having; what problems they may be creating for other departments. They go visit or meet with internal customers to learn about their needs.

Retailing guru Stanley Marcus talks about the importance of listening to customers in retailing and how buyers are doing less—not more—listening. (And this is not just true for retailing.)

> [Y]ou learn something from your customers you can't learn anywhere else. You learn whether they're happy and satisfied. You learn not only what they bought but what they didn't buy—and why. You learn what they came in expecting to buy and expecting to pay. I haven't seen a computer yet that can tell you all that—that can plug into a customer and ask, "Are you satisfied? Have the merchandise and service met your expectations?"
>
> But the danger is that [the computer is] like an addictive drug. You become hooked on numbers to the point that you neglect your products and your people. I've walked into department stores around the country and found buyers sitting in

their offices in sweatsuits. You know what this tells me? It tells me that they have no intention of spending any time on the selling floor. Their whole life is tied to that damned screen.

The idea of listening to customers isn't new. It's a basic marketing principle. Tom Peters and Bob Waterman brought renewed attention to the importance of this principle in *In Search of Excellence*. Peters and Waterman concluded that excellent companies are better listeners than other companies are and that most of their real innovation comes from the market. The authors go so far as to say, "The best companies are pushed around by their customers, and they love it." They cite examples from Procter & Gamble, Levi Strauss, IBM, Bloomingdale's, 3M, Digital, and Wang Laboratories, where new product ideas come from customers, not from inside the organization.

Even when organizations do value customer preferences, ideas, and comments, many organizations don't have regular, systematic ways for frontline and other employees to find out what end users really want. They also lack ways to get that information to people in the organization who need it (such as those in engineering, research, marketing, production, and other departments). Further, most organizations have no regular, systematic way of giving feedback to the front line on what customers value or how employees are doing at providing it.

Companies must increasingly *listen* to their customers, not just "hear" them. Hearing is the mechanical process, and most frontline people do hear. They hear a lot, but they don't listen because they don't know that what they hear is important. For example, when a customer says, "Boy, if only it did . . . ," or "If only it were made this way, then I could . . . ," most employees hear these comments as just another fussy customer complaining about what the product won't do. Most employees take this attitude: "Here's what we have. If you don't like it, don't buy it." Frontline employees continuously hear suggestions from customers, they hear complaints, and they overhear customers talking to each other—but they don't realize how valuable the information they hear is.

Even if employees do *listen*, they generally have no way to pass on what they hear. Managers in most organizations don't encourage or reward feedback or ideas from the front line. Employees don't believe anyone's interested in their ideas or what customers say, and there's no formal process for passing observations on to marketing, engineering, accounting, or other departments. Employees might tell their coworkers over lunch, or tell their spouses at home, but they don't know how to get the information through the organization. Think about how many conversations you've heard—or initiated—that began something like this: "Those jerks. If only they would. . . ." Or think about the lunch or dinner conversations in which you (or somebody else) says, "I spent several days working on this thing, and I've just figured it out. I told my boss, and he said, 'It'll never work. We've tried it before.' "

Now that we've looked at how poorly many organizations handle getting information *from* customers, let's look at how they handle getting information *to* them.

Service quality is largely determined by what customers *perceive* it to be. In many cases, customers aren't aware of everything that organizations do for them. Just because organizations are doing wonderful things for the customers, doesn't mean customers always know about or appreciate them.

Consumer focus-group studies conducted by A. Parasuraman reveal that "making customers aware of . . . 'invisible' service-related standards could improve service quality perceptions. Customers who are aware that a firm is taking concrete steps to serve their best interests are likely *to perceive* a delivered service in a more favorable way." Too many organizations don't bother to tell customers what they've done for them lately.

Communication within the organization.   Now let's shift to communications *within* organizations. I've already talked about how important it is to learn how employees perceive the organization. Employee surveys can tell you what your *employees* expect and what they feel they're getting, just as customer surveys do. Many of the same methods can be used—written surveys, employee focus groups, interviews, and so on.

Sometimes the results of these surveys can be scary. In 1986, MCI Communications Corporation surveyed its employees on a number of issues and found that more than half of them either didn't know or didn't understand where the company was going.

Before doing employee surveys, management must commit to taking some action based on employee recommendations and on problems that surface. Otherwise, employees will feel ripped off. If no action is taken it is a slap in the face. To employees it says, in effect, "Your concerns and ideas don't really matter. We're going to do what we please anyway."

Organizations and their managers are more concerned with having employees follow the rules than with satisfying customers

Many organizations have so many rules and procedures that employees aren't free to exercise any initiative or creativity in meeting customer needs. In most cases, the rules are made many levels away from the customer. Some organizations even have severe negative sanctions for breaking the rules.

A study sponsored by the Southern Governors Association and the Southern Legislative Conference found that 60 percent of all denials for federal assistance programs were denied because applicants failed to comply with procedures. That means that over 1½ million applicants for welfare (Aid to Families with Dependent Children), Medicaid, and food stamps were denied benefits because their applications were incomplete or incorrect; because they failed to produce required documents such as bank statements, proof of rent payments, proof of age for children, or Social Security cards for all family members; or because they failed to produce the required documents by the required date.

One of the reasons for requiring such detailed and complex applications is to comply with federal guidelines and thereby avoid expensive fines imposed by the federal government when state agencies exceed established error rates for determining eligibility. Interestingly, the report also notes that there are severe financial sanctions imposed by the federal government if ineligible applicants are approved for government assistance, but *no* sanctions for denying benefits to applicants who should have been approved. Since applicant errors count against the state agencies, caseworkers are tempted to simply deny applications rather than run the risk of costly penalties. Following the rules seems to be more important than assisting customers (called "applicants" in this case), even if it means denying people life-sustaining assistance.

And sometimes when employees go way beyond the call of duty, they are punished:

In Mountain View, Colorado, a United Parcel Service (UPS) driver unknowingly happened into an armed robbery and hostage situation. When he realized what was happening, he used his truck to pin the getaway car to a fence. Police were able to catch two of the three perpetrators fleeing on foot. Shortly thereafter, a UPS supervisor came to the scene, cursed the driver in front of the police for crashing his truck, and threatened to take away his company good-driving record and discipline him severely. The driver was a hero to the bank and police, but he was punished by his supervisor.

In many organizations, employees are burdened with needless paperwork, forms, reports, meetings, or other tasks that take them away from their real jobs of satisfying customers. Too often people with expertise or skills are kept from using them because they get too tied up in administrative procedures and red tape.

A former Federated Department Store executive says he often spent so much time filling out reports that he lost sight of customers. Albert D. Maslia finally left the company to start his own specialty card store. He now has 11 stores with annual revenues of over $4 million. He says he tries to keep his employees focused on customers by removing red tape.

A Northwest Airlines employee was on his way to work in Detroit on August 16, 1987. He looked up and saw a plane about to crash. It happened to be a Northwest plane. He stopped his car and spent 22 backbreaking hours looking for survivors and pulling bodies out of the wreckage. When he returned to work the next day, he was docked a day's pay for not showing up or calling. He was a hero to rescue workers, crash victims, and bereaved families, but he was punished by his employer for breaking attendance rules. This story about insensitive corporate bureaucracy was reported in the *Detroit News* August 27, 1987, and later was reported in the wire services. Northwest Airlines continues to deny the accuracy of the report and says that the employee received full pay.

Here's another example that illustrates both inappropriate adherence to rules and general insensitivity to customers:

Art Zorka is a professional speaker. He was traveling from Atlanta to a convention in Phoenix. Art's 17-year-old daughter, Juliana, was flying from Miami to Atlanta to meet him so they could fly together to Phoenix. Unfortunately, they got their signals crossed, and Juliana arrived at the Atlanta airport several hours before their flight to Phoenix. When Art wasn't there to meet her, she called the house and found out about the schedule mix-up. Art said, "Go to the Ionisphere Club. I'm a member. I'll meet you there."

A few minutes later, Juliana called Art from the Eastern Ionisphere Club to tell him they refused to let her in. They told her she couldn't wait for her father there because she's not a member and because they serve alcohol there. (They serve alcohol in the entire airport, but they don't keep minors out of the rest of the airport!) Art knew the bar was upstairs, so he asked the receptionist if Juliana could wait *downstairs* in the reception area right near the receptionist's desk. She said no. [This is typical of the attitude of "We're not going to go out of the way for you. We have our rules."]

Art called the Delta Crown Room and explained the situation to the receptionist there. She said, "Fine. We'll be happy to have her wait for you here." Delta welcomed her, even though she wasn't flying with them. Eastern refused to let her wait in their club, even though both Art and Juliana were flying round-trip with them. But that's only part of the story.

When Art got to the airport, he checked the video monitors and saw that their flight to Phoenix had been delayed. It was supposed to leave at 11:15 A.M.; the new departure time was 2:00 P.M. While Art and Juliana were waiting in the Delta Crown Room, they explained to several people what had happened with the schedule mix-up and the delayed flight. A Delta passenger said, "You'd better check your departure time. Eastern has a habit of changing their posted departure times."

At 12:30, Art walked to the other end of the terminal to check the Eastern video monitors. He was shocked to see that Eastern had moved the departure time back from 2:00 to 12:45. It took a mad dash to the gate for Art and Juliana to make their flight.

This example illustrates how little regard some organizations have for customers. Frequently changing departure times shows little regard for passengers who decide to get something to eat, and for people waiting at the other end to meet arriving passengers. In this case it also shows how Eastern's Ionisphere Club employees blindly stick to the rules, even when it inconveniences paying customers.

Excellent service is not recognized or rewarded

Employees at all levels pay attention to what's rewarded. If service is truly important to the management of an organization, rewarding service performance throughout the entire organization is essential. It's important that such rewards are not limited only to those who have direct customer contact, but, unfortunately, this is often the case.

Because so many organizations see service as something that's nice to have—as an extra—it's not taken seriously. And, with so few organizations setting specific service goals or service standards, service performance is rarely measured. If it's not measured, it's hard to reward. (If you don't keep score, how do you know who's winning?)

Very few managers have specific service-oriented goals that are separate from sales, production, performance, or other goals. Even fewer managers are evaluated on their service results or on customer satisfaction. As a result, employees aren't evaluated on *their* service performance or customer satisfaction, either. If no one pays attention to it, makes it part of the appraisal process, or regularly talks about it, service has a low priority or no priority at all. Instead of being a real goal, it just gets lip service.

Sales quotas, production figures, rework or recalls, market share, and other measures all get attention. People's salaries or bonuses are tied to these specifics, so they get measured and rewarded. Many organizations have sales, safety, or productivity contests with prizes such as TVs, microwaves, golf clubs, and vacation trips. People in the organization learn that sales is important. People get recognized and rewarded for performance, but there are very few counterparts in service. Even more rare are service standards, rewards, and recognition for providing service *within* an organization.

Management doesn't know how current service practices affect the bottom line

What's exceptional service worth? What can poor service cost you? Most organizations haven't the foggiest idea.

Several years ago we wanted to have some landscape work done around our house. The people we bought the house from had let the outside go to pot. There were dead trees left standing, and the shrubbery in the front of the house was terribly overgrown. I wanted a few landscapers to come look at the situation, make recommendations, and give me estimates. Many landscapers are small businesses that have owner-operators. They don't have office staffs, so they rely on answering machines when they're out of the office. That's understandable. I called about 12 different landscapers and left messages that I wanted someone to come out to give me an estimate. Half of them never called back—even when I left a message with a live person. I made appointments with six. Two of them never bothered to show up, call to cancel, or reschedule. Of those who came out, I got three estimates in the mail. Only one of those who sent estimates ever bothered to call back to see if I got the estimate, if I had any questions, or if I was ready to start with the work.

The "I don't care if I get your business or not" attitude affects revenues, and little things *can* help some landscapers—and other businesses—stand out from their competitors. "Little things" include showing up for appointments or calling after sending an estimate. The landscaper who got the job has been hired twice since and has earned several thousand dollars from us over several years. Any time I need landscaping, I call him. The others lost out on this business due to their lack of response or attention to the customer.

Sure, some things do make it to the balance sheet, as in the situation described earlier about the department store customer who came back to buy a microwave and VCR. But how do you reflect on the quarterly financial statements the employee who goes out of his or her way for a customer? Or those employees that don't?

A client told us about an incident involving his son, who had just finished college in the Midwest. Following graduation, the lad needed to move all his things to his new home in New Jersey. He planned to leave on Friday night, drive all night, and get to New Jersey on Saturday. He started his new job Monday.

He went to a local U-Haul dealer and told them how much stuff he had to move. The dealer recommended a trailer he could tow. The young man was concerned about his little Nissan 510 being able to pull a trailer full of books, clothes, furniture, and other belongings, especially since the car didn't have a trailer hitch. The dealer recommended a bumper hitch. The day before the move, the dealer installed the bumper hitch and hooked up the trailer.

The lad set out across Route I-70 heading east. As he drove across the country, the weight of the trailer began to pull the bumper away from the car. Eventually, the bumper came to rest on the exhaust pipe. This caused the exhaust pipe to pull away from the car chassis so the muffler ended up next to the rear tire. The excessive heat of the muffler exploded the tire. The car careened wildly out of control because of the weight of the trailer behind it. Luckily it didn't roll over, but there was serious damage to the car: what was left of the bumper was ripped off, there was no muffler, the wheel was damaged, and there was no way to tow the trailer to his destination.

The young man eventually had to rent a car to tow the trailer and also had to pay for repairs to his car. This incident cost him over $1,200. He asked the local U-Haul dealer to reimburse him for at least part of his expenses and repairs since a U-Haul employee had recommended the bumper hitch and installed it. The local dealer refused. The boy's father then had his attorney contact U-Haul's corporate office for reimbursement. The corporate office also refused to make any payment for the damage.

At the time this occurred, our client worked for a large organization that employed about 8,000 people. For years he waged a one-man campaign against U-Haul. He wrote letters to fellow employees telling about this incident, he urged people who needed rental trucks to use Ryder, E-Z Haul, or anybody but U-Haul. He says there have been at least seven or eight opportunities since the incident when he has rented trailers or trucks, but he has never again used U-Haul.

I wonder how much this one customer has cost U-Haul over the years. Probably a lot more than the $1,200 involved. Unfortunately, there's no line item on company accounting forms to account for this loss. And yet, there *are* ways to calculate such losses.

There are many ways to determine the costs of dissatisfied customers. Here's an example from Tom Monaghan's book, *Pizza Tiger*, about Domino's Pizza:

Monaghan tells about visiting one of his stores that had low sales volume and showing the manager why the store couldn't afford to lose even one customer: Even if they delivered 95 percent of their orders within the 30-minute delivery policy, the 5 percent that were late meant 50 orders a week. They knew that about 10 percent of late deliveries resulted in lost customers, so the particular store could lose 5 customers a week. Monaghan multiplied 5 customers a week by 52 weeks, and then by 26 for the average number of times a customer orders from Domino's in a year. He showed the manager that he could have lost 6,760 orders a year because of poor service (being late). From there, it wasn't hard to figure the bottom line cost to that store by multiplying the average price of an order.

The U.S. Office of Consumer Affairs (USOCA) has reported on research performed by several companies and agencies that gives some indication of the cost of poor service. The USOCA research reveals the following:

- ☐ Approximately one in four purchases results in some type of consumer problem.

- ☐ Nearly 70 percent of customers experiencing a problem do *not* complain. One study shows the figure to be as high as 90 percent. This means that for every complaint organizations receive, there are approximately three other customers with problems, some of them serious, that organizations never hear about.

- ☐ Dissatisfied customers who don't complain are the least likely to purchase the offending product or service again. Only 9 percent say they intend to buy again.

☐ For customers who do complain, the *way* their complaint is handled affects their intent to repurchase. When customer complaints aren't handled satisfactorily, up to 83 percent say they'll go elsewhere next time. When complaints *are* handled satisfactorily, the figures are reversed—between 70 and 90 percent say they'll continue to do business with the organization. This means that 60 to 70 percent of all dissatisfied customers will not again buy products from, or do business with, organizations that don't provide good service.

☐ Dissatisfied customers tell twice as many people about their negative experience as satisfied customers tell about their positive experiences. And the more expensive the product or service involved, the more people spread both positive and negative experiences. On average, dissatisfied customers tell nine others about their experiences.

☐ Technical Assistance Research Programs Institute (TARP), USOCA's primary research contractor for these studies, estimates that organization lose one customer for every fifty dissatisfied customers as a result of negative word of mouth.

☐ Dissatisfaction with one product line (from the same supplier or retailer) can have a negative effect on other product lines. If customers have an unsatisfactory experience with one product or service from a company, they stop buying other products or services put out by that company. In resale operations, they also stop doing business with the firm that sold the offending products or provided unsatisfactory service.

☐ It's five times more costly to acquire new customers than it is to keep current ones.

There are many formulas for determining what less-than-excellent service may be costing your organization. Some of the formulas are complicated. Others don't give a complete picture. Below is a simple formula that incorporates the best elements of several formulas and enables you to estimate the dollars-and-cents effects of your current service practices.

To use this formula for your own organization, you'll need three figures:

☐ Annual revenue (Line A).

☐ Number of customers (Line B).

☐ Cost of acquiring and keeping customers. This cost includes sales, marketing, advertising, promotions, discounts, and other costs. Either the actual dollar figure or the percent of sales will work (Line L).

The rest of the calculations are based on the USOCA research and are included in the formula below.

Let's see how this formula works with a hypothetical company. In Example A, let's assume the company has an annual revenue of $350 million and a customer base of 25,000. Let's also assume that the cost of sales is 64 percent, or $224 million. Using these figures in the formula, as done below, we see that this

THE COSTS OF POOR SERVICE

Lost Customer Revenue

A. Annual revenue $_____

B. Total number of customers   _____

C. Percentage of dissatisfied customers   ×_____.25

D. Number of dissatisfied customers (C × B)   =_____

E. Percentage dissatisfied customers apt to switch   ×_____.70

F. Number of dissatisfied customers who will switch   =_____

G. Average revenue per customer (A ÷ B) $_____

H. Revenue lost through poor service (F × G) $_____

Lost Opportunity Revenue

I. Number of other people dissatisfied customers tell (F × 9)   =_____

J. Number of potential customers who buy elsewhere due to negative word of mouth, assuming 1 in 50 told (I × .02) buy elsewhere   =_____

K. Potential lost revenue opportunity via negative word of mouth (J × G) $_____

Customer Replacement Costs

L. Cost to acquire and keep customers—sales, marketing, advertising, promotions, discounts, etc. (dollar amount or percent of revenue: __ % × A) $_____

M. Average cost per customer (L ÷ B) $_____

N. Replacement cost for lost customers (M × 5) $_____

Total Costs

P. Total annual cost (H + K + N) $_____

Q. Total cost over customer's lifetime or 10 years (P × lifetime or 10) $_____

company may be losing over $72 million a year due to poor service. For this company, that's almost 21 cents of every dollar!

The estimates used in lines C, E, I, and J in Example A are based on the USOCA's studies with various consumer goods and services and may not apply to your organization. If necessary, you can adjust them accordingly. For example, if you know for your industry or organization how many dissatisfied customers are likely to switch to competitors, use that figure in Line F instead of .70. Or, if you suspect that the word-of-mouth estimate in Line I is too high or too low for your organization, use your own estimate instead of the one in the example.

The figures can go the other way, too. Providing exceptional service, or even just good service, can *add* to the bottom line. In Example B, let's assume our hypothetical company cut the number of dissatisfied customers in half, improved

Example A

THE COSTS OF POOR SERVICE

Lost Customer Revenue

A. Annual revenue $ _____ 350,000,000

B. Total number of customers _____ 25,000

C. Percentage of dissatisfied customers × _____ .25

D. Number of dissatisfied customers (C × B) = _____ 6,250

E. Percentage of dissatisfied customers apt to switch × _____ .70

F. Number of dissatisfied customers who will switch = _____ 4,375

G. Average revenue per customer (A ÷ B) $ _____ 14,000

H. Revenue lost through poor service (F × G) $ _____ (61,250,000)

Lost Opportunity Revenue

I. Number of other people dissatisfied customers tell (F × 9) = _____ 39,375

J. Number of potential customers who buy elsewhere due to negative word of mouth, assuming 1 in 50 told (I × .02) buys elsewhere = _____ 788

K. Potential lost revenue opportunity via negative word of mouth (J × G) $ _____ (11,032,000)

Customer Replacement Costs

L. Cost to acquire and keep customers—sales, marketing, advertising, promotions, discounts, etc. (dollar amount or percent of revenue: 64% × A) $ _____ 224,000,000

M. Average cost per customer (L ÷ B) $ _____ 8,960

N. Replacement cost for lost customers (M × 5) $ _____ (44,800)

Total Costs

P. Total annual cost (H + K + N) $ _____ (72,326,800)

Q. Total cost over customer's lifetime or 10 years (P × lifetime or 10) $ _____ (723,268,000)

its ability to hear from unhappy customers to 25 percent (so they complain rather than switch), and benefited from normal, positive word of mouth. The company's figures might then look like those shown in Example B.

Many organizations believe that their current service does not require improvement

It's amazing how many companies believe they're immune to suggestions about improving service—that their industry or organization can't improve its current

Example B

Lost Customer Revenue

A. Annual revenue $ <u>350,000,000</u>

B. Total number of customers   <u>25,000</u>

C. Percentage of dissatisfied customers   × <u>.13</u>

D. Number of dissatisfied customers (C × B)   = <u>3,250</u>

E. Percentage of dissatisfied customers apt to switch   × <u>.25</u>

F. Number of dissatisfied customers who will switch   = <u>813</u>

G. Average revenue per customer (A ÷ B) $ <u>14,000</u>

H. Revenue lost through poor service (F × G) $ <u>(11,382,000)</u>
(Although there's still a loss, they've cut their loss by almost $50 million compared to Example A.)

Additional Revenue from Word of Mouth

I. Number of people satisfied customers tell (B × .87 × 4.5)*   = <u>97,875</u>

J. Number of potential customers who buy due to positive word of mouth, assuming 1 in 50 told (I × .02) buys   = <u>1,958</u>

K. Potential new revenue resulting from positive word of mouth (J × G) $ <u>27,412,000</u>

Repeat Customer Business
L. Number of people who return within a year, assuming only 1 in 10 comes back only once (.10 × B)   = <u>2,500</u>

M. Revenue per customer (L × G) $ <u>35,000,000</u>

Reduced Customer Replacement Cost

N. Replacement cost for lost customers (Line N from prior example) $ <u>224,000</u>

O. Reduced replacement costs (N ÷ 5) $ <u>(44,800)</u>

Total Increase

P. Total annual increase (H + K + M + O) $ <u>50,985,200</u>
(This is a net increase of over $123 million compared to Example A.)

Q. Total increase over customer's lifetime or 10 years (P × lifetime or 10) $ <u>509,852,000</u>

* For this example, .87 represents the percentage of satisfied customers (.13 from Line C is the percentage of dissatisfied customers). This example assumes that each satisfied customer tells an average of 4.5 people about a satisfactory experience.

service. The truth is, problems with service aren't limited to any industry or any country.

The ABC News program "20/20" aired a story in January 1988 and another in August called "Does Your Doctor Really Care?" They reported on people's perception that many doctors "have become insensitive, lost their bedside manner, and are as interested in making money as in curing ills."

Interviews with doctors, health care professionals, medical students, and patients uncovered such problems as:

☐ Impersonal care: "All I want is someone to help me. Instead I get passed around like a piece of fruit."

☐ Overbooking: "You sit down in the doctor's office and say to others, "What time is your appointment? . . . Well, mine's at ten o'clock too. . . . You know, everybody's got a ten o'clock appointment."

☐ Doctors' godlike attitudes: (interviewer John Stossel) "Being a doctor . . . tends to make one feel powerful. You've worked hard for your degree. Now people look up to you. Your knowledge is crucial to your customers' well-being. It can go to your head."

☐ Having to wait: "There are always three people waiting [and] it is just assumed that [the doctor's] time is so much more valuable than my time [so] that I can just sit."

A resident at a Massachusetts hospital says, "People lose their names in hospitals because of the volume. You call the next admission a 'hit." Medical students in other hospitals refer to very sick patients as "train wrecks" and unappealing patients as "GOMERS" for "Get Out of My Emergency Room."

Promotional materials for a customer service training film for hospital employees say:

> During the past decade, the health care industry has taken on such gigantic proportions that the human aspect of the patient-hospital relationship has become jeopardized. Accordingly, more and more hospitals are becoming keenly aware of the importance of employee attitudes toward patients.
>
> While they have always tried to indoctrinate their employees with the importance of courtesy to their customers, increased competition in the heatlh care industry is prompting many hospitals to put some organized effort into making their employees' "courtesy conscious."

An article in the *London Sunday Times* in September 1988 about customer service started this way:

> "Our staff treat customers like rabble. They need a good talking to." (Manager)
>
> "If the company doesn't care about me, why should I care about the customer?" (Employee)
>
> "If the staff don't care about me, I'm not coming back." (Customer)

It seems the problems are similar everywhere.

PART THREE

A BLUEPRINT FOR IMPROVING SERVICE

☐ PHASE 1: AWARENESS AND ASSESSMENT

☐ PHASE 2: EXECUTIVE COMMITMENT

☐ PHASE 3: EDUCATION

☐ PHASE 4: ORGANIZATIONAL COMMITMENT

☐ PHASE 5: ACTION

☐ PHASE 6: EVALUATION

☐ PHASE 7: MAINTENANCE AND REVIEW

Becoming a service-oriented organization is similar to building a building: Although specific details such as construction materials, size, color, or height may vary, the process is basically the same, regardless of the type or size of building. You have to lay the foundation before putting up the walls. You build the second story before the third or fourth. You do the detailed interior work after the frame is in place. Finishing touches and landscaping usually come last. Sometimes several activities occur at once, such as laying roofing shingles and doing interior wiring. The process works for practically any building.

The *process* for becoming service-oriented is essentially the same in most organizations. Of course, the details of *implementing* this plan may be different for each organization because of an organization's unique culture, management style, current service levels, desired service levels, commitment and willingness to change, competitive activity, and point of entry,

The process contains seven phases. Each phase usually depends on the previous one, although the transition between phases is often gradual rather than abrupt and there can be some overlap between successive phases. Sometimes activities from several phases may occur simultaneously. The overall process can be easily adapted to work for any organization. The blueprint for the process is shown in the illustration, and the process is described below.

PHASE 1: AWARENESS AND ASSESSMENT

Many organizations aren't aware of the way their current beliefs and practices affect employees, customers, and the overall organization itself. They're also not aware of what's possible. The first step to improving service is for people to recognize the current state of things and to realize that something must change. This realization is often more difficult than it sounds, especially when top management believes, "Everything's fine here; we're very service-oriented." Different strategies may be used for increasing awareness and doing assessments, depending on whether the initiative comes from inside or outside the organization.

In some situations, the need is obvious. Eroding market share, unprofitable quarters or years, increasing competition, and similar factors generally spark some action. Too often, service levels are overlooked as unprofitable divisions are sold, management is replaced, and employees are told to "do better."

In calmer times, awareness of the need for change and the potential benefits can come from inside or outside the organization. The CEO may initiate the process. Senior managers may lobby to get the CEO's attention. Managers or department heads at any level may lobby *their* managers or senior managers.

Outside experts may be called on to help call attention to the situation and arouse interest. Frequently, data on customer satisfaction and employee satisfaction, bottom line figures, and comparisons to competitors are needed to get management's attention.

If the CEO of an organization sees the need and takes the initiative to make the organization more service-oriented, some of the initial steps may be different than if the CEO is unaware or unwilling to act.

PHASE 2: EXECUTIVE COMMITMENT

Unless the CEO sees the need for change, commits to the process, and actively supports new approaches, change will tend to occur very slowly, if at all. For the most rapid progress toward improved service, top management must recognize the value, benefits, and competitive advantages of such improvement.

Ideally, there should be both top-down and bottom-up efforts, and senior management should be involved, but in fact, change can and does occur at all levels. Harvard Business School professor D. Quinn Mills agrees that change *can* come from the bottom up:

> A few years back . . . I was fully convinced—along with other business analysts—that change could come only from the top; none other than the CEO had to be the one to commit to the new participative philosophy. Four years later, I've done a complete about-face. . . . More and more, the impetus for positive change and innovation is flowing in a bottom-up direction. The CEOs who recognize this trend as a competitive opportunity will be the ones who end up with the laurels.

Sometimes the CEO doesn't see the need for improving service, and there are only pockets of interest. Even when a CEO isn't interested, a division manager or vice president can improve service in his or her area. (In a few organizations, there's so little interest in changing that nothing will.) In any organization, a commitment to change should be obtained from the highest level possible.

Many CEOs are uncomfortable with and unskilled at speechmaking, "cheerleading," and other such skills needed to shift the focus, beliefs, and practices of their organizations. Many are unaccustomed to rubbing elbows with frontline employees; coming face-to-face with customers or endusers; or working in their own stores, plants, or offices. Many CEOs need new skills, tactful coaching and reassurance as they embark on a new approach.

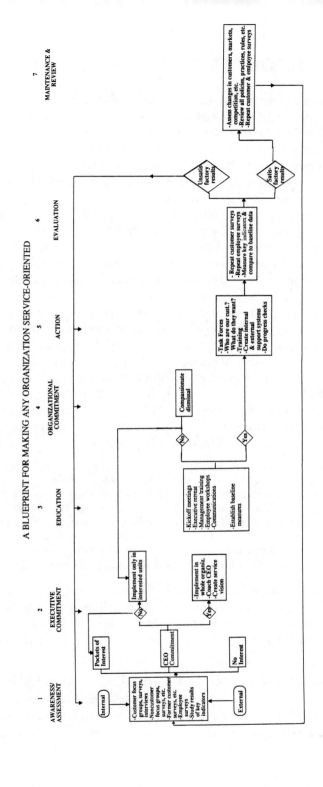

A BLUEPRINT FOR MAKING ANY ORGANIZATION SERVICE-ORIENTED

PHASE 3: EDUCATION

Regardless of where you start, the next phase involves educating employees at all levels about service, customers, performance results, and the changes that will be coming. People need to know that things will be different.

The education phase often begins with senior-level managers, frequently at an executive retreat. Discussions typically involve identifying problem areas, generating ideas for improvement, creating a service vision or philosophy for the organization, and determining next steps.

Once managers are willing to look critically at their own organization and challenge some of their beliefs, they should create a vision of what a customer-focused organization *should* look like. This vision will become the overriding, driving force in the organization. Successful service-driven organizations have clearly defined visions. From this vision comes action in the form of objectives and strategies for achieving the vision.

The next step involves sharing with employees the big picture and the service vision—explaining what's going to happen and telling employees what to expect. For a shift in focus to occur, there needs to be an interruption in the way people in the organization see things *now*. Without a deliberate interruption in current beliefs and practices, things generally continue to be done according to the status quo.

One objective of this phase is to begin examining existing beliefs—beliefs about how the organization should be, who the organization's customers are, what the customers want, how to provide what customers want, and so on.

The message to broadcast in this phase is this:

> Here's our vision for this organization. Here's where we're going. You'll be hearing lots more about it in the weeks and months to come. All of us are going to be examining what we do and how we do it. For now, we want you to know what's going on. And we want you to look at how each of you carries out that vision in your job. There will be meetings, training programs, task forces, and lot of other activities. We want you to participate in all of these. This is not just busywork or something to get excited about for a few weeks. We're talking about a new direction for this organization. We *will* do this. And we want your help in defining how.

Many organizations hold kickoff meetings, rallies, or small group meetings, and they begin an active communications campaign using newsletters. Employees have an opportunity to start shifting their perspective, beliefs, and practices to align with the organization's new philosophy, direction, and practices.

PHASE 4: ORGANIZATIONAL COMMITMENT

Since organizations are compromised of individuals, each employee must accept that he or she is *personally* responsible for achieving the organization's vision.

Each employee must also create his or her own personal vision that aligns with that of the organization. Without this personal commitment, the steps required to achieve the vision will not occur.

Without individual commitment to a new vision, the transformation will die. People must commit to a new organization—to a new vision—often before they know *how* the change will be achieved. This is very difficult for many people. Analytical types will resist, insisting they must know the path before they can agree to the destination.

During this phase, managers also meet individually with each employee to discuss the importance of service and the organization's new direction. Employees must decide if there's still a fit between them and the organization. Some will adapt to the changes easily; some never will.

Managers at all levels must commit to and participate in the process if it is to succeed. Most managers at all levels will need to take on new roles and need to be coached on these. They must also learn how to help their employees cope with the changes that will occur. They need to reinforce new ideas and practices, follow up on and reinforce training, support and reassure people who get discouraged or frustrated during the transition, reward people for wins, and continually remind people of the new approach. Managers should also learn how to compassionately dismiss employees who no longer want to be part of the team.

PHASE 5: ACTION

This phase—implementation—is often the longest. It involves redesigning the organization. The action phase includes the following steps:

- ☐ Defining customers and their needs, expectations, and satisfaction levels; determining what customers really want and how well they think you're providing it
- ☐ Identifying your important points of customer contact (also called "moments of truth"—see Idea 6 in Part Four)
- ☐ Defining what excellent service is; setting standards
- ☐ Creating and running quality service teams and task forces to examine and change policies, practices, systems, forms, or anything else that isn't customer-focused
- ☐ Providing training to improve employee self-esteem, confidence, knowledge, and skills
- ☐ Creating and implementing support systems to keep the process moving, handle problems, and acknowledge and reward employees and work units
- ☐ Doing progress checks to measure results and communicate these to the organization

The action phase also involves shifting the focus of the organization to the customer and giving responsibility for customer satisfaction to the front line. Unfortunately, many organizations start with this phase without doing the previous ones. As a result, they usually have less-than-satisfactory results. Change will also take *longer* to come about if the prior four phases have not been completed.

Employees at all levels must be actively involved during this phase in analyzing policies and practices, serving on task forces, developing and implementing new ideas and procedures, and getting involved in training. It's also critical that task forces and quality service teams cut across departmental and functional lines to begin breaking down these barriers and hasten the process of shifting the focus away from internal concerns to external ones.

PHASE 6: EVALUATION

When the initial transformation has been completed, the organization must be able to evaluate what has been done. Evaluation enables the organization to assess where it was when it started this process, what was done to make a change, and where the organization is now. The evaluation involves measuring key indicators and comparing them to earlier results.

In this phase, it's important to measure the accomplishments of groups and individuals. Group progress should be measured against goals: How well has a branch, a store, or a department done as a team in meeting its service goals? Where possible, measure organizational progress as well: market share, profits, number of customers, customer satisfaction levels, and so on.

Individual performance should be monitored throughout the entire process to determine how well people are meeting goals and working to standards. Where problems exist, they should be addressed through coaching, training, or disciplinary action.

Based on evaluation results, the organization may need to fine tune some of the new activities or return to other phases of the improvement process.

PHASE 7: MAINTENANCE AND REVIEW

Becoming a service-oriented organization is one thing; *staying* that way is another. Customer-focused service is not a "program" that ends after a certain time or after all the training sessions are done. It's an ongoing process. It's like going on a diet: unless you change your eating habits permanently, you'll eventually put the weight back on. For most people, dieting involves a constant vigil. Physicians and nutritionists tell us most people don't keep up with it. Instead, they diet seriously for a while, lose weight, return to old eating habits, gain weight, and then repeat the process.

Organizations often do the same thing with service improvement. They get excited about service for a while, improve service, return to old service habits, and then repeat the process. This final phase is designed to prevent—or at least reduce—this common behavior pattern.

Because customers, markets, employees, products, technology, and everything else change constantly, organizations must change, too. It's essential to have a process for systematically reviewing the vision, policies, procedures, and commitment of the organization so they can be changed as needed. It's also important to continually find ways to renew commitment and energy, challenge people, train people, recognize and reward outstanding performance, and make necessary adjustments in the organization.

PART FOUR

HOW TO IMPROVE SERVICE IN *YOUR* ORGANIZATION

☐ FORTY-FIVE SPECIFIC IDEAS AND STRATEGIES

☐ PUTTING IDEAS INTO ACTION

FORTY-FIVE SPECIFIC IDEAS AND STRATEGIES

Some of the ideas presented in this section can by themselves improve service, but most of them work best in combination with others. A critical lesson from service-oriented organizations is that it's important to apply all of the applicable service-oriented practices in combination. Implementing just one or two ideas—or even the majority of ideas—out of this list will not achieve for your organization the degree of success that service leaders have. There is an enhanced effect that occurs when they're all practiced in combination.

The 45 topics in this section are arranged in a suggested order, but there is no right or wrong way to implement the ideas presented. Progression toward a service orientation is not a rigid, lockstep process. Rather, common sense and practicality dictate that some things come before others. It seems reasonable to start by making a commitment to improving service. Next, it seems prudent to determine who your customers are and what they want before doing too many other things. Creating a service vision and setting standards should come before training, or you may be teaching the wrong things. Maintaining the momentum and measuring results has to occur after there is some movement in a new direction and there *are* some results to measure.

You could argue that almost any topic should come before or after any other topic, or that a certain topic should fall somewhere else on the list, but exact order is not important. The "correct" sequence actually depends on the current situation and the desire to change in each organization; it will never be exactly the same in any two organizations. So it's not essential that you do things in a prescribed order. The second section of this part, entitled "Putting Ideas into Action," will help you figure out the best order for implementing service ideas in your organization and will show you how to get started with the change process.

1. Make a long-term commitment to service

At a seminar on customer service, Don Munson, vice president of Lennox Industries, was asked what single piece of advice he could give organizations that want to become more service-oriented. He said, "Don't start it unless you're prepared to stick with it." He also said, "Expect some additional costs at the bottom line at first. But if you stick with it, the profits will be repaid."

The two important ideas here are *long-term* and *commitment*. To make a difference in your organization, recognize that you can't change it overnight. Improving service is not a one-time thing. You must be in it for the long term. If you're not willing or able to devote several years to changing the focus and practices of your organization, you may be better off doing nothing because at least you won't raise people's expectations needlessly.

Commitment is also essential. It's a necessary first step. Without it, little change will happen. You—and your whole organization—must essentially accept and declare the following:

> I recognize that we must change our approach to focus solely on our customers, and I realize this will require many changes. I also realize what the payoffs will be for doing this and what the prices will be for *not* doing it. I realize this will be a long-term, ongoing process, not a one-time "program." I realize it will be difficult and painful at times. I realize we will end up with a different company in some significant ways. I also realize we can't afford *not* to do this. I am committing all the resources of this organization to the process of transformation. I will personally oversee this process. Further, this effort is much larger than just me; and the rest of the organization has committed to continue this process even if I'm no longer here.

Becoming a customer-focused organization requires a commitment to change. These are not traditional times, so traditional approaches in any area of your business won't guarantee success.

Recognize that changing the focus and activities of an organization requires a shift in the way people think and act. Shifting their focus and changing their beliefs and practices will be a difficult, uncomfortable process for many executives, managers, and employees. It will test management's commitment many times. It will probably mean firing some people who no longer fit or who refuse to change.

2. Accept the responsibility for improving service

In many organizations, no one "owns" responsibility for satisfying customers. Everyone assumes it's someone else's job, so no one does it.

For example, think about what happens when a customer's order is late, or the customer doesn't get what was ordered (maybe it's the wrong model number, size, color, etc.). Customers often say something like, "What's the matter with you people? Can't you do anything right?" And the response is often, "It's not my fault. My job is just to install it/ship it/repair it."

It's critical that all the employees in your organization—regardless of job title or area of responsibility—see that they are "it." Individual employees *are* the organization, and each one is personally responsible for meeting every customer's needs. Responsibility for satisfying customers must belong to *everyone*, from the CEO down. It cannot be delegated to a few people or to a department. Serving customers must be everyone's number-one responsibility.

The following approach must be emphasized to all employees: You can only control what *you* do, so you must act at all times as if you are the *only one* in the organization who can help customers. In everything you do, especially when dealing with customers, assume that no one else in the organization is available at that moment to help you help the customer. You have to do what is right for the customer and what is best for the company. You're *it*. It's your responsibility.

The customer-focused, service-oriented way of accepting responsibility for an incorrect delivery might sound like this: "I'll bet that really put you in a bind. Let me take care of that for you. As I understand it, you were supposed to get 20 model A widgets, but you got 36 model B widgets instead. You can count on me to straighten it out for you. I'll call you before lunch today to tell you when to expect the model A's you ordered. Don't worry, I'll take care of it." And wouldn't it be surprising if this came *not* from a customer service representative or a sales or marketing person, but from an accountant, a mail-room employee, or a custodian, because that person understood that his or her real job is to take care of customers (even if that's not what that employee spends most of the time doing in a normal day).

3. Identify your customers

Your customers may be called clients, citizens, patients, passengers, tenants, taxpayers, students, voters, guests, members, parishioners, or some other name. Whatever they're called in your organization, they're all people whose needs must be served. In many cases, there are several *different* "customer" groups. For example, in order to survive, a college must serve its board, its alumni, its faculty, its donors, its students, the legislature in some cases, the parents of students, business and industry, and the community it's in.

Before you can serve your customers, you must know who they are—which is often not as easy, or as obvious, as it sounds. There are many ways to classify customers. I use five broad categories: internal customers, external customers, potential customers, former customers, and stakeholders.

Internal customers.   Identify the people, departments, divisions that depend on the products (results, outputs) or services (expertise, knowledge) you provide. Determine who you "sell" your products or service to inside your organization.

External customers.   If you or your department deals directly with customers, identify who your customers are. Do you sell to intermediaries before your product or service reaches the end user? If so, identify all of these. Who buys your products or services? How often? Your external customers may be:

□ Direct personal customers: Individuals you sell your products or services to directly for their personal use.

□ Indirect personal customers: Individuals who buy your products or services through another party (someone else actually buys your products or components from you to resell to end users). For example, car manufacturers sell to dealers, a restaurant franchiser sells to a franchise owner, and many insurance companies work through independent agents.

□ Businesses: Organizations that use your products or services to create other products to sell either to individuals or to other businesses. Makers of electrical components sell to car manufacturers. Candymakers such as Mars, Inc., may sell their products to wholesalers, who sell them to retailers, who sell them to consumers.

□ Combination customers: Organizations, such as airlines that sell directly to individuals and businesses, as well as indirectly, through agents.

Potential customers.   Most of the books, films, and seminars today talk about service to customers. They emphasize the importance of finding out what *customers* want by means of surveys, interviews, comment cards and correspondence, and other methods. While all this information gathering is essential, it is somewhat myopic. These activities only tell you how to get better at what you're doing with people who are *already* customers.

Very few programs mention *potential* customers or prospects—people or businesses that have never been customers but could be if you offered something they wanted or needed, if they knew about it, and if they could afford it. And the books and programs don't say anything about how to attract, and retain, those customers who are *not* doing business with you.

In *Service America!*, Ron Zemke and Karl Albrecht tell about an art museum that wanted to attract more customers. To learn about its customers' interests, the museum surveyed customers who visited the museum. Although the survey results proved enlightening to the museum's management, I think the museum was approaching the wrong people. To find out how to attract more people to the museum, the survey should do more than just ask the people who are already *there* why they came in. It should also ask people who *don't* visit the museum why they don't and what it would take to get them there. It is important to identify people who are not customers but could be.

Former customers.   We know that approximately one in four customers may be unhappy with some aspect of your organization at any given time. And as many as 70 percent won't tell you. They'll just take their business elsewhere. Many organizations don't even know they're losing that many customers each year. And they don't know why.

Identify those customers who have stopped doing business with you or who are doing less business than they once did. Then find out why. Idea 5 (below) will give you some suggestions on what to ask these customers.

Stakeholders.   Stakeholders are people or groups who have a sincere interest in your organization and in whether it succeeds or goes out of business. Stakeholders include customers and employees (internal customers), as well as the following:

Owners/stockholders

Governing boards

Government agencies

Regulatory agencies

The public (local communities)

Consumer affairs groups

Special-interest groups

For example, the members of the board of directors of a university aren't actually customers (unless they have children who are students or family members who are university employees). But they do have a significant interest in the institution and the service it provides. If it's a public university, the state legislature also has a vested interest. And usually the local community has an interest. In fact, decisions that may be popular with customers—i.e., students—may be unpopular with other stakeholders.

If appropriate for your organization, you may also want to identify your stakeholders and learn what each expects.

4. Find out what your internal customers need, want, and expect from you

Every person, department, and company is both a customer and a supplier. If you're a parts assembler in a manufacturing plant, your "supplier" is whoever makes the components you get. Your "customer" is the next person in the manufacturing process. If you're in the finance department, you're a supplier of credit to other departments. You're also a customer of the data processing department, benefits department, and other departments. If you're a secretary, you supply phone messages, correspondence, files, and other "products" or "services" to others. You're also a customer of the mail room.

An internal customer is anyone for whom work, products, or services are produced or intended. This customer can be another person, your boss, a group of peers, another department, or another division. Internal customers buy various products and services, just like external customers do.

Employees must learn who their customers are and who the end users are, and what both want. Employees also need to see how they fit in to the whole picture. They should know what happens to their work when it leaves their work area—how their customers use it and/or how the end user uses it.

Employees or organizational units should be encouraged to "call on" their internal customers, just as salespeople call on external customers, to find out what the internal customers expect. Some areas you can pursue with internal customers are as follows:

What are their priorities, major projects?

What problems are they facing?

How can you help them with these problems?

How can you make their lives easier?

If they had to go outside to get the service or products you provide, what would they want from a supplier?

How do you stack up in providing the products or services they need?

What would they like you to keep doing? Stop doing? Do more of? Do more often?

Do you respond in a timely manner?

How well do you meet their needs?

How's your communication?

Are there times you don't meet their needs?

What happens when you don't meet their needs?

What suggestions do they have for improving that situation?

Are you usually friendly and helpful?

Then, just as in an outside sales call, explain what *you* can provide in the way of information, technology, people, equipment, or other resources.

Employees and work units should also identify their internal "suppliers" or "vendors" and should establish standards and clarify what they expect from these vendors. Some organizations have people visit or work in other departments to "live in the other person's shoes" awhile.

5. Find out what your external customers and end users need, want, and expect from you

The same applies for external customers. It's not always easy to know what customers want. One bank executive we know says there are two kinds of bank customers. Customers of one type demand highly personalized service and want bank employees to be all smiles, to recognize them, to call them by name, and to treat them like family. These customers will tell you *everything* that's happened to them since they were in last (which was probably yesterday).

The other customer type cares only about speed and convenience. These customers want to deal with banks that are close to where they live or work and that are fast, efficient, and inexpensive. They want to get in and out quickly. They don't want to "visit," they just want to bank. These people love automatic teller machines and would be happy if they never spoke to a teller.

The next few pages present some specific ways to discover what *your* customers want.

1. Conduct market research.   Determine:

☐ The most likely buyers or users of your product or service.

☐ What customers expect when they buy the type of product or service you offer.

☐ What customers expect from the products or services you offer, regardless of who provides it. For example, what do hotel guests expect from *any* hotel?

☐ What's most important to customers.

☐ What's least important to customers.

☐ What customers would be willing to pay a little extra for.

☐ How you are doing at providing these extras and where you can improve.

☐ How you compare to your competitors.

☐ What customer buying motives are—why would someone buy what you're offering?

☐ What else is available that could meet those same customer needs.

2. Create a prototype and test it.

☐ For new products or services where there is no customer awareness or perceived need, use focus groups, prototypes, and test markets to gauge the desirability of the item or service.

☐ Use interviews or focus groups to talk to potential customers. Include people you think would be most likely to buy the product or service, as well as other types of people in case your initial assumptions are off base. Ask people who are *not* part of that group questions such as: If this product or service were available, would you buy it? Why? (Use their answers in your advertising.) How much would you pay for it? How does the name strike you? What other features would you like to see in this product or service?

☐ Use test groups or begin offering the service on a limited basis in a controlled market. See what works and what doesn't and make changes as needed. (Some automobile companies create clay models of cars before building prototypes and ask customers for their reactions and ideas.)

☐ Be prepared to shift your original ideas, concepts, or design radically if necessary, based on feedback from potential customers and test-market users.

☐ Be prepared to drop the product or service and move on to something else if it doesn't fly. Try lots of things. Get them off the drawing boards and out where the customers can make judgments about them. If they work, fine. If not, rethink them or drop them. Try another idea, get it out the door, test it, and keep the process going. Tests don't have to be large-scale or involve a lot of time or capital. Keep them controllable.

☐ Don't forget about former customers. You might want to ask: Why did they leave? Whom are they doing business with now? What do they like most about those they do business with now? What would it take for them to come back to doing business with you?

3. Define a key customer group.   Identify a group of people whose opinions you value and who do business with you on a regular basis. Ask them to notify you of good and bad experiences they have had with your organization. Offer them something in return—discounts or something else that expresses your thanks for their assistance. You can also rely on this group as a sounding board for new products, services, promotional ideas, or pricing issues. If possible, get them together periodically for a brainstorming session. Make a big deal of it.

Weyerhaeuser regularly invites some of its best customers to attend in-house seminars as "students" and to provide input to the company. The sessions are frequently attended by the Weyerhaeuser executives and managers who want to hear customers tell them what the company needs to do to be more customer-focused. Charley Bingham, CEO of the Forest Products Company, says, "Understanding customer needs is everybody's business . . . not just [the business of] the marketing people. Our only reason to exist as a company is to serve customer needs, and we need everyone in the company pulling on the oars together to do that."

AT&T includes several key managers from its major customers as part of its executive development program. AT&T makes it clear to customers that this program is not a sales meeting. The invitation letter says, "We need your help in gaining a better understanding of the needs of our customers; what you see as our major strengths and weaknesses; and your recommendations for how AT&T can improve customer relations with clients in general and you in particular." The letter goes on to say: "[B]e as candid and critical as you like. Our objective is to see ourselves as our customers see us."

And Xerox invites senior representatives of major customers to make presentations at its week-long executive development program on what they like and don't like about Xerox.

4. Go visit customers.   Get out of your office and go where the customers are. See how they use your products. See what problems they may be having and what new ventures they're working on. Also, instead of sending only executives or managers to visit customers, also send the frontline people who actually make the product or who have the most contact with the customer.

Disney requires every executive (including the president, finance people, personnel managers, and others) to spend at least 1 week a year in the park working shifts. The executives take tickets, sell hot dogs, drive monorails, unload buses, and do similar tasks.

Nordstrom requires buyers in each department to spend half their time on the sales floor so they can learn what customers want.

Managers at the Southland Corporation must each work at least one full shift in one of their 7-Eleven stores. Managers also regularly go with franchisees to knock on neighborhood doors, giving residents coupons and comment cards to send to corporate headquarters. (Some companies open a small number of retail stores for the sole purpose of getting close to customers.)

5. Invite customers to see you.   Invite customers to see your operation and to meet the frontline people who make the products or deal with them most frequently. Make your frontline people your ambassadors—let *them* conduct the tours and explain their operations. Many managers report that these visits frequently result in ideas and suggestions from customers about improvements and new products.

6. Use "shoppers."   There are several ways to have your business "shopped." The easiest is to call or visit your own organization; or you can have your spouse or friends do this and record their impressions.

There are also companies that hire shoppers. Such people have been used for years to thwart shoplifting. Many companies are now using shopper services to measure their own service levels.

Shoppers may order food at a fast-food restaurant and clock how long they wait, buy gasoline at filling stations, test-drive new cars, place orders for flowers, or shop for televisions or stereos to see how well they are served as customers. Most shopper services use a checklist that is developed in conjunction with the client, so shoppers evaluate specific things about specific businesses. For example, one of our clients, a restaurant chain, asked us to develop training programs for them. We helped them define what their servers, bartenders, and hostesses should do and how to do it. Then we developed a shopper checklist so the shoppers could determine if people were doing what they had learned in training.

An Atlanta-based company, Sertec, has taken the idea of using shoppers even further by relying on customers to provide information. Sertec provides in-store messages that encourage customers to call an 800 number to complain, or praise, almost any type business—a cleaner's service, a trucker's driving, a restaurant's food or service, and so on. The idea behind the 800 number is that many people are more willing to pick up the phone and call about poor service than to write a letter about it. If they do neither, management often doesn't know about customers who were dissatisfied because they just go away and in many cases don't come back.

Sertec president George Zimmermann tells about a regular customer at a restaurant who called the toll-free number when she'd been locked out of the restaurant after arriving one minute after they locked the doors for the evening. In the process of the call, Sertec learned that the woman was elderly and diabetic. She had eaten at this restaurant every day for the past several years, spending approximately $3,000 a year. This information was quickly passed to the company's management and a fast phone call to the store enabled the manager to rectify the situation before the woman got to her car, thus saving an important customer. Without the service, she may have just become upset and taken her business elsewhere.

One Sertec customer, a restaurant owner, verifies the usefulness of the 800 number: "I like the instantaneous response. It obviates the reply card. By the time it's filled out and mailed, the trail is cold. It's too late. If I get a call about a restroom or bad food, I can call immediately and have it checked."

Sertec also helps its clients learn what customers like (and don't like) by tabulating the complaints and compliments it hears and then reporting to clients which products and services customers like and don't like.

---

6. Identify your "moments of truth"

Every organization has a series of events that make up its service cycle. These events are easier to spot in some organizations than others, but all organizations have them.

For instance, a simplified service cycle for an equipment manufacturer might be as follows:

1 Prospects are contacted by phone.
2 Sales calls are made.
3 Customer places order.
4 Equipment arrives and is installed.
5 Employees are trained.
6 Adjustments are made, if needed.
7 Invoice is sent.
8 Payment is received.

For a hospital stay for appendicitis, the cycle might go like this:

1 Check-in at admitting office
2 Completion of forms and paperwork

3 Checking into room and orientation

4 Initial tests and blood work

5 Meals

6 Prep for surgery

7 Surgery and recovery

8 Recuperation and follow-up tests

9 Discharge from hospital

10 Invoice

11 Payment

For each event, there are many opportunities for customers and the organization to interact. These opportunities are called "moments of truth." Jan Carlzon, president of Scandinavian Airlines System, is credited with coining this term. He says a *moment of truth* is any event in which a customer comes into contact with any aspect of the organization, however remote, and has an opportunity to form an impression.

Here's how Carlzon explains it:

> Last year, each of our 10 million customers came into contact with approximately five of our employees, and this contact lasted approximately 15 seconds per time. Thus Scandinavian Airlines System is "created" in the minds of our customers 50 million times a year, 15 seconds at a time. These 50 million "moments of truth" are the moments that ultimately determine whether our company will succeed or fail. They are the moments when we must prove to our customers that our company is their best alternative.

These moments of truth provide thousands of opportunities to provide good, average, or poor service. Rick Johnson, manager of business seminars for Walt Disney World, asks: "How many times will your people on the front lines be tested today? And how many times will they succeed in earning or renewing the respect and loyalty of another customer or client? Your organization's reputation, its investment in facilities, products, services, and staff, even its prospects for the future, are all on the line every time your people deal with your customers."

Keep in mind that moments of truth include *any* contact customers have with your organization. This includes your ads, your people's appearance, your correspondence, your owner's manuals, your invoices, how your people sound over the phone, how competent and helpful your employees are, and so on.

All of these encounters with your organization provide opportunities for customers (or potential customers) to form an impression. And these impressions are largely based on customer *perceptions*. So if your correspondence is sloppy—if it contains errors and typos—people may believe your products are also of low quality. If your office or reception area is dingy and dirty and has worn furniture, people may have a hard time believing you can provide them with state-of-the-art products, technology, or information.

Most organizations don't have a common understanding of their service cycle or moments of truth. They haven't identified all the planned and unplanned opportunities to make an impression. The result is that service just sort of "happens," instead of being planned and managed. On the other hand, service-oriented organizations *manage* the customer's experience.

Here's an example of what one company did as a result of identifying its moments of truth. Most visitors to the Disney parks are amazed at how clean they are. If you've ever visited any of the parks, you may recall seeing cast members sweeping streets and sidewalks and picking up trash. While keeping the parks clean is part of their job, their main job is to give directions and assistance to park guests.

Disney management knows that in a setting like their parks, with so many people visiting, there are lots of opportunities for people to ask directions, need restrooms, get first aid, or find lost children. They also know that most people don't mind interrupting the work of someone performing a noncritical, low-status job to get help or ask directions. So Disney puts lots of these cast members out on the streets.

However, first Disney gives them 3½ days of training. They learn about the Disney culture, and they learn where all the attractions are and how to get to them; where first aid stations are; where the restrooms are; what to do if they see a lost, crying child; and so on.

Those seemingly unplanned encounters with a Disney employee are not unplanned. Disney knows what it means to manage every moment of truth—even something as simple as asking a street sweeper for directions.

So the first step in managing your moments of truth is to identify them. You must know what the normal, routine cycle of events is whereby customers come in contact with your organization. And you must know what the out-of-the-ordinary events are likely to be.

So far, we've talked about normal, routine, planned moments of truth. There are also unplanned moments of truth: special requests, unusual situations, unexpected breakdowns or delays. These are the ones that can cause you the most serious problems, especially if your training focuses on following the rules. These are the situations that "what-to-do-if" training doesn't cover. And these are the moments of truth that help distinguish service leaders from the rest of the pack.

Traditional companies believe they have little or no control over what customers think or do. They frequently take the attitude that customers should automatically recognize what makes their products or services better than those of their competitors. Customer-focused companies, on the other hand, believe *they* are responsible for communicating their differences to customers. They make sure that every employee knows what those differences are—what makes their products or services better.

In *your* organization, you must define your service cycle. It might help to think of your service cycle in terms of six basic activities:

1 Attracting customers (advertising; visual appeal of your products, place of business, stationery; telephone manners)
2 Taking the order (paperwork, time, accuracy of ordering information, handling of special requests)
3 Processing the order (shipment or delivery time, stock conditions, back orders)
4 Delivering the product or service (time, accuracy, damage)
5 Following up (billing, installation, training, service)
6 Handling problems (errors or problems with any of the above; also repairs, breakdowns, or adjustments)

Then, for each step in your service cycle, identify the moments of truth. For each moment of truth, ask yourself: Is it planned or unplanned? How long does it last? What do customers expect? What are all the ways it can go wrong (meaning we deliver less than the customer expects)? How can we prevent things from going wrong? Finally, ask yourself: How can we improve our moments of truth?

Answering these kinds of questions is not something you can do tomorrow over your morning coffee. It takes time. Get input from many people, especially at the front lines. Keep in mind there are also service cycles and moments of truth *inside* your organization. Each department should also define its service cycles and moments of truth, just as the organization as a whole does for its external customers. For example, what are all the possible points of contact with other units and departments in the organization? What are all the ways other people or units can form an impression of you or your work unit? (See Part Five for some additional examples of moments of truth, in organizations such as Burlington Coat Factory, Walgreen's, and Sears.

7. Take your pulse. Find out how you're doing now

You won't know what to change unless you know where the problems are or what areas can be improved. In many organizations, top managers really don't know how well they're doing. Of course they look at quarterly reports and other financial indicators, but there's more to an organization than its bottom line.

Development Dimensions Inc. surveyed over 2,000 customers and customer-contact people in *Fortune's* Industrial 500 and Service 500 companies. The survey identified 9 customer service skills and 17 competencies important for frontline employees, and it asked both customers and employees to rate frontline employees on these 26 categories. On every item, customer-contact people believed they were providing better service than customers did. *You* may think you're doing better than your customers think you are.

In many organizations, the "facts" that tell managers how well they're doing are largely assumptions, guesses, or hoped-for conditions. Many managers really don't know the facts, but if they don't they should find out what the facts are.

There are 11 critical areas that affect your service levels and service quality. They are:

1 The business, industry, or field you're in
2 Your organization (company, association, etc.)
3 Your products or services
4 Your philosophy and beliefs
5 Your customers
6 Your competition
7 Your suppliers
8 Your people
9 Your systems, policies, and procedures
10 Your service orientation
11 Your results

Appendix A contains an organizational self-assessment that will help you to determine how well you're doing in each critical area. To get the most benefit from this assessment, you must be absolutely, totally sure of the answers—no guessing, estimating, wishing, or hoping for answers is allowed. You must be absolutely certain of your answers, and in many cases, you must know *how* you know. If you can complete the survey in Appendix A without talking to anyone else in your organization or gathering information other than what's in your head right now, you're probably guessing, hoping, or lying.

There are many ways to take your organization's pulse. You can use the survey in the appendix, create your own, or hire a consultant. The important thing is that you do it.

8. Meet and exceed customer expectations

Service quality is largely determined by customer perceptions—their beliefs about what they're *getting* compared to what they *expected* to get. Perceptions are highly subjective. They may not be logical, accurate, or fair, but they're real and they're powerful.

One of the challenges we all face is that customers today expect more than ever before. People expect products to work. They expect to get what they pay for. They expect to get the desired *results* from products. They expect to look better, feel better, do their work easier and faster, or experience whatever results the product or service promised to deliver. They expect services such as health care, transportation, and financial advising to meet their needs.

One aspect of customer expectations is embodied in the old adage that "you can never go back." Once they've experienced great products, restaurants, cars, or service, most people won't tolerate anything less.

I travel a lot in my business. Over the years, I've stayed in countless hotels and motels and eaten in innumerable restaurants. I've experienced the good, the bad, and the ugly. Once I've had certain amenities and had a certain level of service, I subconsciously set a new standard. Once I've seen what's possible, I begin to compare every subsequent hotel or restaurant with the best I've had. Others who travel frequently have the same experience. They tell me their image of "the best" becomes a composite of all their experiences and, like many things, can become distorted. The image may be better or worse than reality, but that doesn't matter. All that matters is that the image *is* the standard. And you can never go back, because anything less just doesn't measure up.

Of course, many customers have certain minimal expectations. In a hotel or restaurant, people *expect* certain levels of cleanliness, speed, and quality of food. When you pick up a telephone, you expect to hear a dial tone.

A storm shut down Southern Bell's directory assistance system for 8 hours in the northern part of Georgia recently. Customers had no directory assistance. One Bell operator commented on customers' reactions: "Its unreal! We go out for a few hours and get called every name in the book!"

Once we get used to a certain level of service, we expect it.

Theodore Levitt, a professor at Harvard, has an interesting way of describing expectations. In *The Marketing Imagination*, he describes four levels of attributes for both tangible and intangible products: generic, expected, augmented, and potential.

Generic.   This level describes the bare minimum necessary to do business, meet customer needs, or provide a service. These are the "table stakes." Without these you're not even in the game.

For example, the bare minimum needed to open a retail store might be a room with merchandise, racks or tables, and a cash register. The bare minimum for a hotel might be rooms with beds, dressers, lamps, sheets, and towels. And the bare minimum for a medical practice might be a license to practice, an office, and the basic equipment (chairs, stethoscopes, etc.).

Without this generic "product," you have nothing to offer. But the basics alone are not enough. People also have minimum expectations that exceed the generic product or service.

Expected.   These are the minimum expectations or purchase conditions that go beyond the generic product or service. They can include such things as right price, delivery, installation, post-purchase service or maintenance, and training.

In retail, most customers expect reasonable and convenient hours, the right selection or merchandise mix, reasonable prices, and clean merchandise neatly displayed. In a hotel room, most people expect heat and air conditioning, a phone, and a television. They also expect the room to be clean, have no bad odors, have no bugs, etc. And most people going to a doctor or dentist expect the office to look like a doctor's office, to be clean, and to have magazines; they expect staff to be dressed like health care professionals; and they expect to be seen within a reasonable time.

Augmented.   Many organizations offer just what customers expect and little else. But as competition increases, organizations must distinguish themselves from others by improving their products or services. Augmented products (or services) go beyond what the customer expects by offering more than customers think they need or have been accustomed to. I think of augmented products or services as those that make people think (or say), "Boy, this is really nice!"

Augmented service in retail might include unique merchandise; enough salespeople so customers don't have to hunt for items; staff who are knowledgable and friendly, and who approach customers first; early notification of sales; refreshments for customers; and a personal phone call from a salesperson to tell you about some item you'd like.

Augmented service in a hotel might be larger-than-normal rooms at no extra cost, movie channels available in each room at no extra charge, in-room check-out, hot tubs, 24-hour room service, hangers that don't lock in, beverage bars in rooms, bathrobes, hair dryers, movie rental, restaurant and lounge on premise, pool, workout rooms, and so on.

In a doctor's office augmented service might include no waiting or a phone call if the doctor is more than 30 minutes behind schedule, juice or coffee for patients, telephones you can use while waiting, toys for kids, and so on.

Unfortunately, the augmented product or service can become the expected. Beverages and meals on airplanes, drive-through cleaners, 24-hour groceries, payment by credit card, and free TV in hotel rooms were all first offered to augment what customers expected. Now these amenities have become what is expected. So organizations must continue to augment their products or services. Otherwise, customers become jaded—they either become price shoppers or they switch to someone who's offering something new or different. (However, Levitt says that not all customers want all augmentations—some would rather pay a lower price than have the "extras.")

Potential.   Levitt makes the distinction that "augmented" is everything that has been done or is being done to attract or keep the customer, while "potential" is anything that could be done but isn't being done yet.

The sky's the limit for potential services. And potential for one organization may already exist as part of augmented service in another organization.

In retail, live entertainment or a van that brings items to customers (instead of customers' going to the store) may be possible. Potential service may also be coming to *you* if they mess up your order.

Or how about a hotel that rents rooms for 24 hours starting from time you check in, so late-arriving guests don't have to check out at 11 A.M. (a convenient time for hotels, but not for guests). Guests could leave their luggage and come back after a meeting or sightseeing to shower and change. A Dallas hotel already uses this check-out schedule. And a Chicago hotel has a "blizzard kit" for guests who get stranded in the Windy City during the winter. Kits include toiletries such as deodorant, toothbrush, razor, and underwear. The hotel even has separate men's and ladies' kits.

What if doctors sent flowers to surgery patients or had Saturday or evening hours? Some do!

Every customer has expectations. They have them as customers of restaurants, dentists, hospitals, retail stores, and other firms they do business with. They have expectations in business dealings, too. A customer's expectations of your organization are a result of many factors, including previous experience with similar organizations, previous experience with your organization, awareness of your advertising, word of mouth about your organization and its output, and promises by your employees.

Over time, these cumulative evaluations create an image of your organization, its products and services, its credibility, and its reputation. And, as the TARP studies showed, people's satisfaction (based on their perceptions) of one product can affect the sale of others.

Simply put, customer satisfaction is the difference between what customers expect and what they get. When organizations exceed customer expectations, service is perceived as being good; when organizations fail to meet expectations, service is perceived as being poor, (see illustration).

Parasuraman and his associates confirmed this in their study of service quality. Their research shows the importance of discrepancies in expectation and perception in six areas. The wider the gaps, the less likely it is that customers will be satisfied. And the more areas that are involved, the poorer service will

How Perceptions and Expectations Affect the Quality of Service

What's
expected

_____

↑
gap   Poor service
↓

What's
delivered

_____

The larger the gap between what's expected and what's
delivered, the poorer the service is perceived to be.

What's   What's
expected   delivered _____ Acceptable service

When what's delivered is the same as what was expected,
service is perceived to be acceptable.

What's
delivered

_____

↑
gap   Exceptional service
↓

What's
expected

_____

The more service exceeds what was expected, the better it is
perceived to be.

be perceived to be. If there are only small gaps in all but one or two areas, service is likely to be seen as good. If there are large gaps in four or five areas, service is likely to be perceived as poor. The service quality "gaps" are listed below:

What management thinks customers want	What customers actually expect
What management believes customers expect	Management's ability to set guidelines and standards for providing what it believes customers expect
The service guidelines and standards of the organization	Actual delivery by employees
What the organization tells customers to expect	What customers actually get at point of delivery
What employees actually do at point of delivery	How customers perceive what employees do
What customers expect	What customers perceive they get

The real issue here is that, like it or not, customers are always evaluating your products and service. Sometimes the evaluations are done consciously, sometimes unconsciously. Sometimes there are clear-cut expectations ("You said it would be here at 10:00 Tuesday"), and sometimes the expectations are more intangible or emotional ("This looks like a nice place to eat," or "I just don't think this will fit the bill"). And the scorecard we all use is based on our individual expectations and our perceptions.

How important are customer perceptions? A study at the University of Minnesota Medical School showed that patients decide how much confidence to place in a doctor based on the doctor's appearance. Although such perceptions have nothing to do with a doctor's medical competence, many patients apparently *think* they do.

Unfortunately, as Parasuraman's study showed, what customers perceive is often not what organizations intend to deliver. The message is: It isn't good service unless the customer says so. It's not good just because engineering designed it well or production made it expertly with the best materials. You may have a well-designed, highly crafted product that is made to the highest standards, and customers still might not like it or want it. Remember the example earlier in the book about the electric components company whose switches were so good they outlasted their customers? Great product, but not what the customers needed.

Unfortunately, customer perceptions aren't always logical. For example, Donald Burr, former president of People's Express Airline, once said that passengers believe if there are coffee stains on the fold-down tray tables, the airline does sloppy engine maintenance. We know that's not logically true, but we're not dealing with logic. We're dealing with perceptions. It may not be logical, or even fair, to make assumptions like that, but people do it anyway.

I was sitting in a doctor's waiting room not long ago. I noticed several of the plants were wilted and dying. I heard one patient say to another, "Look at the way he takes care of these plants. I hope he takes better care of his patients." Such thinking may not be logical, but many people think that same way. And most of the time they (and we) are not even aware of it because it occurs at a subconscious level.

Of course, you can't *control* people's perceptions, but you can *influence* them. The reputation for good service at companies such as American Airlines, Deere & Company, Maytag, American Express, and others comes largely from meeting, and exceeding, people's expectations. These companies consistently deliver what customers expect—and more.

A reputation for good service also comes from helping to shape people's perceptions. Service-oriented organizations continually remind customers and prospects of their service. Federal Express' customers and potential customers know that their package will be there overnight. IBM customers and potential customers know that if the system goes down, a team of service people will appear within hours. Disney customers and potential customers know they can escape to a fantasy world for clean, fun, wholesome entertainment.

The way to begin exceeding your customers' expectations is by learning what your customers want, as described in Idea 5 above. What exactly do they expect from the products or services you offer? Once you know what customers expect, find out how well you're doing in meeting those expectations. Where can you improve? How do you compare to your competitors? Answer these questions and then adjust your products or services to meet and exceed customer expectations.

This approach seems simple, but it's really difficult to implement. Perceptions don't change overnight. People have come to expect poor service from many industries. They've come to expect that certain organizations don't promise very much *and* don't deliver very much.

In one of our workshops on service, there's an exercise in which participants go out for lunch in teams. They're given an assignment to complete before reconvening. After lunch, teams discuss their lunch experience.

I remember one team discussing a waitress. Someone had asked her to bring salad dressing on the side; another wanted extra lemon for iced tea. She did both things. The group realized they didn't *expect* her to do either, and they were delighted when she did, without having to be reminded. They concluded that, in many restaurants, just getting what you ask for is exceptional. They also realized that their appreciation of getting what they asked for was subconscious; had they not been thinking about it and discussing it in a workshop, they probably wouldn't have been aware of it.

Service-oriented organizations also realize that exceptional service is not what *they* think it is, it's what the customer perceives it to be. And it's not always easy to create positive perceptions for the customer.

A participant in Parasuraman's study explained that his bank refused to cash his paycheck from a "nationally known" company because it was postdated by 1 day. Another focus-group participant, who worked in a bank, explained why the bank legally couldn't cash his check. Since no one at the participant's bank explained that to him, he saw them as *unwilling*, instead of *unable*, to cash his check.

If you expect a car repair bill to be $95 and it turns out to be $350, you're probably going to be less than satisfied. If you expect a shipment to arrive on Tuesday and it comes on the following Friday, you probably won't be very happy. However, if the shipment comes a day *early*, the supplier is likely to gain a few points.

Another problem with meeting and exceeding customer expectations involves ownership responsibilities. According to a report produced by Learning International, many people either don't read, or else misinterpret, product warranties and guarantees. People often assume that certain items will be covered, but they're not. A common example is car warranties. Customers often assume that, if a car is under warranty, they won't have to pay for any parts or repairs. Customers are frequently upset when they're charged for parts that aren't covered, or charged for things like oil, brake fluid, and other items.

The same holds true for assembly and operating instructions. Most people don't read them. Many consumers operate under the philosophy "When all else fails, read the instructions." It's often too late by that time. Many companies report that many service calls and warranty claims could be averted if customers had read the product literature *before* tinkering with the product. The key point here is: Customers *expect* things to be easy to assemble, they *expect* to know how to operate them, and they *expect* you to be there to help them if the product doesn't work or they botch things up. Such expectations may not be logical, fair, or prudent, but they are a fact of business life.

Recognize this fact and be prepared to deal with it. Manage customer expectations by presenting honest, reliable messages about your products and services—what they can and can't do. Communicate with customers in many different ways. Set up service centers. Use toll-free lines. Train people to do troubleshooting and repairs.

Also avoid giving customers unrealistic expectations and then failing to meet them. You've probably experienced such situations yourself:

You and an associate stop for lunch. It's noon. You have an important meeting with your boss's boss at 1:00. It's a 10-minute drive to the office. The server comes to the table. After placing your order, you say, "We're in a hurry. We've got to be out of here by 12:45. How long will it take for what we ordered?" The server says, "Uh . . . well . . . it shouldn't be too long. They're not real backed up right now." Twenty minutes later your lunch still hasn't come.

The nurse at your doctor's office says, "The doctor will see you in a few minutes." Thirty minutes later, you're still sitting in the waiting room.

You go to a popular restaurant—one of those that's so busy they don't take reservations—where there's always a wait for a table. You put your name on the waiting list and ask the hostess how long it'll be for a party of four. She says, "About twenty minutes." An hour later, you're still not seated. You ask, "How much longer?" She says, "You're next. It should only be a few more minutes." Fifteen minutes later, you're still not seated.

Don't make promises you can't keep. It sets up false expectations.

A study by Milind M. Lele found that exceptional service providers ensure they meet and exceed customer expectations by creating products and services that will satisfy the most demanding customers under the most demanding conditions. Lele tells about Swissair hiring its own baggage-handling operation in Bombay, India, because the airport's regular service wasn't fast enough. Swissair only had one flight a day to Bombay! Maytag builds the same washers and dryers for home use as it does for laundromats; one has a coin slot and the other doesn't.

Go beyond what's expected.

A participant in Parasuraman's study told about a repair person who fixed her broken appliance and then explained to her the problem and how she could fix it herself if it happened again. She rated the quality of this service as excellent because it exceeded her expectations of simply getting her appliance fixed.

The New York Hilton surveyed all its employees (over 400) to find out what languages they spoke. It turned out that the employees spoke 30 different languages. Employees now wear special lapel pins showing guests what languages they speak. That's going beyond what's expected.

While preparing for a speaking tour overseas, I called the U.S. offices of the tourism bureaus for the countries we were going to visit. I wanted information about visas, shots, places of interest, and so on. I called one office and got a recorded message that said, "We're not available right now, so your call is being taken by our automated message service. Please leave your message at the tone." I left my message and phone number on their tape. About 3 hours later I received a call. A nice young man said, "I'm a little confused. This is the Carson-Pirie-Scott telephone order department. You called and left a message on our machine. I wanted you to know you didn't reach the party you were calling. I thought you'd want to know right away so it doesn't mess up your travel plans."

Apparently, I had misdialed and reached the order department of Carson-Pirie-Scott department stores. The young man who called me, Kevin Murphy, could have figured I was so stupid that I called a department store to ask about passports and visas, and he could have just ignored the whole thing. Instead, he took the trouble to let me know I had not reached the place I was calling. That's going beyond what's expected. And I'm not even a Carson-Pirie-Scott customer—yet.

---

9. Make customer satisfaction a way of life

Unless excellent service is the norm, is ingrained in the culture, is the lifeblood of your organization, and is the primary topic of conversation in your organization, service won't improve very much for very long. In customer-focused organizations, everything the organization does is focused on the customer. Your location, facilities, ease of access, procedures, policies, and paperwork should all be designed, planned, and carried out with the needs of the *customer* in mind instead of the convenience of the employees. Ollie Stiwenius, a Scandinavian Airlines Systems executive, put it best when he said: "The organization exists to support the people who serve the customer. It has no other meaning, no other purpose."

Employees must communicate this message to customers: "We're here to meet your needs and keep you satisfied." If everyone shares that common goal, there will be more teamwork and cooperation. People will be less concerned about building or maintaining "empires" and more concerned with serving customers.

Nothing should get in the way of providing service to customers. If a supervisor or manager gets in the way, the front line should be encouraged to go around that person—directly to the top if needed. No one should be allowed to interfere in a moment of truth. If there's some disagreement or a different way to handle the situation, the issue can be discussed *after* the customer has been satisfied.

10. *Demonstrate* your commitment to service

Improving service is a lot like having a million dollars: everyone wants it, but few are willing to do what it takes to get it. Most people sit around hoping someone will give it to them.

Actions speak louder than words. You must actively, visibly demonstrate your commitment to the changes necessary to become a customer-focused organization. H. James Harrington, author of *The Improvement Process*, said, "A corporation takes on the personality of its top management. So, if management doesn't believe the company can do better, the company shouldn't even try the improvement process. That process starts with top management, will progress at a rate reflecting managements' demonstrated commitment, and will stop soon after managers lose interest in the process."

Demonstrate your commitment via time and money. Remember, your actions speak louder than your words. That means avoiding what Ken Blanchard calls Seagull Management, "where managers fly in, make a lot of noise, dump on everyone, and then fly out."

Put service first on the agenda at every meeting to communicate that it's important. "What's the latest customer (or member) survey show? How many complaints/compliments did we get this week? How can we get better?" Get your direct-reports to do the same. Put service reminders and customer-focused suggestions in pay envelopes. Communicate that you're serious and this emphasis on service isn't going to go away next week.

Examine your policies, practices, and benefits. Are there useless policies and procedures that have been in place forever? Sacred cows, such as making customers "take a number" when there's no one else in the place, or completing paperwork or keying in data while customers are waiting? Be willing to change. What has worked in the past may not work today.

Create task groups or service teams made up of managers, supervisors, and frontline employees. Include people from different departments and functional areas on each team. Direct these teams to assume everything being done now may be wrong. Nothing is sacred. Give teams the authority to question everything. They are not to be concerned with cost, feasibility, history, long-standing policies or practices, politics, or anything else except how they can serve customers better. Their guiding question is: "Given our vision, if we were truly serving our customers, what would we be doing in this area?"

Managers should spend part of their time regularly working with customers. Not selling, but visiting them, talking with them, and asking about their needs. Sometimes managers are so busy managing, they forget about customers. Service 1st Corporation surveyed over 80 companies of all sizes about their service practices and found that 66 percent of senior managers spend less than 25 percent of their time with customers.

The customers managers spend time with should not be limited to other managers in the carpeted executive suites of attractive, big-volume customers. Customer contact by managers should include the whole range of people who come in contact with the product or service. These may be the people on the shop floor or the people your organization deals with on the phone or face-to-face. The bigger your organization, the more important this effort is, because managers may be far removed from the front line and may have no concept of who the customers are and what they really want.

Find other ways to make sure your managers are visible to employees and customers. Not to snoop, check up, or "catch," but rather to say, "I believe taking care of our customers is important enough for everyone to do it. How can we help you do it better?" Managers might periodically relieve employees at the front lines, especially on the not-so-desirable shifts like weekends, holidays, or nights. Upper-level employees pitching in at the front lines sends a strong message to customers and to other employees about the importance of service.

Take rude, crusty, sour people out of customer-contact positions. Offer them a chance to work elsewhere in the organization or get rid of them. Chances are, if they're rude, insensitive, or sour with their internal customers, they'll be the same way with your external customers. They may not be the players you want on your team. Weeding out these people also sends a message through the company that you're serious about the way you treat customers.

11. Offer a 100 percent service guarantee

One of the best ways to demonstrate your commitment to service is with a 100 percent service guarantee. Although warranties on products such as cars, computers, and stereos are commonplace, very few are 100 percent money-back, no-questions-asked guarantees. Most have some conditions ("does not apply to all models"), stipulations ("must have a receipt"), or restrictions ("within 90 days"). Many are difficult for customers to collect on.

It's hard to find guarantees for such services as a hotel stay, dry cleaning, legal services, or haircuts. Hard, but not impossible.

"Bugs" Burger Bug Killers (BBBK), a well-known Miami pest control company, guarantees its customers, many of whom are hotels and restaurants, that the customer won't pay anything unless *all* pests on their premises have been eliminated. And, if a guest sees a pest, BBBK will pay for the guest's room or meal, send the guest a letter, *and* pay for a future meal or room. If a customer is ever dissatisfied with BBBK's service, the company will refund the fees paid up to one year *and* pay the fees for another exterminator of the customer's choice for the following year. And if a customer's facility is ever closed down because of pest infestation, BBBK will pay all fines, all lost profits, *and* $5,000. (BBBK's name has been changed to Prism, but many people are familiar with it as BBBK.)

L. L. Bean, the renowned Maine mail-order company, guarantees all of its products:

> All of our products are guaranteed to give 100 percent satisfaction in every way. Return anything purchased from us at any time if it proves otherwise. We will replace it, refund your purchase price, or credit your credit card, as you wish. **We do not want you to have anything from L. L. Bean that is not completely satisfactory.**

Holiday Inn hotels guarantee meeting planners that meeting rooms will be set up on time and according to the planner's specifications, that coffee breaks will be ready on time, and that audiovisual equipment will work. If there's a problem with some part of the service and the hotel personnel can't fix it on the spot to the customer's satisfaction, that aspect of the meeting is free.

Herman Miller, the office furniture company, gives warranties on its products and guarantees that office equipment and furnishings will be delivered and installed by the agreed-upon date.

Pentel Corporation, makers of pens and pencils, guarantees its products for the life of the product. I had one of Pentel's mechanical pencils for several years. One day, the lead would no longer come out. I sent it to Pentel. Pentel couldn't repair it, so the company sent me a new pencil—free. The new pencil was accompanied by the letter reprinted on page 117.

Service guarantees are not limited to huge corporations. Jim Thorpe Transportation Company, a family-owned bus company in a small Pennsylvania town, offers a 100 percent money-back guarantee on its tour packages. And *The Service Edge* newsletter tells about a small hamburger stand in Lexington, Kentucky, that was facing stiff competition from McDonald's and Burger King. The hamburger stand started a "Meal a Minute" policy. If a customer doesn't get the ordered meal in one minute, the next meal is free.

Even a company as small as ours guarantees our programs. If a client is not satisfied with one of our seminars, we'll refund the program fee.

Christopher W. L. Hart wrote about the "Power of Unconditional Service Guarantees" in the *Harvard Business Review*. Hart says that virtually every business can offer guarantees, regardless of its products or services. Hart describes six characteristics of a good service guarantee:

1 *It's unconditional.* There are no *ifs, ands,* or *buts.* No excuses. No (or very few) conditions or restrictions. And the *customers* decide if they're satisfied.

2 *It's easy to understand and communicate.* It contains, clear, precise, simple terms like "30 minutes or $3 off" (instead of "fast delivery").

3 *It's meaningful.* It guarantees things that are important to customers (lowest prices, 15-minute service, etc.).

4 *It puts the organization's money where its mouth is.* It calls for a significant payout when the promise is broken, and it does pay off. Guarantees that involve no risk for the organization offer little value to customers.

5 *It's easy to invoke.* It doesn't put customers through time-consuming procedures, hassles, and paperwork to get satisfaction. And employees don't make customers feel guilty for invoking the guarantee.

6 *It's easy to collect on.* The customer shouldn't have to wait long or work hard to collect on the promise. Payoff should be easy and quick—on the spot, if possible.

Sound extravagant? It does to many. But Hart offers sound reasons for implementing service guarantees:

☐ *A guarantee forces you to focus on customers.* This means you *must* know what customers expect from the products or services you offer. You must know what customers think is important. The organization is forced to concentrate on delivering what customers say they want, not what the organization wants to give them.

☐ *A guarantee sets clear standards.* A clear, specific service guarantee tells your customers and employees what the organization stands for and what to expect from it.

☐ *A guarantee helps all employees accept responsibility for service.* Significant payouts provide strong incentives to deliver on the service promise. Managers, work groups, and individual employees who must bear the costs of foul-ups work hard to prevent them from recurring.

☐ *A guarantee generates feedback.* We know most dissatisfied customers don't complain; they simply take their business elsewhere. And the offending business rarely knows why. With an unconditional, easy-to-understand, easy-to-invoke service guarantee, more customers are willing to complain, thus providing you with valuable information.

PENTEL OF AMERICA, LTD.

11 Kulick Road, Fairfield, New Jersey 07006   •   **Phone (201) 575-7525**

January 10, 1989

Jeff Disend
2137 Mt. Vernon Road
Atlanta, Ga 30338

I have received your Pentel mechanical pencil which you have
sent to our Quality Assurance department. I have examined
the pencil and have found that I am unable to repair it.

Since I have been unable to repair your pencil, I have replaced
it at no charge. If you should have any questions regarding any
merchandise Pentel manufactures, please contact my office.

Pentel welcomes feedback from its valued customers. I would like
to thank you for writing Pentel regarding your complaint.

Thank you for your patronage with Pentel products.

Sincerely,

Corliss Hubay
Quality Assurance

Enclosed; 1 each P225A pencil

☐ *A guarantee forces you to examine obstacles to improved service.* In developing your service guarantee, you must examine the failure points in your current system. You must identify and eliminate problem areas and limitations.

☐ *A guarantee boosts your marketing efforts.* It encourages new customers to do business with you by reducing their risks. It also builds loyalty with existing customers.

Many people say, "That sounds good, but what about the risks?" The most common concerns expressed about service guarantees are the following:

Uncontrollable variables. Hart concedes that there are some things that can't be controlled, such as the weather. But many of the things managers cite as uncontrollable really are controllable—employees, equipment, training, supplier problems. The key is to take a hard look at those things you *can* control. Even though it may not be easy or inexpensive, it is important to control whatever you can.

Also of great importance is how the organization and its people react to things they *can't* control. Do they go out of their way to take care of customers when things go awry? Do they make amends? Things happen that may not be in your control. The key is to find out how to minimize or reduce these events and to determine how you'll handle them if they do occur.

Cheating. There are always people who will take you up on your guarantees. That's the point. You want them to. The number of times you need to pay off can tell you how you're doing. Payoff also communicates to most customers that you're serious about providing the service you promise.

Of course you don't want people to take *unfair* advantage, but it may happen. However, most service-oriented companies concentrate on the majority and don't worry about the few who will cheat them. Hart relates the perspective of Phil Bressler, a Domino's Pizza franchisee who owns 18 restaurants. Bressler says customers cheat only when *they* feel cheated. He says, "Companies create the incentive to cheat, in almost all cases, by not providing value."

Service-oriented companies take a long-term approach. Bressler also tells about college students who used to call in pizza orders to addresses that were hard to find. It was a game to get free pizzas. Bressler's attitude is that the short-term lost revenue was a long-term investment: "They'll be Domino's customers for life."

High Costs. This concern also stems from a short-term perspective that views service guarantees as a *cost* rather than an investment. Service-oriented companies don't make cost-versus-customer comparisons. Of course, if your products or services are inferior in some way, a guarantee could be financially disasterous in the very short term.

12. Recognize that providing excellent service is a person-to-person activity

Providing exceptional service to internal or external customers is the willingness to do something for the customer as a *person*. This willingness requires seeing customers as people—as thinking, feeling human beings with needs. This means finding out how they feel and what influences them to make certain decisions. It means putting yourself in customers' shoes and anticipating their needs. It means getting every employee to ask themselves about every customer: If I were this person, what would I want? What else might this person need? How can I do things better for this customer?

Craig Johnson, a zone vice president with Frito-Lay, tells a story about one of the company's route drivers:

The driver's customer was a grocery store. Outside the store, one of the grocery's customers (thus a customer of a customer) had a broken heater hose in her car. Bobby Tye, the Frito-Lay driver, got a new hose and put it on the woman's car. Did he have to do it? Does the Frito-Lay training program say, "If a patron of one of your customers has car troubles, you should stop and do minor car repairs?" Of course not. He did it out of concern for another *person*.

This kind of service must come out of caring and sincere interest in customers. Unless your employees care about customers, they're likely to just go through the motions. And if they don't believe in, or care about, your products or services, they won't get very excited about selling them.

Customer-focused organizations have discovered something that traditional ones haven't: A company is not a customer. *People* are customers. Acme Manufacturing is not the customer; Bob Smith, its plant manager, is. Mercy Hospital is not the customer, but its maintenance engineer is. Delta Airlines is not the customer, but the person who buys or leases its airplanes is. Companies don't make decisions—people do.

Customer-focused organizations also realize that these people were *people* long before they were plant managers, maintenance engineers, or purchasing agents. Traditional organizations tend to forget about the human side of things. They try to deal with people like they're all business. Customer-centered organizations know that this all-business approach doesn't work.

A former neighbor of mine was an IBM service manager. When IBM customers had problems with their computers, Eddie got the call. When he arrived, customers were often angry, frustrated, and under pressure to get the system running again. Eddie used to tell me, "First I take care of the customer. Then I take care of the computer."

Since every human being is unique, every customer (and the organizations the customer represents) has unique needs, feelings, preferences, and biases. That means your customer-contact people must have the confidence and skills to handle each customer and each situation on an individual basis. That's why "what to do if" training isn't very effective: it can't cover every situation every human being may present.

Rather than trying to anticipate every situation an employee might encounter, service-oriented organizations concentrate on creating an *environment* in which customers are valued and providing good service is the norm; one in which people are ready, willing, and able to go beyond what's expected to serve the customer. This kind of service happens best when employees find *personal* reasons to commit themselves to serving customers. Sadly, the typical organization wants people to do things for the *organization's* reasons. This never works. However, organizations *can* create an environment that encourages employees to regularly go beyond what's expected because the employees believe in doing so, not because they were *told* to. Bill Marriott Jr. says, "You cannot order anything from anybody. They've got to do it because they want to do it."

Sometimes this is as simple as just liking people. This attitude is evident in the piece that promotes the Crested Butte, Colorado, ski area.

What's needed is not necessarily heroic or spectacular. It doesn't require acts that would make people stop and think, "Wow! That person really went out of their way for me!" Often it's only the difference between giving directions by grunting and pointing versus explaining directions in a way that shows you care about the customer and his or her needs. It's the difference between seeing the customer as a person and seeing the customer as a number ("Number 47. Does anyone have Number 47? OK, Number 48!"), or a condition ("the green lube job in the corner" or "the appendectomy in Room 402"), or an interruption of other work.

The Ritz-Carlton hotels understand this. During a training session for new employees at one of the new Ritz-Carlton hotels, the general manager said, "Service, ladies and gentlemen, means this: If someone asks for help, drop what you are doing and *take* them where they want to go, *get* the iced tea, *move* the chair. And when you're finished, say, 'Thank you. Good morning. My pleasure.' That's it."

Two examples from restaurants further demonstrate the difference:

Kay and I stopped in a Wendy's restaurant one evening. My seat faced the counter. Just behind Kay was the stand with the condiments, napkins, and utensils. There was a teenager standing there slowly pushing napkins into the pop-up napkin dispenser.

She didn't look like a Wendy's employee, and she wasn't dressed in a Wendy's uniform.

HALF THE FUN OF A VACATION IS
MEETING THE
NATIVES

And meeting them in Crested Butte is as easy as enjoying our wide open, sunny skiing. The snootiness you've heard about in the big, glitzy resorts just isn't here in Crested Butte. This is a place that's real friendly. Real casual. Real comfortable. In fact, we like to say that Crested Butte is the Real West – as in kicked back and relaxed.

Tuck's a good example of that. He's the guy in the middle of the picture. Everyone knows him. He's got personality and character that won't quit . . . just like Crested Butte.

You might say Tuck's a cowboy-poet. When the snow melts, you'll find him wrangling and trail guiding, then composing ballads and acting in local theatre.

Wintertime, when you ride his bus . . . more on that later . . . he's singing songs on the radio or humming one of his own. But, for all those brains, Tuck also packs the brawn of a karate black belt.

When you ask Tuck why he came to Crested Butte, you begin to get a clue as to the spirit of the place: "What I liked was the welcome I received. This place builds bridges for the people who come here."

About the bus. You'd have to agree it's rather colorful . . . not your typical ski resort bus. You see, one day we unleashed all the artists in town on our buses. Now they're all hand-painted, individual works of art, mobile too. They get lots of comments from guests, and start many a conversation with drivers, like Tuck. The buses are another comment on the spirit of Crested Butte . . . irreverent and about as different from the stuffy look and feel of other resorts as you can get.

So, come on and make a friend in Crested Butte. And while you're doing that, you'll get all the skiing you'll ever want. And an unspoiled Victorian town with plenty of wining and dining in true Western tradition. But we bet what you'll remember, and come back for, is our hospitality.

CRESTED BUTTE
COLORADO

1-800-544-8448
or call your local travel agent

She had on tight black pedal-pusher slacks, high-topped black shoes, white calf-high socks, and a wrinkled white blouse. Her hair was straggly and falling down over her face.

I was intrigued with her because of what she was doing and the way she was dressed. It looked like her body was there but her mind was on Venus. She was moving very slowly and methodically—as though she was in slow motion. As she stood there slowly stuffing napkins, her body was moving like she was listening to some great music, but she wasn't wearing a Walkman!

She was facing the door. By turning her head slightly to the left, she could see the ordering line. Within a 3- to 4- minute interval, several groups of customers came in. They all got into the "snake line." I could see that the behind-the-counter person was not there. Soon there were 10 people in line, and the line actually snaked back to where the girl was standing, still stuffing napkins. She never knew those people were there. I figured that since she didn't work there, it didn't matter.

One of the people in line leaned over to her and said "There's no one at the register. Can someone take our order?" Still in slow motion, she put down the napkins and disappeared. I thought she went to find someone who could take their orders. The next thing I knew, she was behind the counter and entering orders into the register. I was stunned! She really *did* work there. (Well, sort of.) This was quite a moment of truth for those customers.

Here's a different example of what service can look like when it's person-to-person:

Kay was in Houston for a speaking engagement. She met her hosts in the restaurant of the Four Seasons Inn on the Park where the program was being held. When they sat down, there was a lot of noise coming from the kitchen—the restaurant was apparently remodeling—and it was difficult to carry on a conversation at the table. Their waiter, Bob, appeared and, before anyone could say anything, apologized for the noise. Kay said, jokingly, "It sounds like there's an elephant giving birth back there." He laughed and excused himself. He went into the kitchen and told the workers what Kay had said, and the construction crew cracked up. Then he said, "If a customer thinks it sounds like there's an elephant in labor back here, it's entirely too loud." The crew quit working.

When Bob returned to the table for drink orders, Kay asked if they had a chardonnay by the glass. They didn't but he went to the dining room, brought back a bottle, opened it, and poured her a glass.

Kay is allergic to onions. There was a combination salad plate on the menu that came with three salads: tuna, chicken, and shrimp. Kay asked if any of them was made with onions. Bob checked and said they weren't, so she ordered the salad plate. When Bob brought the meals, Kay had two scoops of tuna, two scoops of chicken, and no shrimp salad. Bob explained that he had called the chef who made the salad just to be sure and had found that the shrimp salad had onions in it. Rather than interrupting the conversation at the table, Bob had just given her two scoops of each of the other salads.

During the meal, Bob learned that Kay is a professional speaker and was in the hotel to do a program in a few hours. At the end of the meal, he tried to interest them in dessert, but they said no, they'd come back after her program.

Several hours later, they did come back. Bob remembered them—by name. He asked Kay how the program went. He remembered the chardonnay Kay was drinking; also, without asking, he brought the dessert tray to their table. Quite a different moment of truth. Bob obviously brought his mind and body to work, was alert to conditions around him (a noisy kitchen), respected customer requests (chardonnay, no onion), and cared enough about customers to talk to them. Kay says this was one of the best restaurant experiences she's ever had.

13. Change what people think about

Psychologists tell us that what we think about and believe becomes our reality and that our behavior is the result of our beliefs. When people believed the world was flat, very few dared to sail out past the horizon. When people believed illness was caused by bad body fluids, they practiced bleeding and used leeches to cure illness.

The Inquisition was about beliefs. If those who were not in positions of power or influence held different beliefs, they were imprisoned, murdered, or tortured. Clearly, beliefs do affect behavior.

Take something as simple as a diet. Ask a dozen people how they've lost weight and you'll probably hear about a dozen different methods. Some believe in the grapefruit plan, some in the water plan, some in Weight Watchers, some in protein regimens and so on. Dieters' beliefs (or hope) in a certain diet affects their behavior—what they eat. If a dieter believes that eating cactus needles and hot rutabaga juice helps take off weight, guess what that person will eat—even if there's no valid evidence that such a diet works.

In many ways, beliefs are habits of thought. We like to stay in our familiar, safe thought patterns. And habits can be both good and bad. They can save us time; for example, our ability to develop habits keeps us from having to relearn how to tie our shoes, drive a car, balance a checkbook, fry an egg, take a shower, or get to the office. Once we have learned them, we can do these things automatically.

The bad news is that this ability also tends to limit our ability and willingness to see new ways of doing things. We like to stick with things that are familiar and comfortable. Change can mean increased discomfort or anxiety. As a result, habits are hard to break. We get caught up in a routine, a certain way of doing things. We have a comfort zone for dealing with customers or handling transactions. We do these things a certain way because they've worked for us in the past and we've been rewarded.

Beliefs also affect behavior in organizations. There's a belief in some organizations that quality is the responsibility of supervisors or of the quality control department. This belief affects organizational structure, job tasks, and reward systems. In these organizations, people who deliver the product or service don't believe it's their responsibility to inspect for quality because that's someone else's job. So they don't inspect for or worry about quality. Other organizations believe that quality is everyone's responsibility. In these organizations, there are often no inspectors; line workers do their own inspections. Instead of only a few people looking for problems, everyone does.

Many organizations also hold certain beliefs about the roles of managers and employees. There are certain things they believe each group should and shouldn't do. Management is supposed to interview and make hiring decisions, do performance reviews, decide on raises, assign work, and set production goals, among other things. Traditional organizations believe that frontline employees can't and won't do these things. So only managers do these things, and an elaborate set of policies, rules, and unwritten codes is established to "keep employees in their place." In some organizations, managers maintain the following attitude: "Employees are out to get us. They'll rip us off every chance they can. We have to protect ourselves."

A similar belief exists in some organizations about customers. Top managers in some organizations believe that the majority of customers are out to rip them off and take advantage of them. They pass these beliefs on to their employees formally and informally through the organization's training, culture, policies, and practices. They set up elaborate, time-consuming, expensive procedures and paperwork to protect the organization from customers. They see their relationship with customers as a battle. I've even heard top managers say, "You just have to keep beating them over the head with it [the service or product]." They set up an "us against them" mind-set. If you've ever tried to get a refund and been told you *must* have a receipt, been told to fill out numerous forms, been told you can't return an item because you bought it at one of the company's other stores, or been told a refund would take 4 to 6 weeks to process, you know what I'm talking about.

There are other organizations which believe just the opposite. They believe that most customers are honest, want value for their money, and are willing to pay for what they get.

L. L. Bean customers and employees relish telling the story about a customer who called and said he had a pair of L. L. Bean boots that had fallen apart. The employee who spoke with him asked how long he'd had the boots, and the customer said 26 years. Without hesitating, the employee apologized for the inconvenience and promised to send another pair that day. At no charge.

A Nordstrom employee reportedly once took back a pair of tires and gave the customer a full refund, with no questions asked. And Nordstrom doesn't even sell tires!

Whether such stories are true or not, reported incidents like these reflect the beliefs of these two companies. L. L. Bean, Nordstrom, and other service-oriented companies like them are not naïve or stupid. They know that a few people will take advantage of them. But they believe that the goodwill and repeat business from the majority of their other customers will more than make up for those few. They spend their time, money, and energy trying to satisfy the majority of customers rather than protecting themselves from the minority.

Here's the key point about beliefs: If you make no effort to influence what people in your organization think about, or if you have not made a conscious, concerted effort to help shape people's beliefs toward being service-oriented and customer-focused, people will create or maintain their own beliefs—and these may be contrary to what's needed, what's important, and what customers want. When employees believe that their jobs require them to follow the rules at all costs, process forms correctly and on time, do as they're told, or move merchandise from here to there, customers get "I only work her" and "Those are the rules" service.

Changing organizational beliefs is, of course, easier said than done; but that doesn't mean it *can't* be done. The important thing is to begin getting people to think, believe, and act in the customer's and the organization's best interests.

Very often, there needs to be an interruption in the way people in the organization currently see things. Without an interruption in current beliefs and assumptions, things usually continue along the same old path. But once employees can look at their organization—and their part in it—from a different perspective, they can begin to shift their focus.

Creating change requires moving away from the comfortable and familiar. Doing this is usually uncomfortable at first—like the feeling you had when you learned to drive, or learned a new sport, or moved to a new city.

Many organizations, indeed many industries, have had to change the way they see themselves and their relationship with their customers. For example, Kay and I have done a lot of work in the health care field. Many administrators tell us essentially the same story: "For years, we just sat here and waited for people to come to us. If they were hurt or sick, they knew where to find us. We treated them and then billed their insurance carrier. Everybody was happy. Now the game has changed. Reimbursements are limited by schedules. There are clinics and other providers competing with us. People are more health conscious and concerned about wellness. We've actually had to go out and start marketing in our community just to survive."

Colleges and universities tell us the same thing. Marketing and recruiting for faculty, students, and grant money is now a way of life. Faculty members are lured to other institutions by promises of grants, bigger and better labs or other facilities, secretaries, reduced teaching loads, and other perks. The stakes are high because the ability to recruit and maintain high-caliber faculty enables many schools to recruit better students, who often bring scholarship money with them.

An organization can also shape what people think about by deciding what business it's in. That may sound naïve and blindingly obvious, but many organizations don't have a clear picture of this. The business you think you're in affects what your organization does, how it's organized, and what your people do. Identifying an organization's primary business provides focus and direction.

Defining the business you're in helps shift people's beliefs and behavior because it focuses attention on the real business, not on the products or services offered. For example, IBM says its business is providing business solutions, not selling computers. If IBM's business were selling computers, all the company's energy, direction, and focus would be on making and selling "boxes." Instead, people at IBM are focused on finding good business solutions for their customers. The computer is a means to that end.

Jan Carlzon of Scandinavian Airlines System (SAS) says that when SAS realized it wasn't in the airline business, but *was* in the transportation business, the company changed its focus. When management and employees saw that their real business was getting people safely from one place to another, that changed their focus away from airplanes, hangars, ticket counters, and computers and toward making air transportation as easy, convenient, and safe as they could.

It may take some tough, analytical thinking to discover your organization's real business, but it's worth it. Consider the services and/or products of the organizations listed in Chart 4 and then consider their real business—the one that shapes their thinking and activities. Think how different these organizations and their people are because they see themselves as being in the business listed on the right instead of the generic business listed in the middle column.

Defining a group's "real business" works inside organizations, too. In *Peak Performance*, Charles Garfield tells about a California aerospace company:

A vice president asked Garfield to explain why a certain group of the company's maintenance engineers at one of its plants had such good attendance and excellent productivity and morale. The executive told Garfield the job was basically glorified plumbing work—it involved keeping pipes and gauges operating in the company's thermodynamics plant. (It was important to keep the pipes and gauges running within specs to protect the expensive parts being tested.)

Garfield went to visit the plant. He asked the supervisor why all his people were wearing green surgical smocks. The supervisor explained that he had gotten the smocks from his son, a heart surgeon. He explained that the people on his maintenance crew are like surgeons. Their job is to take care of the pipes of the plant, just like his son takes care of the pipes in people. The foreman had even had "Dr." stenciled on each engineer's locker. Garfield concluded that knowing that their real business was to "take care of these pipes the way a doctor takes care of your heart" gave the workers in this crew a sense of purpose and importance.

CHART 4   WHAT BUSINESS ARE WE REALLY IN?

Organization	Business or Product	Real Business
IBM	Computers	Business Solutions
Coca-Cola	Soft drinks	Refreshment, nostalgia
Revlon	Cosmetics	Hope
AAA road service	Emergency car repairs	Security ("One phone call away")
Car manufacturers	Cars	Reliable transportation; ego reflection on wheels
Executive Suites	Hotel suites	A convenient, clean place to stay away from home
Georgia State University Continuing Education Department	College courses	A vehicle for people to improve their lifestyles and feel better about themselves

Decide what business *you're* in. And if that business doesn't involve providing something—usually something intangible and highly personal—to customers, you haven't defined it right yet.

Providing outstanding service to *every* customer *every* day requires a transformation in the way most organizations operate. That transformation means a change in behavior, which requires a change in beliefs. The key is to change what people think about and to get everyone thinking about customers, fellow employees, and service in the same positive ways.

14. Create or redefine a service vision for your organization. Describe what service should look like, sound like, feel like

Here's a little parable:

Years ago, in the ancient, mystical kingdom of Lipett, it was rumored that the way to happiness, success, fame, and fortune was to find the mythical Terces. In all of history, it was said that only a handful of people had ever found it.

Legend has it that finally a young businessman named Ceo ("Seeyo") set out to seek the Terces. Ceo told his friends that if he found the Terces, it would bring him everlasting happiness and untold wealth. He'd be known across the land. Ceo told his friends that he knew just where to look and what to do and that surely he would be rich and famous in no time. His friends reminded him that they'd heard the same story from many others before him.

Undaunted, Ceo started his search. He asked everybody, "Are you the Terces?" He tried to get others to believe in his dream and help in the search.

Ceo soon learned that finding the Terces wasn't as easy as he'd thought it would be. Some people *said* they shared his dream and wanted to help him (so they could share the wealth and success), but most of *them* lost interest quickly. Others couldn't be bothered, saying things like, "Hey, I have my own work to do." Still others questioned his dedication and commitment, but he'd always reply, "I'm really serious about this. I'm committed to it. I've dedicated my career to this. I won't give it up."

Eventually, Ceo persuaded some friends and a few employees to join his glorious quest. They went all about the countryside asking everyone they saw, "Are you the Terces? Do you know where to find it?"

Over the years, they tried many different ways of finding the Terces. They looked in many places. Every time people would go out to search, each person would bring back something different. And the person would always say, "This is what *I* thought it looked like." But Ceo and his helpers were always disappointed in the end. There were even a few times they were *sure* they had the Terces, but each time it escaped after only a few months.

When Ceo was in his middle years, he went on a trip to another land called Cigamon. He was elated (and a little envious) to learn that the people of Cigamon had found the Terces. Everyone he talked to in Cigamon knew about the Terces and loved to talk about it. Ceo learned that the people of Cigamon had managed to keep the Terces for many, many years—and that they always had to work very hard to keep it from getting away.

Ceo *had* to know their secret, so he sought out the oldest and wisest minds of that land and asked them to meet with him. When they were all assembled, the first wise one asked Ceo, "Are you sincere, 100 percent committed, willing to stick with it, never give up, and never abandon it once you have it, no matter what?"

"Oh, yes," replied Ceo.

The wise one appeared satisfied with that response. He smiled slightly and said, "Good, because that's the first step. Without that kind of commitment and dedication, you might as well not go any further."

The second wise one asked Ceo, "Do you know what it *looks* like?"

Ceo replied, "Well, no. But I'll know it when I see it."

The next wise one asked, "Do you know what it *sounds* like?"

"Well, no, but I'll know it when I hear it," Ceo answered.

The next wise one asked, "Do you know what if *feels* like?"

"No," Ceo said, "but I'll know it when I have it."

And another asked, "Do you know where it lives?"

"No, but I'll know it when I *find* it."

The wise ones asked him questions for hours. After everyone had asked all their questions, the room got very quiet. At the end of the table sat the oldest and wisest of them all. He hadn't said anything yet. Finally, he looked patiently at Ceo and asked, "Now do you know the secret?" Ceo thought for a long time, and finally he quietly said, "No." The wise one explained, "The biggest secret is that there *is* no secret. You see, we discovered a long time ago that if you don't know what it looks like, you won't know when you've found it. And other people can't help you find it if you're all looking for different things."

Ceo listened intently as the old man continued: "We also learned that keeping it once you get it is even harder. And, most important, we learned that it doesn't live *any*where—it lives *every*where. It lives in your people."

This tale is really about service. We *talk* about it, *say* we're committed to it, *search* for it, and do lots of things to *court* it; but unless we know what it looks like, sounds like, and feels like, how will we know when we have it? And if *you* don't know, your employees surely won't. And, like the Terces, we'll lose it unless we keep working at it.

Many organizations do not have a powerful, commonly understood, commonly shared vision. When this situation exists (and it does in most organizations), it's like having several highly dedicated, committed players show up to play, but one shows up to swim, one to play tennis, one to play football, and so on. The result is that no one really knows why the group has been assembled. There's nothing to unify the players and give them direction. They all do their own thing, often competing with each other for attention and resources.

Having a common vision, a common purpose, and a common understanding of organizational service is an important first step in changing what people think about. It gets them all thinking about the same things—how to satisfy customers.

In *Service America!*, Zemke and Albrecht make the following point:

> Of all the things we have said and will say about service, the most important is this: Unless shared values, norms, beliefs, and ideologies of the organization—the organization's culture—are clearly and consciously focused on serving the customer, there is virtually no chance that the organization will be able to deliver a consistent quality of service and develop a sustained reputation for service.

A common vision is important for several reasons. First, it gives the organization a philosophical framework—a context to operate in. People can ask themselves, "Is this decision consistent with who we are and what we stand for? What's the best decision on this policy, budget expenditure, new product, or customer refund, in view of our guiding principles?" Walt Disney reportedly once said, "When your values are clear, decision making is easy."

The senior managers interviewed for the Citibank study introduced in Part One said they established a set of values for their organization that expresses "the way we do business with our customers." Many executives saw this set of values as being so important that they took personal responsibility for developing and implementing it. Over half them reported having an explicit *service* mission statement that expresses the company's *service* philosophy so all employees have the same understanding, awareness, and behavioral guidelines to follow.

Second, a shared vision acts as a unifying force, giving everyone in the organization a common goal and direction. Making this point, I'm reminded of the movie *Bridge on the River Kwai*, in which the American and British prisoners in the Japanese prison were dying because they had no reason to live. When the British major convinced the Japanese commandant to let the prisoners build the bridge, it gave the men a common purpose. They developed a sense of energy and teamwork. Their energies were focused on completing the bridge.

Walter Wriston, former CEO of Citicorp and later chairman of the President's Economic Policy Advisory Board, was once asked about the role of vision in organizations. He remarked, "All the good companies have one. It covers how people are treated. Many of the successful companies have created a sense of fairness and a sense of family. When Pfizer, which is an enormous company, talks about the Pfizer family, they mean it. At Citicorp, people talk about the logo being tattooed on them." At The Coca-Cola Company, people talk about having Coke in their veins instead of blood.

Even our founding fathers recognized the need for a clear, concise, written statement of philosophy on how the nation would conduct itself. We know this statement as the Declaration of Independence.

Third, a shared vision provides clarity in uncertain situations. Usually when an organization faces a crisis or moves in a new direction, there are few or no precedents—and no clear paths to follow. People need guidelines for their day-to-day actions and decisions. They need to know what's expected. A clear, commonly shared vision provides this guidance. The shared vision is like a beacon that guides travelers in the right direction. Even if they can't see the path or if there are obstacles they must steer around, the beacon keeps them heading in essentially the right direction.

James E. Burke, chairman of Johnson & Johnson, credits his company's credo (included in Appendix B) as having the "single most important role in our decision making" during the Tylenol crisis in 1982. The first line of the credo says that the company's first responsibility is to the people who use its products and services. The credo also states Johnson & Johnson's responsibility to the communities its employees live and work in. These beliefs strongly influenced the company's quick action to notify the public and remove Tylenol from the shelves. During the crisis, many Johnson & Johnson managers in many different departments and geographic locations had to make important decisions quickly and under a lot of pressure. Their shared values enabled them to make essentially the same decisions.

So how do you create, or redefine, your organization's vision—what it should look like, sound like, and feel like? The good news is that there's no "wrong way" to do it. Much has been written recently about vision, mission statements, strategic planning, operating philosophies, values, strategies, and the like. All of it can be pretty confusing. Below are my definitions of some of these terms:

Mission.   The organization's purpose or reason for being. The mission usually makes a statement about the business the company is in and the results the company wants to achieve. The company's mission is permanent—it could be carved in stone over the front door.

Operating philosophy.   Also called guiding principles, values, code of ethics, or similar terms. The operating philosophy defines the values, beliefs, responsibilities, and priorities of the organization. It also describes how the organization chooses to do business and treat others. The operating philosophy is also relatively permanent and doesn't change much over time.

Strategies.   Includes all the goals, plans, and actions necessary to accomplish the mission (in accordance with the operating philosophy). It's the "how to" for achieving the vision. Strategies can include goals for expansion to new countries or markets, new product lines, new manufacturing facilities, increasing market share, and so on. Strategies can—and should—change as needed to reflect changes in competition, markets, customer preferences, and other factors.

Strategies often include the major decisions a firm must make in order to survive, grow, and achieve its vision. The strategies combine to form a plan for delivering the products and services of the organization to customers in ways that customers see as valuable and that differentiate the organization from its competitors.

Vision.   As I see it, vision includes all of the terms defined above. Vision describes an ideal to strive for without necessarily describing how to accomplish that ideal. It's literally a mental picture of the organization's mission, ways of doing business, and strategies.

Some writers believe that vision statements should express lofty spiritual and idealistic dreams. I'm more down-to-earth than that. I believe that the clearer the picture in everyone's head, the more focused the organization will be in moving toward achieving its mission. It's sometimes hard to picture lofty and idealistic concepts. Some may disagree or find fault with these definitions. That's understandable. I don't think it really matters what you call these concepts or how you define them. What *does* matter is that you create—or reshape—your organization's vision, or mission, or purpose, or whatever you choose to call it. The process of *doing* this creating or reshaping is what's important.

I also believe it's important to define—or redefine—your values; your ways of doing business; and your ways of treating customers, employees, and suppliers. It's important to create a picture of how you want people to interact with each other. The *end result*—a clear, written picture—is critical here. How you achieve the picture is up to you, and the picture will look different in every organization. I'll give you some suggestions shortly.

Finally, I believe it's important to communicate your vision and your values to all the members of your organization and to your customers. Again, how you do this will vary. The key is to do it continually and in as many ways as you can. Later I'll go into more detail on that topic, too.

CHART 5   GUIDELINES FOR CREATING A SERVICE VISION

The formula I suggest for vision statements is MUSICAL:

Meaningful. Communicates something important, not just hype or flowery rhetoric. Stuff, not fluff.

Understandable. Easy to grasp and explain to customers and employees.

Stated in present tense. Stated as givens, as though these things have already been accomplished.

In writing. If it's important enough to do, put it in writing. This makes it visible and easily communicated.

Comprehensive. Broad enough to cover virtually every situation employees may encounter but without prescribing specific behaviors or decisions so it doesn't limit people's actions or decisions.

Actionable. Easy to put into action on a day-to-day basis. Not abstract or theoretical, and not so unrealistic people can't live up to it.

Lasting. Communicates enduring values, not just passing whims or fads.

How do you define or redefine your vision? Start by taking a group of key executives off site to a retreat for a few days. Resolve to hammer out the answers to the questions provided at the end of this section. Add other questions that address your organization's needs and existing conditions. Be prepared for heated discussions. Encourage them. I recommend using an outside facilitator to help keep the sessions flowing, keep them focused on the topics, and keep personalities out of the discussions.

Also, convene focus groups of employees from different levels, departments, and locations. Have them answer the same—and other—questions. Use outside facilitators if at all possible.

Then combine the best from both groups. You'll probably find some discrepancies and widely differing points of view on some issues. Such discrepancies often indicate problem areas, and you'll need to discuss and resolve these.

Chart 5 provides some guidelines for formulating a service vision. See Appendix B for sample vision statements from several organizations. As you construct or redefine your organization's vision statement, here are some issues you should consider:

What business are we in?

What is the organization's purpose?

What sets us apart from our competitors?

What do we value? What's important to us?

How do we perceive (think about) customers?

How do we perceive fellow employees?

What do we want customers to know about us?

What do we want employees to know about us?

How do we deal with our suppliers?

What do we expect from employees?

What do we expect from suppliers?

How do we handle conflict and disagreement within the organization?

What kind of competition or cooperation do we want between organizational units?

How do we view enterprising individualism versus teamwork?

How far do we want employees to go in doing whatever it takes to satisfy customers?

What's our role in, or responsibility to, our communities?

What's our responsibility to our employees?

What's our responsibility to our customers?

How do we recognize and reward our employees (celebrate wins and milestones)?

How do we handle people who don't fit in to our culture?

How do we want our customers to be treated?

How big or small should we be to accomplish our mission and uphold our values?

How should we be organized to best accomplish our mission and uphold our values?

What obstacles do we face in achieving our mission?

15. Communicate the vision

Once your organization has a clear, written vision, you must communicate it. One of the major problems with vision statements is getting them out of the executive suite and into the organization. Numerous executives say to us in our seminars, "I have a clear vision of where we're going and how to get there. How do I get it out to the rest of the organization?"

A study sponsored by Learning International and conducted by Louis Harris and Associates, Inc., may shed some light on.this problem. The findings indicate that most efforts to communicate vision and strategy involve primarily one-way communication such as speeches, annual reports, newsletters, and business plans. While these are important and necessary tools, they're often inadequate. This study also reveals that executives don't use other means, such as rewards or recognition, to help spread the vision. Only 11 percent of the surveyed executives reported using recognition to reward managers for communicating the vision to others.

Executives in customer-oriented organizations report that they continually remind employees that every customer contact can make or break the company, and that every contact with every customer is the most important contact of every day.

Develop a concise, hard-hitting message or theme that communicates the values of your company to your customers and employees. This message should convey what your organization does, how it is unique, and how customers will benefit from doing business with you. The message also reminds *employees* about what's important.

- [ ] State Farm Insurance says, "Like a good neighbor, State Farm is there."
- [ ] Federal Express says customers can count on them "When it absolutely, positively has to be there overnight."
- [ ] John Deere strives to "Keep the Customer Running."
- [ ] Publix, a Florida-based supermarket chain, tells customers and employees that Publix is "Where shopping is a pleasure."
- [ ] McDonald's emphasizes QSCV: Quality, Service, Cleanliness, and Value.

Keep in mind that the process of communicating the vision and indoctrinating all employees with a customer-focused perspective begins during the employee selection process. A job interview provides the first opportunity for a prospective hire to hear about a company's culture, standards, and expectations. When employees who conduct hiring interviews understand and believe in a customer-focused mission, they will paint for candidates a different picture of the organization than will interviewers who see the organization as selling products alone.

Learning International reports that "many senior executives may fail to realize that a number of their best managers have a personal vision to share, but aren't communicating it because they're given little incentive or reason to do so." In addition to not rewarding or recognizing managers for helping to spread the vision, many organizations inadvertently punish managers for doing so. Executives and managers at all levels should look at how people are rewarded for delivering better-than-average service. Are your managers praised or punished when their employees go out of their way for customers? What if employees bend the rules a little? What happens if someone in your organization sacrifices short-term gains for long-term customer satisfaction?

If it's important, reward it. *And* make sure you're not punishing the very behavior you're trying to foster.

16. Develop your own service mission or theme to align with the corporate vision

Regardless of your job title or area of responsibility, create your own service vision to align with the larger vision. If you're a department manager, repeat the process described above: define or redefine the mission, values, and ways of doing business for your department or work unit. Go talk with your internal customers. Learn their needs, problems, and time restrictions. Learn what happens if you don't serve them well. Even if you're a one-person department, it's worth doing this. Your "work unit" means you and those who work with you in your department, section, team, or whatever.

Here are some things to consider when developing your personal service vision:

☐ *Why am I (and this unit) here?* What's my personal mission? What's the purpose of this unit? If you don't have a clear purpose, write a mission statement for your unit.

☐ *How does my mission fit in?* How does what I see for myself and my unit fit with the organization's overall direction, strategies, values? Are we in synch?

☐ *How do others think I'm fulfilling my mission?* Do your internal customers believe you're meeting or exceeding your mission?

☐ *What value do I add to the organization?* What bottom-line value do you contribute? If somebody were to look at you and your unit as an investment opportunity, what return would they get on their investment of salary, benefits, desks, and supplies?

☐ *What would happen if I (or my unit) weren't here?* If you or your department were eliminated today, how would that affect your organization? Try to keep your ego out of this one. What *measurable* effect would there be? Can the organization get the output, information, or services you provide for less somewhere else? If nothing would be lost, you may not be pulling your share.

17. Make service everybody's business

In *Service America!*, Zemke and Albrecht observed:

> It's one thing to get the front line people into a customer-oriented mode. It's quite another to sell that gospel to people in noncontact roles. . . . Inside people become preoccupied with inside concerns . . . like information, procedures, forms, and reports. Their point of view is often, "It's somebody else's job to take care of the customer. My job is to make sure these reports get in on time."

Zemke and Albrecht also say, "When inside people lose their sense of being connected to the customer . . . they become bureaucrats. They can no longer see how the results they produce help the company meet the wants and needs of the market. It telegraphs a profound misconception when a person says, 'I don't have anything to do with customers.'"

A director of a customer service department once asked Tom Peters how to get a greater commitment to service in his department. Peters' reply was:

If you really have guts, you should lobby to get rid of the customer service department. . . . For customer service to be successful, it must be everyone's business—in indirect functions far away from the firing line or the retail floor itself.

Because I'm not likely to talk you into that, I suggest that you radically shift the application of your resources from doing customer service to training people throughout the firm to provide better customer service.

It's important that people who don't have regular, direct customer contact think of themselves as providing service. This includes people in finance, purchasing, data processing, engineering, manufacturing, contract administration, and the like. In some organizations, these people see the role of handling customers as "beneath" them—something for less-qualified, untrained, lower-paid, lower-status people to take care of. They see their own jobs as the "real work" of the organization. There's a caste system in many organizations, and frontline people are frequently at the bottom of the heap.

Zemke and Albrecht had it right when they said that the message everyone in the organization needs to understand is this: "If you're not serving the customer, you'd better be serving someone who is."

At Stew Leonard's Dairy, when office workers notice long lines at the checkout counters they stop what they are doing and take the initiative to help bag groceries to speed things up. They do this without being asked because they understand that their real job is serving customers. Whatever else they do is only a means to that end.

However, the service leaders represented in the Citibank study acknowledge the difficulty in stimulating a service orientation in employees who do not have regular customer contact. They agree that this is something that requires constant attention. Their recommendations follow:

☐ Indoctrinate *all* employees with a service orientation.

☐ Make sure all employees see how their jobs fit into the organization, how their jobs affect customers, and how their errors affect others in the organization.

☐ Provide incentive programs for service-related activities aimed at noncontact employees.

☐ Encourage and reward managers of noncontact units to instill service orientation in their employees.

You can also indoctrinate and continually reinforce in employees the idea that they *do* make a difference—that, regardless of their job responsibilities, they contribute to serving customers and meeting customer needs.

You should establish clear standards for service in every position. Make them measurable and incorporate them in the performance review system. If service is not part of everyone's job, from the top down, people won't give it much attention. Everyone must be held accountable for setting and reaching service-related goals, in addition to sales, production, or other job-specific goals.

Have each employee and organizational unit describe the benefits of what they do for both internal and external customers. You might want to use this format:

I/we _____ (verb) so that

_____ (external customers) and

_____ (internal customers) will

have _____ (benefits).

Have each employee and organizational unit write simple, measurable goals that relate to service; for example:

☐ Reduce turnaround time by 10 percent (or 2 days) within 90 days

☐ Reduce complaints by 5 percent in 30 days

18. Establish strict service standards and stick to them

Service-oriented companies recognize the need for establishing service standards so both customers and employees know what's expected. You must do more than tell employees to be more customer-focused or tell them to provide better service. You must define exactly what better service means in your organization. Without specific, well-understood standards for what exceptional service is, employees will interpret it themselves.

Having clear service standards sends a strong message to customers that you're serious about meeting their needs. It also sends a strong message to employees. Here are a few examples of clear, specific service standards:

☐ Boeing tells its customers it will have a part to them in 2 hours, even if it has to take the part off a plane on the assembly line to get it to them. This standard tells customers like United, TWA, and others that Boeing is willing to go to great lengths to keep its planes in the air, where they make money. It also tells employees how serious Boeing is about meeting its commitment to its customers.

☐ Domino's Pizza says you get your pizza in 30 minutes or you can take $3 off.

☐ Federal Express says your package will be delivered the next day or you don't pay. Everything the company does is geared toward meeting that standard, and everyone in the company—telephone operators, drivers, freight handlers, pilots, accountants—has the same goal.

☐ McDonald's has a 700-page manual that describes all its procedures for making food, smiling at customers, cleaning the stores, and practically everything else.

☐ Marriott has Standard Operating Procedures (SOPs) for every task. The SOPs are detailed instructions concerning such things as how to open the pool each day, how chefs are to make each recipe, how food is to be arranged and garnished on plates, what bellhops should do when escorting guests to their rooms, and so on.

Be creative as you set service standards within your organization. Some companies state that their phones will be answered in at least three rings. Others set standards that every customer complaint will be resolved by the end of the same business day. Think about the kinds of standards your customers will appreciate.

Standards also help ensure consistency, even by non-customer-contact employees. Standards ensure that anyone performing a function—whether it's taking an order, serving a meal, or preparing a shipment—does the task in the same way. The larger the organization, the more important this consistency is. Having consistent standards eliminates, or at least reduces, the chances for omissions, errors, and people doing things their own way because they weren't sure how the things were supposed to be done.

Allowing employees to know what's expected and to work within well-defined guidelines enables people to go outside or beyond these guidelines when necessary to meet customer needs. Lack of standards prohibits "beyond the call of duty" service. When people don't know what's expected, they tend to do as little as possible to call attention to their actions for fear of reprisal. Or they think of ways to justify their performance or actions in case they're questioned. People who know what's expected of them have a frame of reference, and thus decision making is easier for them.

Traditional companies set standards based on *management's* needs and perceptions. Service-oriented companies rely on heavy input from customers and top performers in every job to help set the standards. Invariably, standards set by the front line are tougher and are achieved more often than are those handed down without any input.

There are two primary dangers inherent in standards. One is the danger of becoming too codified, regimented, and rule-bound by setting rigid, arbitrary standards and goals. The other is the danger of providing too *little* guidance, so that every employee must constantly create his or her own standards. In this case, customers eventually end up getting arbitrary, inconsistent, and usually inferior products and services.

Some issues you might want to consider:

☐ Under what circumstances are refunds given, or returns or exchanges accepted?

☐ Are there differences for different customers? For example, do the same policies apply for an established, loyal, high-volume customer who pays its bills on time and for a new, slow-paying, low-volume customer?

☐ What are some alternative actions or remedies people might use in various situations?

19. Recognize the importance of frontline employees

The quote below was in a Disney brochure promoting a workshop called "The Disney Approach to Quality Service":

> How will your front line staff deal with the next person they encounter? How can you be sure that the contact will be satisfactory? How can you be sure that your valued client will complete the transaction, satisfied that he or she was properly served, with the intention of returning again and again?
>
> Of course, there is no assurance beyond the confidence you have that your staff will do the job that is expected of them. To build that confidence, a compelling and lasting commitment to service must be established.

Let's put this concept into dollars and cents. If you've already figured the value of an average customer, you can also calculate the value of the assets your frontline people handle every day. Let's say an average customer spends $1,500 in a year. And let's say an average frontline person talks to 20 people a day. Then each frontline person is responsible for a potential $2,400,000 in revenue per year (20 customers/day × $1,500 × 240 days). Do you see your frontline people as $2-million-a-year account managers or as $20,000-a-year order-takers, receptionists, or customer service representatives?

We've all heard the old adage, "Your people *are* the organization." It sounds good, but most organizations don't do much to demonstrate this either to the people at the front line or to customers.

And the larger the organization, the more important this concept becomes. If your organization has only a handful of employees and only a few locations, managers can personally visit the locations, manage quality and service, and train and coach employees. When there are thousands of employees, and dozens—or even hundreds—of locations, managers can't be around to ensure quality during every moment of truth. Service-oriented organizations realize this.

Clearly, then, hiring the right people and training them properly is essential. Just as important is the trust and confidence you place in your frontline employees. Can the managers in your organization say to employees, "You are the company to our customers. You make an impression on customers, meet their needs, and handle their problems every day. We can't always be there to make decisions for you or show you where to find information you need. But we have complete confidence in you to do what's best for our customers and this organization." Can managers and executives say this? Do they?

20. Hire service-oriented people

Becoming more customer-focused also means hiring service-oriented people. Technical skills are only part of the picture. You have to start with people who have the experience, skills, and aptitude for their jobs, and then train them. In this section, we'll look at five major aspects of hiring service-oriented people:

1 Why hiring service-oriented people is important
2 Who is responsible for hiring service-oriented people
3 Basic characteristics of service-oriented people
4 How to select service-oriented people
5 Where to find service-oriented people

Why hiring service-oriented people is important.   The kinds of people you hire, promote, or transfer into customer-contact positions is critical. Hiring is also important for non-customer-contact positions.

To be service-oriented, companies must hire people who naturally care about people. Distinguishing such people from a pool of job applicants is sometimes difficult, because so many applicants say they "love people." Yet some people would much rather work with *things* (cars, computers, paint, etc.). There's nothing wrong with that preference; however, such people shouldn't be on the front line where constant people contact is essential.

Some people seem to have a chip on their shoulder. They come across as angry or bitter, even if they're not. Some people like working alone, some need to be the center of attention, and some need always to be right (even if they're not). Some people are comfortable only when they can work at their own relaxed pace. Others can work only in an orderly, predictable environment where things don't change much. These kinds of people often don't do well in service-oriented organizations.

Service-oriented companies define the experience, skills, and temperament required for customer-contact positions. They hire people who are empathetic, caring, and intelligent; who are concerned about customer comfort and satisfaction; who understand the customer's point of view; who keep their promises; who are willing to go the extra mile; who remain pleasant, smiling, and agreeable; who show *real* appreciation for the customer's business, not just with a perfunctory "Thank you for shopping here."

A service-oriented disposition is not a training issue; it's a hiring issue. It is very difficult (if not impossible), time-consuming, and expensive to "teach" sour, grumpy, negative, insensitive, complaining people to be caring, sensitive, positive, and friendly. These attributes aren't learned skills; they're approaches to life. You must hire (or promote) people who have the temperament you desire.

Frito-Lay's Craig Johnson says, "You can't force people to be committed to service. You must hire people who are interested in what your organization is about."

In order for your organization to become more service-oriented, your recruiting practices may have to change. You must identify the skills and characteristics of successful performers. Then you must find people with those skills and traits. Hire them, promote them, or transfer them to the front lines. They may also need to be trained, paid, coached, supported, and motivated differently than they are now.

Although today we're more sophisticated in defining employee characteristics and doing employee profiles, none of this is new. In 1917, hotel magnate E. M. Statler sent the letter (next page) to the managers of all his hotels.

Statler recognized over 70 years ago that hiring and promoting "pleasant, cheerful people of good disposition" was good business and that he needed to get rid of grouches, people with sour dispositions, and people who felt sorry for themselves.

But it's not a one-way street. Potential employees should also have the opportunity to decide if yours is the kind of organization they want to work for. Do the organization's values, mission, working conditions, work hours, and related factors align with a potential employee's values and needs? Several years ago, in *Training* magazine, Deede Sharp, a training manager at Disney World, described how Disney views this process:

> During our recruiting and selection cycle, we make the importance of service and our expectations very clear. We do a one-hour presentation on what Disney stands for, what our values are, and what working for Disney is like. We want people to back out before they ever see a guest if there is any doubt that they will like this kind of work.

Ronald H. Dunbar, executive vice president of human resources at Ryder Systems, told *Human Resources Executive* magazine that Ryder's job applicants are interviewed extensively by peers, supervisors, and even subordinates. He says the interviewers also do "extensive reference checking and give people realistic previews of what the work and the Ryder culture will demand of them."

Who is responsible for hiring service-oriented people.　The responsibility for recruiting and training should rest with managers, not with people in a human resources or personnel department.

In her book *No One Need Apply*, Lee Bowes reports that many personnel officers in companies of all sizes are female, minority, or both. More than two-thirds have been promoted from some lower-level position not related to personnel. About half have been with their organization for 15 years or more, and very few have any training in personnel work or related fields. Many people end up in personnel because they were pushed upstairs, were asked to handle a tough situation, or just fell into the job. Once in personnel, they rarely go out to work in other departments as do other up-and-coming managers.

"Hire Only Good-Natured People"
Hotelman's order 60 years ago just as applicable today

(In 1917 E. M. Statler sent to the managers of all his hotels the following letter.)

From this date you are instructed to employ only good-natured people, cheerful and pleasant, who smile easily and often. This ought to go for every job in the house, but at present I'll insist on it only for people who come in contact with guests.

It does go, from this day, for all department heads, front office people, cashiers, captains, elevator men, porters, telephone operators and other employees who have to deal directly with patrons.

And it isn't only a case of hiring. That policy is to guern all promotions; and you are to begin, right now, to measure your present staff by it.

If it's necessary to clean house, do it. Don't protest. Get rid of the grouches, and the people who can't keep their tempers, and the people who act as if they were always under a burden of trouble and feeling sorry for themselves. You can't make that kind of person over; you can't do anything with him profitably, but get rid of him. Let the other fellow have him, and you hire a man who can be taught.

You want to lessen complaints, don't you? You want your organization more efficient, don't you? Well, I've been studying this idea for months, and I'm convinced that it will help solve several problems we have—of complaints, of competition, of handicaps we've had in certain spots. Not immediately, perhaps; not tomorrow, or the middle of next week; but there will be noticeable improvement just as soon as it gets along.

Unless—unless you and your department heads are indifferent or antagonistic, in which case you'll want to go on just as before, without giving it a trial.

But I've decided on this, and I'm going to do my very most toward seeing that it does get a fair trial, and that it gets the same attention and respect and adherence as any other basic principle of this organization.

Which is exactly what it is—a basic principle! Hire pleasant, cheerful people, people of good disposition, and reject everyone who isn't.

It isn't enough to be courteous to 74 patrons and pert with the 75th. It won't do to be cheerful 58 minutes of the hour and disgruntled the other 2. It isn't sufficient for 10 employees to give service and the 11th to go slack on his job.

In another hotel another clerk may have sold the guest just as comfortable a room, another bellman may have handled his bag just as deftly, another waiter may have served him piping hot dinner just as promptly, but the thing that made the impression on the guest was that these latter employees seemed "glad to do it,' they seemed interested in him personally.

Gracious service means more than "perfect" service. The guest will wait an extra minute for his chops if the waiter brings him a newspaper and explains the delay pleasantly.

Every hotel employee is a salesman. He must satisfy customers with the only thing he has to sell—service—and he must please them with the way he sells it. I believe that a majority of the complaints in a hotel are due more to the guest's state of mind than to the importance of the thing about which he complains.

—E. M. Statler

Bowes concludes that these factors produce long-term, trusted employees who have a knack for keeping their noses clean and fitting into the organization's fabric. They do what's asked of them and don't make waves. They tend to lose touch with what's needed in the organization. Until recently, they've not been known for making significant policy decisions on their own. When tough-minded corporate executives make decisions, those in the personnel department are rarely consulted.

This is all the more reason to put the responsibility for hiring, training, and firing with line managers who must be accountable for the activities of their people and the results of their work units. In its mission statement for the 1990s, The Coca-Cola Company says:

> The responsibility for developing people cannot be delegated to training courses, academic exercises, or professionals in the area of human resources. Those have a role to play but do not constitute an adequate process. *The development of our best people is the personal responsibility of Management.* It requires each manager to see his or her most important responsibility as teaching or developing people. Our charge is simple—recruiting and training the best talent by the best managers. As that talent grows and develops, they become the next managers capable of and responsible for developing new talent, thus perpetuating a strength.

Hiring practices are also affected by beliefs. Some organizations believe that hourly and frontline employees can and should be involved in the hiring process. Companies like Ryder, Johnsonville Sausage, and Hewlett-Packard have peers involved in the interview process. And, a few highly innovative organizations, such as Worthington Steel and the General Motors plant in Fitzgerald, Georgia, even leave hiring decisions up to employee work teams. Now that's putting responsibility for hiring with the people who are most accountable for results!

I believe that the closer to the front line you can place hiring decisions, the better. Such an approach usually eliminates personnel departments from all but the initial screening of applicants. Of course, placing the hiring decision with line managers, supervisors, or employees usually means that those doing the hiring may need some training and lots of confidence building. They may need to learn *how* to interview and *how* to make good hiring decisions. They probably also need to believe they can and should be involved in hiring.

Managers may also need to take a larger part in defining the skills and requirements needed for various positions. Because personnel departments frequently have no idea what traits and skills are actually needed in a particular job, job descriptions written by them are often as bad as the hiring decisions they make. When personnel does both the job description and the hiring, it's often a prescription for disaster.

Basic characteristics of service-oriented people.   Before managers—or anyone else—can make good hiring decisions, they have to know what to look for.

If you don't know what you're looking for, you probably won't find it. Unless you define the skills, experience, background, and temperament best suited for positions in your organization, it won't matter who does the interviewing, because they'll all just be playing recruiting roulette; that is, they'll meet with lots of people and hope they're lucky enough to find a good one once in a while. The roulette odds are about as good as they are in Monte Carlo. In most cases, organizations are merely playing to avoid *losing*—that is, to avoid hiring too many people who don't work out.

Service-oriented organizations go to great lengths to define what they're looking for before they begin the hiring process. For General Electric's Answer Center—the company's 24-hour, toll-free hotline for handling customer questions and complaints—GE identified the personality traits essential for successful telephone agents. When hiring such agents, GE screens applicants carefully. Out of 500 applicants, the company typically hires only about 15. Once selected, applicants go through an initial 5-week training period followed by another 100 hours of training each year to maintain and improve their skills.

Before describing the kind of people you'd like to hire or promote, consider the jobs themselves. I'm talking primarily about customer-contact positions, but this process applies to *any* job. First, describe the purpose of every job in terms that include satisfying customers. Too often, customers aren't even mentioned. For example, the job of a plumber might be described as "installing or repairing plumbing," but the description could be made more customer-focused by adding "so that customers are satisfied and will call us for their other plumbing needs." The specified purpose of a retail sales position might be to "help customers select what they desire or need so they are satisfied with their purchases and will return in the future."

Describing the purpose of any job and including customer satisfaction is also important for positions inside organizations that have little end-user contact. Some examples:

Data-entry clerk: To provide accurate, timely, and necessary information to client departments so they can serve customers more efficiently.

Warehouse shipping associate: To process customer orders so customers get what they order, on time and undamaged, and so they will continue to order from us.

Accounts receivable supervisor: To support the receivables staff in processing payments so that customers receive accurate statements on time.

Next, consider the job itself. Below are some areas to consider which will help you determine the skills, background experience, or education you'll want in a position. Decide which of these are important and how important they are for each job. Add your own if you like.

☐ What *knowledge* does the job require?

Industry terminology, jargon

Technical know-how

Specialized knowledge (law, medicine, etc.)

☐ What *skills* or *abilities* are required (specific job-related skills such as how to use computers, repair cameras, sell, run cash registers, do inventory, complete an invoice, etc.)?

☐ What are the *physical requirements* for the job?

Eye–hand coordination

Manual dexterity

Eyesight

Hearing

Tactile sensitivity

Strength

Stamina/endurance

Speed

Agility

☐ What *communication skills* are needed?

Listening

Grammar

Pronunciation

Accent

Telephone

☐ What are the *working conditions* of the job?

Location

Hours

Safety

Travel

☐ What is the *nature of the job?*

What's the pace and pressure?

Are tasks structured and well-defined, or loose?

Do tasks change or stay the same?

Are job-holders responsible for product, equipment, facilities, money, etc.?

Whom do they have most contact with: other employees, suppliers, customers, general public, or others?

Do they handle confidential information?

How closely are they supervised?

Whom do they report to?

What kinds of decisions must employees in frontline positions make? How often?

What are the size, scope, and consequences of employees' decisions?

Once you've defined the job itself, you can look more objectively at the educational level, courses of study, experience, and other indicators most likely to predict success. Determining these requirements is relatively easy. The harder part is defining the personality characteristics and interpersonal skills necessary for customer-contact people. One of the best ways to define these skills and characteristics is to analyze a sample of your top performers. Once you've defined the job, try to isolate the skills, experience, and characteristics of those who are most successful in that job or a similar job.

Another key is to make a distinction between those things someone needs to bring with them and those things that can be learned. Hire for those traits and attributes people can't learn on the job, or for the knowledge or skills it takes too long to learn. Teach people the rest once they're on board.

Below is a list of some traits and characteristics to look for when hiring service-oriented people. It's not an all-inclusive list, and you may want to add some or delete others to fit your needs. Each position may require different combinations of these and greater or lesser depth. For example, people in positions at the front line may need more sensitivity than organization and planning skills. Positions with less direct customer contact may require other skills and traits. Also, the same traits may have different meanings for different positions. For example: Creativity may be a critical skill at the front line and could be defined as "the ability to come up with unusual ways of solving customer problems." In product design, creativity is also critical and might be defined as "the ability to come up with innovations in product design features, packaging, or materials." Those doing the hiring must decide, for the organization and for each position, which skills and traits are important and how they are defined.

Alertness: Attentive to situations and conditions, including subtle or unspoken cues. Sees the big picture; puts things in perspective.

Analysis and inference: Identifies essential elements of situations, makes accurate inferences from available information, and suggests workable solutions or takes appropriate actions.

Appearance: Is clean and well-groomed; dresses appropriately for organization's working environment and situations.

Assertiveness: States position tactfully but forcefully, even in the face of opposition; able and willing to stick by decisions; not unduly influenced by power, prestige, or status of others.

Coaching/counseling: Assists others in clarifying problems and seeking their own solutions; provides positive or negative feedback in helpful, caring ways.

Common sense: Applies good judgment to situations, policies, and practices to reach sensible, practical solutions. Able and willing to "bend the rules" if necessary as situations warrant.

Concern: Is caring; demonstrates sincere concern for the problems, needs, and well-being of others. Does not become robotic and just "go through the motions."

Coping skills: Handles job- or self-imposed pressures well; functions effectively in the face of deadlines, inadequate resources, anger, rejection, dangerous or unpleasant working conditions, interpersonal conflict, etc.; remains calm in stressful situations.

Creativity: Comes up with novel ideas or innovative solutions to problems; develops ideas or solutions that go beyond the established rules and the ways things are always done.

Conformity: Operates within established guidelines, rules, policies, and procedures.

Decisiveness: Able and willing to make decisions and take action on the spot; when necessary, makes decisions based on limited information and without requiring advice or approval of others.

Dependability: Delivers on promises; follows through on commitments. Can be counted on to be there (rarely late or absent). Willing to come in or stay late when needed.

Empathy: Sees situations from other people's points of view; able to put self "in the other person's shoes."

Energy level: Demonstrates and communicates a sense of vitality and importance through actions and speech. Demonstrates appropriate zest, vigor, and friendliness in voice and actions. Able to work at a fast pace if the job requires it.

Flexibility: Can quickly adapt to changes in the environment, procedures, or other areas with minimal inconvenience, disruption, or resistance; able to quickly recognize changes in customer needs, moods, or priorities and to respond appropriately.

Independence: Works effectively and productively without close supervision; knows what to do and does it; is a self-starter.

Initiative: Able and willing to go beyond the minimum expected; without prompting, looks for and employs ways to improve own performance.

Integrity: Has sound ethical principles; is honest; can be believed and counted on; is genuine, not phony or put-on; easily admits to a mistake.

Interpersonal skills: Deals effectively with others, including establishing a rapport, listening, and adapting behavior and communication styles to best communicate with others; able to let others be "right," even if they're not.

Leadership: Earns the respect of others; influences the actions of others; exercises good judgment in working with others; gets willing support from people who don't work for (or report to) them.

Listening: Maintains attention when customers air grievances, listens for the real issues, and hears both facts and feelings when others are speaking. Lets others talk.

Oral communication: Present ideas and information clearly, concisely, and correctly over the phone or in person, even in the face of negative or hostile listeners; speaks clearly; uses appropriate business vocabulary and voice.

Organization/planning: Organizes, prioritizes, and schedules work; deploys resources to company's best advantage; recognizes the importance of timing in situations and responds appropriately.

Patience: Remains calm in stressful situations. Willing to repeat instructions (several times, if needed) or continue a conversation without belittling or demeaning others.

Persistence: Able and willing to perservere and to see things through, even if tasks are unpleasant; finds alternative ways to resolve problems or obstacles.

Positive outlook: Maintains a warm, friendly, upbeat outlook and communicates this to others where appropriate. Likes people.

Prevention orientation: Able and willing to go beyond just solving problems. Analyzes and researches situations to determine causes and takes actions to prevent them from recurring.

Problem-solving ability: Gathers necessary information, separates symptoms from possible causes, determines the dimensions and consequences, and suggests workable solutions.

Sensitivity: Recognizes and interprets verbal and nonverbal cues to understand the needs, feelings, problems, and concerns of others; recognizes and responds to situations, pressures, and conditions of others.

Standards: Demonstrates high standards for self and for others. Does not accept average or "good enough." Strives for excellence in everything.

Teaching/training: Communicates knowledge, skills, and procedures to others so they can easily understand and use them.

Teamwork/cooperation: Able and willing to work with others, to work as part of a group even if it means sacrificing personal desires or comfort to benefit the group or organization, and to let others be the center of attention.

Tolerance of ambiguity: Functions effectively in situations where there may be inadequate information or conflicting demands, absence of guidelines, and no right or wrong answers or ways to do things.

Written communications: Writes clearly, concisely, accurately, and correctly; reads and interprets written materials efficiently and well. Able to write effective business letters if written replies are called for.

How to select service-oriented people.   Once you've defined what you're looking for, you need an effective way to screen applicants to determine which ones meet most of your criteria.

Job-placement experts tell us the traditional interview is the poorest predictor of future job success. Both candidates and interviewers tend to present distorted views of their good qualities while minimizing problems. Also, job searches and interviews require certain skills and abilities. People with good job-search and interviewing skills may not have the skills needed for the job in question. Nevertheless, interviews are still the most widely used recruiting and hiring practices.

There are better ways to find qualified employees. They take longer and require a little more preparation, so many organizations don't use them. They prefer to stick to the traditional job interview approach of "Tell me about yourself," "Why do you want to work here?" and "What are your strengths and weaknesses?"

One approach to hiring is based on the premise that the best predictor of future performance is past performance. Approaches such as conceptual questions, mini cases, and role plays are based on this premise. Another approach maintains that actual performance in real or simulated situations is the best predictor of actual abilities and of future performance (assessment centers, in-basket exercises, interactive video, and job-related assignments are examples of this approach). Both approaches may be right, and it's possible, even advisable, to use a combination of the past-performance approach and the simulated-situation approach. I'll describe each briefly and give examples.

The conceptual questions approach (also called patterned or structured interviews) involves identifying job-related tasks or situations and asking candidates how they've handled these situations in the past. Of course, questions should be tailored to the needs of the job, which is why identifying those needs is an important first step.

If tolerance for frequent procedure changes and making quick decisions on the spot are important, you might ask questions like, "What did you like best about your last job? Least? What's the biggest frustration you faced in your last position? Give an example. How did you handle it? Describe the most difficult situation you faced there and explain how you handled it."

If the applicant says, "I like to know where I'm going each day, have a work station, and keep things pretty orderly," or if his or her most difficult or frustrating experiences involved handling people, the applicant probably won't be happy in a customer-contact job, won't be productive in such a position, and won't stay very long. People like this are not inferior just because they're not comfortable with lots of changes. They just won't fit into a customer-contact position. There are many other positions for which that temperament is perfect and will contribute to a person's success.

If tight deadlines and last-minute changes are a large part of the job, call candidates a day before their interviews and ask them to do something—write something, describe something, or complete a task—and bring it with them. Then talk in the interview about that assignment.

Other conceptual questions that might be helpful in an interview include the following:

☐ "Tell me about the most difficult situation you've had with a customer. How did you handle it? What happened? How did it turn out? What's the ideal way of handling a situation like that?"

☐ "Tell me about a time when you had to make a quick, on-the-spot decision for a customer. Describe the situation and what you did. Why did you handle it that particular way? How did it turn out?"

☐ "What do you think is the proper balance of employee freedom versus supervision? Give me an example of when you felt you had too much supervisory control. How did you react in that situation?"

☐ "Describe the kind of work environment in which you feel the most productive."

These conceptual questions indicate how attentive applicants are to situations they've experienced, how they perceive situations and reflect on them later, and the mental processes they've used to resolve problems.

There are several limitations with these kinds of questions. A major limitation is that they rely on the candidates' *descriptions* of what they did, so there's room for embellishment. Another is that some people tend to ramble. Some interviewers confuse wordiness with insight when there may be none. Even perceptiveness and insight in verbal descriptions may not translate into the behaviors you want on the job.

Another selection approach involves mini case studies typical of situations applicants might find themselves in if they were hired. These situations enable interviewers to assess an applicant's ability to think on his or her feet; exercise judgment, tact, and flexibility; and come up with appropriate solutions to different situations. Using the same cases with each applicant also enables direct comparisons that conceptual questions don't allow for. Of course, specific cases should be developed for specific positions.

Here is an example of a mini case: "A customer approaches you with an expensive item he wants to return. He has no receipt, and you're not sure if the merchandise is really your company's. What would you do?"

Mini cases have drawbacks, too. There's still a lot of emphasis on verbal skills—applicants describe what they *say* they would do in a given situation. And some interviewers may listen more for the words than for the applicant's overall intentions in the way they handle the situation. There's also a tendency for applicants to give answers they think the interviewer wants to hear. And pressure to respond quickly may cause some applicants to give hasty answers that aren't well thought out.

Other selection methods involve simulations, role playing, in-basket exercises, and similar activities in which applicants don't *talk* about what they'd do in situations, they actually *do* it. For these selection methods, it's also important to first identify the skills, temperament, conditions, and decision-making abilities necessary for the job.

In role playing, applicants are given a brief description of a situation ("You're a restaurant manager" or "You're a telephone sales representative for an office products company") and a few factual details about the situation. The interviewer, or someone else, plays the part of a customer. Sometimes the role plays are videotaped.

A video variation of this has been developed by companies such as the Jackson Smye Company of Toronto, Canada. In this method, an applicant watches a videotaped vignette. The vignette ends leaving a situation unresolved, and the applicant then "handles" the situation by talking directly to the people on the video screen, as though it were a live situation. Observers assess the applicants' responses.

There are drawbacks to these methods as well. Customized video vignettes can cost $200,000 or more. Even video vignettes of "generic" situations can be costly, and developing role plays requires time to develop scripts and prepare to enact them. With role plays, stress levels for applicants (and interviewers) are often high. Some say this isn't bad, because it simulates the stress in real, on-the-job pressure situations. But although these approaches come closer to real job conditions, they're still not actual situations.

The ways I've just described for selecting service-oriented applicants are all designed to improve your ability to predict who's going to perform on the job the way you've defined it. Even with their limitations, these methods are certainly better than the "tell me about yourself" kind of interview.

However, the best predictor of future performance is not past performance, it's *current* performance. I suggest using the above methods to find the person or people you think will work best. Then add a step to your selection process: have applicants actually *perform* job-related activities or tasks. This gives you information on what they can actually do, not what they *say* they'll do.

Of course, this approach isn't practical or even advisable for every job. You wouldn't want to burn down a building just so you could observe a firefighter applicant's ability to put the fire out. In reality, a combination of the predictive methods described above and real-time performance is the most feasible approach.

However, there are some practical ways to observe current performance:

☐ *Student internships.* Many organizations have summer interns. Others have students work part-time or full-time for a semester. This is often a good way to identify talented people who'll fit into your organization. It also gives them a chance to see if *they* want to work for *you.*

☐ *Temporary employees.* "Temps" are usually hired for a specific time period or a specific project. Many businesses hire them during peak periods or when key employees are on leave. They're often hired through employment agencies. If a temporary employee doesn't work out, most agencies are willing to send another. Although there can be tax and labor-law implications associated with using temps on a long-term basis, using temps can be a good way to find qualified people. If an opening occurs, a good temp can be contacted and offered a permanent position.

☐ *Leased employees.* This is a relatively new, and growing, concept, especially for businesses with fewer than 100 employees. Depending on how it's organized, leasing can be similar to hiring temps for recruiting purposes. If you lease employees from an agency and some employees don't work out, the agency will generally send replacements.

☐ *Use of a probationary period.* Such a period gives you a chance to observe people on the job in order to assess their performance. It also gives *them* an opportunity to determine if they like the organization, the job, the hours, and so on. During the probationary time, employees can be observed and "shopped."

Where to find service-oriented people. The labor force is shrinking, and more skills than ever are needed for the jobs organizations seek to fill. The most common cry I hear from managers and executives in the United States is, "I can't find people." In most cases, using traditional sources and means of attracting qualified, talented people won't work anymore.

To attract and keep today's work force, your organization may need to change some of its views and practices. You need to look in unconventional places and offer more than the traditional pay and benefits package. Many organizations are holding brainstorming sessions with employees at all levels to come up with ways to find qualified people and to make their organizations more appealing to them. You should, too. Don't worry if some of the ideas you come up with sound impractical, even outlandish. These are not traditional times. Below are some ideas some organizations are using. Adapt them or expand them to work in your organization.

Consider hiring

☐ Your own full-time employees to take on second, part-time jobs in your organization.

☐ Teachers, especially in summer, on weekends, or on holidays. Many teachers are people-oriented, are patient, and have good communication skills.

☐ Students. Many students want meaningful work experiences as much as they want money.

☐ Retirees. After a year of retirement, many people are bored and eager to come back to work. Most only want to work part-time.

☐ Military people who are retiring or are being discharged.

☐ Women (or men) with school-age children. Many are willing to work as long as they can be home when their children get home from school; such people can often work 4 to 5 hours a day.

☐ Women (or men) with older children. Many are interested in returning to the work force when their children are grown.

☐ Recently widowed or divorced people. These people sometimes want something to "take their minds off the situation." They, too, may only want to work part-time at first.

To attract these people, you may need to do some of the following:

☐ Offer more. Many of today's high-school and college-age workers don't "need" a job like such workers did several generations ago. They're also more picky about the kind of organization they work for.

☐ Make sure your organization treats people with respect and makes them feel like part of a team. Be sure to involve families.

☐ Offer good wages.

☐ Play up what you have to offer. The Kentucky Fried Chicken Company frequently runs blind ads (ads that don't identify the company) describing what it offers to employees. A steel company we know of uses 25 percent of its advertising space to publish its corporate values: "Respect for the individual, a safe working environment, equal opportunity, employment security, integrity in all our undertakings, encouraging ability and ambition in all our people."

☐ Offer flexible hours. Not everyone can work 9 to 5. There may be talented, qualified, willing people who can work at different times.

☐ Create multiple job-holders—two (or more) people who hold the same job and fit the work into their individual schedules.

☐ Offer child care.

☐ Offer scholarships (or contribute toward scholarships) for younger people.

☐ Offer benefits—insurance, health care, profit sharing, etc.—to part-timers. These benefits appeal to younger workers, housewives, and retirees, many of whom may not be eligible themselves or may be underprotected. Consider offering partial benefits for part-timers.

☐ Provide a definitive career path. Show people how they can take on greater responsibility and gain status, pay, and experience. Build in additional areas of responsibility, making people crew leaders, shift coordinators, trainers, and so on.

☐ Provide transportation to and from work. Some employers who are not on public transportation lines, or whose employees don't have cars, operate van pools.

Here are some ways to find qualified service-oriented people:

☐ Employee recruiting. For example, if someone referred by an employee is hired, the employee who made the referral gets a bonus. If the new person stays for 6 months (or whatever period you decide), the referring employee gets another bonus.

☐ Recruiting at job fairs in shopping malls, chambers of commerce, colleges, and universities.

☐ Recruiting in related industries. Several country club clients of ours recruit food and beverage people from restaurants, hotels, nursing homes, hospitals, and other businesses that have food service operations. Be creative.

☐ Recruiting in areas of high unemployment. Consider recruiting in places like the northeastern United States, Houston, or other such areas for positions in places like Orlando and San Diego, where the labor pool is smaller.

21. Get rid of people who don't fit in—but do it compassionately

Most people fail in their jobs because their value systems, ways of solving problems, and ways of getting along with others don't fit in with the organization. Technical skills are rarely the problem. In fact, research by Drake Beam Morin, Inc., an international career management firm that specializaes in both selection and outplacement, shows that the major reason people leave jobs or get fired is not the inability to perform the work, but the inability to fit into the organization's culture and style.

There's an old story about two bricklayers who were asked what they were building. One said, "A wall." The other said, "A cathedral." The first one was merely doing job. The second bricklayer had a vision and saw how he fit into it.

In the bricklayer example, "management's" vision is a cathedral. Not a bridge or an inn. Each bricklayer is free to align or not align with that vision. If he chooses not to build cathedrals, he can take his skills and abilities and go build bridges.

The people in your organization should have the opportunity to choose whether they want to align with the company vision. Some may do so right away; some may never align. That doesn't mean they're bad people or even bad employees. It may simply mean that their values and personal missions do not align with the rest of the organization or that they've chosen not to play in a particular game anymore.

In *Moments of Truth*, Jan Carlzon says,

"Some employees may not see or fully understand the vision and goals at the beginning. The leader must resist the urge to dismiss those people, and, instead, work with them, give them additional information, and attempt again to make them understand. Of course, there will always be those who refuse to be persuaded. From them, he must demand loyalty, if not emotional commitment, to the goals. Otherwise, they should be asked to leave.

The importance of the organization's culture cannot be underestimated. According to Peters and Waterman in *In Search of Excellence*, "The excellent companies are marked by very strong cultures, so strong that you either buy into their norms or get out."

According to V. Clayton Sherman, author of *From Losers to Winners: How to Manage Problem Employees and What to Do If You Can't*, people know when they're not performing well. I believe they also know when they don't fit in with the organization's culture. People in these situations suffer stress and emotional trauma. The difficulty is that people in these situations often lack the self confidence to believe that they can do well somewhere else, so they stay. It's easier to stay where they are than to risk leaving. Most human resources experts agree that allowing people to stay in these situations does them a disservice.

Transferring such people to another position or location often compounds the problem. Too often, people who aren't performing well or who don't fit in are moved around, in hopes of finding a place where they'll fit, or at least do minimal damage. Sometimes they're actually put in sales, marketing, telephone work, or other areas that have high amounts of public contact.

Transfers can be effective in some situations. For example, it is wise to move insensitive, negative, rule-bound people *out of* customer-contact positions, but that usually doesn't solve the real problem. It just transfers the problem to another department and another manager. Outplacement specialist James E. Challenger observed, "Internal transfers, unless they are clearly a promotion, are often seen as a penalty for unsatisfactory performance and can be more humiliating than a discharge."

It's far more humane to fire people than it is to allow them to stay in what they see as a losing situation. Just do it with compassion. In fact, surveys show that, a year after being fired, many people say, "It was the best thing that ever happened to me."

Ryder's truck division exemplifies this. Ryder's Ronald H. Dunbar says, "If you perform well at Ryder, you'll be paid well. But those who don't won't be around too long. We don't keep people who don't perform." Ryder also seems to have mastered the concept of compassionate firing. The company provides outplacement services for people and makes sure that the outplacement firm is available to outplaced employees 7 days a week, 18 hours a day, and for the rest of the person's career.

Contrast that to a company I once worked for:

The APC Skills Company is a management consulting firm with clients all over the United States. Every Sunday night, consultants fly from their home cities to the clients' job sites, and every Friday night, they fly home. Supervisors and managers fly almost every day, going to different jobsites. Each employee is issued an air travel card (ATC) in the company's name, and each employee makes his or her own travel arrangements and pays for any required airline tickets.

The way this company fired people was to wait until an employee was on the airplane on Friday afternoon, heading home. Then the person's supervisor would ask for their ATC card, and that was it. Employees had no notice, no severance pay, no continuation of benefits (this was before the COBRA laws), no outplacement services, no job on Monday, and no income. That's *not* a compassionate way to fire someone who no longer fits in!

Identify unhappy people in your organization—people who don't seem to fit in. Talk to them coach them, counsel them if necessary. Give them a chance and a choice. If they still can't or won't fit in, you must decide for them that they'll probably be happier and more productive somewhere else.

There's also another dimension to this idea of fitting in: It's a two-way street. Managers and executives can—and should—consider how well *they* fit into the organization's culture, mission, values, and ways of doing business. If *their* values, mission, purpose, and business ethics don't mesh with the organizaton's, they should leave and find an environment in which they'll be happier and more productive. No, it's not always easy, but it may be necessary.

Tom Knaub is a registered landscape architect. Several years ago, he just wasn't happy in the company he worked for. Tom realized that his company's mission was to make enough money so the six partners could retire at age 45. As a result, the pressure was intense. The firm got involved in projects it couldn't handle. Some of the tactics for winning bids were questionable. Tom wasn't comfortable in that environment. His values were not compatible with his organization's. He changed companies and prospered.

Lisa Birnbach, author or *Going to Work: A Unique Guided Tour through Corporate America*, has identified several factors to look for in attempting to find the fit. After studying what it's like to work at over 50 different companies, she reported in an article in *Parade Magazine* that many people look for more than just money—they're also concerned with how their jobs satisfy other needs.

Using her findings as a basis, here are some things you might want to consider about your own fit with your organization:

☐ How important is it to you to be a part of something important or worthwhile (like medical research, cutting-edge technologies, or helping the less fortunate)?

☐ To what extent is your organization involved in these kinds of activities?

☐ How important is it for you to be creative, to come up with new ideas, and to have a way to have your ideas considered?

☐ To what extent are you able to use your creative abilities in your current organization?

☐ How important is it for you to like the industry or business your organization is in?

☐ How much do you like—and get excited about—the industry or type of business you're in?

☐ How important is it for you to work with others, to be a part of a team?

☐ To what extent do you feel you're part of a team?

☐ How important is it for you to maintain a life away from work (time for family, hobbies, and other interests)?

☐ To what extent do you feel you're able to keep your work and private life separate?

☐ To what extent do you feel you can be yourself at work?

☐ How do you like to be supervised?

☐ Do you get the kind of supervision you need to help you perform at your best?

22. Eliminate needless bureaucracy

Invert the pyramid. There's been a lot of talk recently about inverting the organizational pyramid to improve service. I agree with this approach. Inverting the pyramid means shifting the focus of the organization by looking at the organization in terms of who is important to its success and survival. Flattening the pyramid means eliminating unnecessary or redundant levels of management. In traditional companies, the pyramid looks like the one on the left in the diagram on page 158.

In traditional organizations, the five *P*'s—*P*restige, *P*ay, *P*erks, *P*erceived importance, and *P*ower—increase toward the top of the pyramid. In this hierarchy, most people in the organization believe that they "work for" the level or levels above them. The closer to the top of the pyramid you are, the more weight you carry. In many organizations, physical surroundings—such as plush offices, limos, reserved parking spaces, and executive dining rooms—and excessive attention to title, rank, and protocol reinforce this hierarchy by drawing attention and focus up the organization rather than out to customers.

A major national retail drug company based in Pittsburgh, Pennsylvania, was so preoccupied with titles and other trappings of rank that all managers and executives were always addressed as "Mr." in print (there were no female managers), and names were always listed on memos or distribution lists in descending rank: the president first, then vice presidents, then department heads, then supervisors, and so on. To make this work, everyone in the organization had to learn and use the pecking order. Many new managers and secretaries were reprimanded for unknowingly violating the hierarchy!

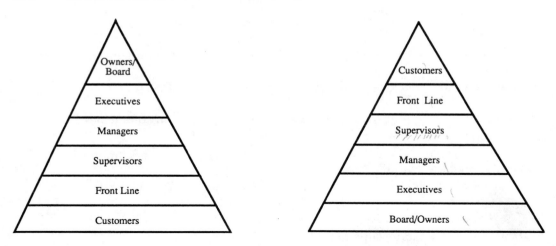

In this same organization, the senior vice president decreed that he was the *only* person allowed to use a red pen to edit or correct correspondence, rough drafts, press releases, or any other written material.

In customer-focused organizations, the pyramid is exactly the opposite (diagram at right, above). In these organizations, the people most important to the success and survival of the company *aren't* the owners or executives; rather they're the customers. The customer is the real boss, and these organizations recognize that fact. The people in the organization believe they "work for" the customer. The customer has the highest status, importance, and power.

Former IBM corporate marketing vice president Buck Rodgers tells about the time IBM CEO Thomas Watson Jr. called a 3:00 meeting with all his senior managers. Rodgers was already on his way to see an out-of-town customer when Watson called the meeting. Watson would not start the meeting unless everyone was present. When Rodgers returned to the office at 6:30, Watson and the managers were still waiting to start the meeting. Rodgers told Watson he was with a customer who had a serious problem. Watson replied, "You have the right priorities." Then he turned to the others and started the meeting.

Next in importance in service-oriented organizations are the people who have the most contact with customers—that is, the people on the front line. Next are frontline supervisors, whose job it is to support the frontline employees in getting what they need to best serve customers. The focus and attention of people in the organization are on serving customers, not on internal trappings of power, prestige, and importance.

Invert the pyramid in your organization. Make customers, not executives and managers, the focus of attention.

Flatten the pyramid.   The number of levels in organizations can vary. Many organizations have 15 or more levels between the customer and the CEO. Regardless of the number of levels, the higher you are in the organization, the less likely you are to have contact with customers. In addition to inverting the pyramid, many organizations also need to flatten it by removing needless layers of management and getting people closer to customers. Jan Carlzon talks about flattening the pyramid:

> Any business organization seeking to establish a customer orientation and create a good impression during its "moments of truth" must flatten the pyramid—that is, eliminate the hierarchial tiers of responsibility in order to respond directly and quickly to the customer's needs.
>
> "Managing" is thus shifted from the executive suite to the operational level where everyone is now a manager of his own situation. When problems arise, each employee has the ability to analyze the situation, determine the appropriate action, and see to it that the action is carried out, either alone or with the help of others.

Break down organizational barriers.   Look for and try to reorient managers who are "turf builders"—who build empires in order to be more powerful personally, rather than to further the interests of the organization or to serve customers better. Break up empires.

Find ways to help individuals and organizational units work together to improve service; for example:

☐ Create project teams or task forces that cross organizational boundaries. Reward people for serving on these teams.

☐ Relocate entire work units or offices to different floors, buildings, or cities; or temporarily transfer some managers (or others) to other departments or locations.

☐ Reassign managers' office space; remove walls.

☐ Hold events that give people from different areas a chance to meet and mingle.

Create small organizational units.   Large organizational units often require more rules, regulations, and time than smaller units do. Many experts recommend keeping organizational units to about 100 people. When units get bigger than this, reorganize and spin off new units. Communication, resources, vitality, familiarization of people and resources, response time, and decision making are all more manageable and responsive with smaller units.

Customers can get more efficient and personalized service from a company with fewer people and organizational levels. Smaller units are usually able to react faster to customer needs and requests, as well as to changing market conditions.

Eliminate blind obedience to rules.

A friend of ours got married recently. Several couples decided to go in together to buy a gift. Two people volunteered to pick out the gift for all of us. They found some unusual china pieces that were "perfect" for this couple. The pieces cost over $300. Before buying them, our shoppers wanted to make sure these pieces would complement the pattern the newlyweds had chosen. They asked if they could use the store phone to call the bride's mother. The clerk told them that customers were not allowed to use the store phone; they'd have to go outside and use the pay phone. Our shoppers were shocked and indignant! The result: a lost sale, no chance of future business from any of us, and negative word of mouth. We figure our two shoppers told at least 35 people about how poorly they were treated at that store.

Based on an average $50 sale and five purchases over a 5-year period, we figured that the clerk's blindly following the rules cost that store at least $1,300.

Examine every policy, procedure, practice, system, form, and building lay-out. Ask yourself if they help or hinder the way you serve your customers. If they're absolutely necessary (and most aren't, but we've just come to think they are), how can they be improved or streamlined? Remember some of the examples given earlier in the book about employees who were customer-focused but whose company's policies and practices punished them? Look into how your organization reacts to employees who go out of their way for customers.

For many managers, inverting the pyramid and eliminating the rules and bureaucracy that has given them power and prestige is difficult. For some it is simply inconceivable. Some may not know how. Others may not be willing. And if they are unwilling or unable to do so, they may no longer fit what's needed in your organization, and the organization may have to compassionately fire some managers.

23. Take care of your employees

Service-oriented companies believe that employees are superstars whose talent is waiting to be unleashed. Such companies have shown that employees at any level can do anything and everything—set standards, set quotas, check quality, manage budgets, interview applicants, train people, and handle tardiness and absenteeism by coworkers. They have proved that if employees feel important and responsible, they can be trusted. They have seen that people closest to the customer can and should have the freedom to make decisions on the spot about how to satisfy customers. Their managers have learned how to support decisions made by frontline people, rather than making decisions for them. Rules and practices that are designed to control people or that unintentionally (or intentionally) demean people or hinder their ability to serve customers have been eliminated. The rest of this section presents six major ways to take care of employees.

Believe in and trust employees.   Organizations are only as good as their people. Ford Motor Company CEO Don Peterson says, "You will provide the best products and services *only* if your people are the best." For change or growth to occur in an organization, it must occur in individual employees first.

Bob Small has built a global reputation for creativity and quality in the hotel industry. He has earned the coveted Five-Star rating for four hotels he has managed. Small firmly believes that only 10% of a guest's experience is based on what Small calls "mortar and brick," that is, the beautiful facilities. He believes that the other 90 percent is based on the hospitality and service provided by the employees. And *that* depends on how employees feel about themselves.

According to Citicorp's Walter Wriston,

> It's very, very simple and yet everybody wants to make it complicated. I just say hire the best people you can find and treat them like human beings. I don't know of a better way to motivate people.
>
> Anybody can form a corporation. The talent you have is what is opposite the customer. It's the only thing that distinguishes one company from another. If you have very good people, they will come up with answers to customers' problems.

How companies view their employees—and, what is more important, how they *act* toward employees—largely determines how well employees serve customers. There are several reasons for this. Perception and beliefs are key elements here, and the flow in organizations is usually from top to bottom and from inside to outside. If employees *believe* that they must not deviate from the rules (whether or not this is what management intends), they'll take a "that's our policy" attitude. If, however, employees have internalized the idea of service, believe they have an obligation to customers, and *believe the company will support them*, there's no limit to what they'll do. I love the story about the Federal Express employee who, without seeking management approval, used his personal American Express card to rent a helicopter, flew to a mountaintop in a severe storm, and personally repaired fallen communication lines to get his company back in business!

Certain specific skills (handling customer complaints, listening, resolving conflict, etc.) have always been needed by people at the front line; however, for the pyramid to be successfully inverted, people at the front line must develop greater confidence and self-esteem as well. They must understand who their customers are and what the concept of meeting customers' needs is all about. Frontline people must also see that the organization values them as people, not as employees, and is willing to help them grow as people. This means that if a shift is to occur in the organization, it must occur in the individuals first. People must grow and expand in order to realize their ability to handle greater responsibility. Remember that employees are people first, and cashiers, sales clerks, engineers, accountants, vice presidents, or customer service reps second.

Employees must first see themselves as capable, trusted, worthwhile *people*. Once a person's confidence and self-esteem improves, he or she can handle greater job responsibilities and provide better service. Bashful, unassertive, timid, wimpy, uncertain people don't rent helicopters to fix power lines—they don't go out of their way or perform heroic deeds for their customers. Heroic service acts occur when employees *believe* in doing whatever it takes to satisfy their customers and when they know their organization not only supports these kind of acts, it expects them.

It is management's responsibility to set the tone and create the environment that encourages people to go beyond what's expected. The first step is to see people as people, not as numbers. Recognize their untapped potential and believe in them. They will respond. There are scores of studies that demonstrate that people will behave just about the way they are expected to. If employees are treated like trusted partners who can and will accept responsibility for their own staffing, schedules, productivity, quality, budgets, and service, most will respond. Show employees you care about them and respect them as people and as employees by providing them with clear standards and expectations, adequate training, and the tools and resources they need.

Jan Carlzon says there were four basic principles underlying everything he did at Scandinavian Airlines System:

1 People need to know and feel they are needed.
2 Everyone wants to be treated as an individual.
3 Giving someone the freedom to take responsibility releases resources that would otherwise be concealed.
4 An individual without information cannot take responsibility; an individual who is given information cannot help but take responsibility.

Those are pretty good principles to follow in *any* organization!

Survey employees. Many times managers *think* they know how their employees feel about the organization, its products or services, their training, their resources, and so on. However, even when management makes a conscious effort to take care of employees, employees may not see the effort or its effects. It's a question of perception.

An article in *Industry Week* described a situation at the Ford Motor Company. Ford had been working diligently since the early 1980s to change its corporate culture by becoming less hierarchical, reducing autocratic management practices, and increasing participation at all levels. Management thought it was on the right track with employees. "We thought we had created the right environment; we thought people felt free to speak out. We also thought we had got everyone to cooperate on design projects," says retired vice president Donald F. Kopka. "Instead, we found [from our survey] that our environment wasn't working. We were fighting the old system where the boss was supreme." In effect, employees still saw managers as mini-dictators busy building or protecting their own empires. Employees believed management didn't want to hear their ideas or suggestions. Employees felt frustrated and powerless. "The [survey] results were devastating. We thought we were good managers, but that's not exactly how our employees perceived us."

As with customers, it's not what you do that matters, it's what employees *perceive* that counts. If you don't do some kind of surveys, you could be deluded into thinking everything's fine, just as Ford did.

Employee surveys can tell you what your employees expect and what they feel they're getting, just as customer surveys do on the customer level. Many of the same methods can be used—written surveys, employee focus groups, interviews, and so on. Some organizations survey their employees at least every 2 years.

When doing surveys, make it clear to employees that (1) their responses will be confidential, (2) individuals cannot be singled out, (3) they will get feedback on the results. To do otherwise breaks trust and causes employees to be (more) suspicious the next time a survey is taken.

One executive interviewed in the Citibank study said: "Employee attitude surveys must be a way of life, not something used to fix known problems. Yet when problems are sensed, this may be the time to escalate surveying frequency."

Keep employees informed. Customer-focused organizations believe that the more employees—in any job and at any level—know about the organization, its history, culture, values, traditions, products, strengths, and weaknesses, the better able they are to represent the organization to their internal and external customers. Making sure all employees are well-trained and well-informed helps avoid the "I don't know, that's not my job" approach to customers. When employees feel they're kept up on things and feel more a part of things, they're more able—and willing—to help customers. This applies to non-customer-contact employees, too.

People in organizations need to know where to go for help when they need it. They must feel they'll get the resources they need when they need them. Resources include people, money, technical expertise, tools and equipment, supplies, and information. People also should be informed as to how their unit, department, or team is doing. Post these results and customer reactions.

Decide what information employees need to know. If you're not sure, err on the generous side. People need to know what's going on. Provide full information on the financial status of the company, including sales, income, and profits. Also provide information on problems, issues, growth and successes, setbacks and failures, and upcoming changes—not just once in a while, but continually. Employees on Harley-Davidson work teams are given access to *all* the numbers, and they use these to set their own standards and track their own productivity and profitability.

This sharing of information is very difficult for many organizations because of traditional beliefs about what information employees "should" have. When employees are kept informed, instead of projecting an attitude of "I just work here" or "They don't tell me anything," employees come across to customers as "I can help because I'm in the know." Remember, employees treat customers the way they are treated.

And get information to people quickly. Use monthly, weekly, even daily newsletters, bulletins, meetings, flyers, and other means. Overcommunicate rather than undercommunicate.

Make the organization a desirable place to work. In some organizations, management attitudes such as these are typical, even if they're not always verbalized:

"Our customers are all out of town, so they never see our customer service area. Why worry about how it looks?"

"In this company, only managers have nice big offices. All customer service people need is a desk, a chair, and a telephone."

"You don't live here; you just work here. What do you expect?"

If employees are cold or cramped, if they work in dirty conditions, and if they generally feel like second-class citizens, they're not likely to give first-class treatment to customers. It boils down to respect for the individual. Because service is a person-to-person business and customer relations mirror employee relations, employees who don't believe they are respected and treated fairly won't make sure that customers are respected and treated fairly.

You may want to examine your policies, practices, working conditions, and benefits to be sure they show that you care about the health, welfare, and growth of your employees as *people*, not just as employees. It's really very simple. Provide a clean, safe, suitable working environment that enables them to do what they're supposed to do. Call them by name. Make requests, not demands. Say "please" and "thank you." Employees are people, not robots. Listen to their side of things. Back them up. If they're on the phone with customers a lot, provide a reasonably quiet area with few distractions so they can give their attention to customers. Make sure that they're not too hot or cold, that they have enought light, and that they have comfortable chairs.

Elevate the status of frontline positions. In many organizations, customer-contact positions are entry-level or exit-level positions with low pay and low status. Look for ways to upgrade the prestige, pay, recognition, importance, and visibility of these positions. Make the people who deal with customers feel important.

Make a big deal about important events. When new people join the company, do something special to make them feel important. Hold rallies, meetings, celebrations, and other special events to keep people informed, to recognize and reward individuals and teams, to celebrate wins, and to remind people of their service mission.

Make people part of the process. Japanese automakers who operate plants in the United States make a practice of involving employees in decisions about work schedules, overtime, and job rotation.

Federal Express, Hallmark, Procter & Gamble, IBM, and others show ultimate respect for employees with their policies of internal promotions and no layoffs. Federal Express has a Guaranteed Fair Treatment Program whereby any employee can get a hearing from higher-level managers on any matter without fear of retribution. There's also a review board of peers and an executive board for appeals to a higher level. Pitney Bowes has similar programs with regular employee meetings. Any employee can submit a question to management and get an answer. Employees also elect coworkers to represent them on the Council of Personnel Relations, which also has management members. Employees can bring issues or concerns before the Council to be resolved.

Home Depot is the nation's largest chain of do-it-yourself stores. I know from personal experience how service-oriented these stores are. CEO Bernard Marcus and president Arthur Blank have recognized the importance of the well-being of their employees. According to Blank, "We want to help people lead the most productive lives they can, not only at work, but in terms of their own feelings of self-worth and self-esteem. We think we have a responsibility to offer not just facilities and an environment, but a whole way of life that encourages people not only to take care of customers in our stores, but to take care of themselves and their families."

Not entirely altruistic, Blank also says, "If our employees are in fact doing all those things, they'll be more productive for the company. I think someone who has a balanced life is a much more productive and effective employee than someone who is just focused on one portion of his life, whether it's work or something else, so that things are out of kilter."

Home Depot offers its employees the following amenities:

- [ ] An outdoor wilderness-type program to help them learn how to handle stress under difficult situations
- [ ] A $150,000 fitness center
- [ ] A company-sponsored wellness program
- [ ] Educational programs on stress management, weight loss, and smoking
- [ ] Free health fairs with various health tests available
- [ ] Company-sponsored softball, basketball, and bowling teams
- [ ] Company-sponsored runners
- [ ] Incentive programs that pay employees to participate in health-related activities

Home Depot employees receive strong management support when they participate in the various available programs. Both Blank and Marcus encourage health and fitness activities with their presence and with the company checkbook. They believe in investing in fitness centers, classes, sports teams, and so on, and they attended the opening ceremonies for the fitness center. Blank and Marcus typically send letters of support to employees who enroll in smoking classes.

As you consider making your organization a good place to work, pay special attention to policies and practices related to women and minorities. You may be missing potentially good employees who can't afford to work for you because of your policies or practices. Women now make up over half the work force. In many industries, there are more women than men in frontline, customer-contact positions such as retail clerk, reservationist, receptionist, and telephone sales.

U.S. Labor Department statistics indicate that 75 percent of all working women are in their childbearing years, and of this group, 80 to 90 percent will become pregnant. Most of the women who have children will return to their jobs. Women are increasingly concerned about how their employers will support them in being good mothers as well as good employees. They're looking for more in areas of fair pay, opportunities for advancement, maternity leave, day-care support, flextime, and job sharing.

Prevent contact overload in frontline employees.   Employees who have frequent, direct contact with customers, either face-to-face or over the phone, are highly susceptible to contact overload. When employees have continuous or intense interactions with customers, it's often emotionally draining. This is especially true for employees who frequently handle customer problems, customer complaints, or upset customers. Some psychologists even refer to an "emotional labor" aspect of certain jobs. Frontline people in restaurants, hotels, airlines, and hospitals are particularly vulnerable. So are flight attendants, receptionists, and switchboard operators. Some call it "reservations fatigue."

Some managers have noted that frequent customer contact tends to exhaust employees, or at least decrease their sensitivity to customers and thereby decrease their effectiveness. For example, some managers report that when people on the front line handle the same problems and complaints day after day, they tend to get callous and go on "automatic." They hear the beginning of a complaint and assume they know what a customer is going to say. They respond with an unemotional, programmed response.

Overload often results in fatigue, hostility toward customers, apathy toward the job or customers, and other symptoms. Sometimes employees take it out on the customer. Employees who are tired and overworked and have just handled three irate customers in a row are not in the best condition to deal with more customers.

Psychologist and trainer Dr. Terry Paulson tells of an incident that illustrates what the effects of contact overload can be:

Paulson was standing in line to check his bags at New York's Kennedy airport. The customer in front of him was terribly rude and obnoxious to the ticket agent. When the customer left, Paulson commented on the abuse the agent had taken and asked, "Do people talk to you that way often?"

"Oh, yeah," the agent said. "You get used to it around here."

Paulson said, "Well, I don't think I'd get used to it."

The agent replied, "Don't worry, bud. After all, the customer's always right."

Being an astute psychologist, Paulson suspected that the man didn't really mean that. He told the agent, "Well, I don't think he was right in this case."

"Don't worry," the agent said. "I've already gotten even. He's on his way to Chicago. His bags are going to Japan."

It is important to recognize that contact overload does exist and that some of your frontline people may be experiencing it. Identify positions with high potential for contact overload, and expect higher turnover in those positions.

Certain things can help lessen the effects of contact overload, but there is no real way to eliminate it altogether. Here are some suggestions for preventing and handling contact overload:

1 Define the personality types and characteristics best suited for high-contact jobs. Staff such positions with people best suited to handle them.

2 Restructure customer-contact jobs if possible to reduce some of the pressure and hassles.

3 Shift veteran employees and new hires who don't have the proper customer-contact temperament but who may be otherwise qualified into permanent positions without as much contact or stress.

4 Rotate people out of high-contact jobs periodically. Every 3 to 6 months, shift them to less stressful but necessary jobs.

5 Provide frequent breaks so people can get off the firing line for a while.

6 Provide longer than normal time away from the job, like some 3- or 4-day weekends periodically, to allow frontline people to recuperate.

7 Require frontline employees to take time off every few months.

8 Increase staff levels. Hire enough people so you can rotate them, have shorter shifts, and give time off. This also ensures that you won't get caught shorthanded if people are sick or quit.

9 Provide ongoing training on self-esteem, diffusing emotionally charged situations, communication, being customer-focused, and similar topics.

10 Provide lots of encouragement and recognition.

11 Provide paid weekends at resorts, hotels, Disney World, or similar locations for employees and their families.

12 Provide a paid dinner, theater tickets, a weekend at a hotel, or some comparable extra as a way of saying, "Nice going! We know you're often in a pressure cooker and get dumped on a lot. We appreciate what you do for us and our customers. Have a nice time on us."

13 Teach supervisors how to support frontline employees who are susceptible to contact overload. Show them how to assist (not take over for) an employee who is having difficulty with a particular customer.

14 Allow supervisors to provide time-outs for their people. When there's a greater likelihood of getting irate customers on an unpredictable schedule, or if a customer is upsetting someone on the front line, allow for people to step out for 5 to 10 minutes to compose themselves. With large pools of contact people (phone banks or ticket counters), it may be advisable to have several employees who can fill in when others need a break.

Eliminate demeaning practices. Get rid of policies and practices that are internally focused and that get in the way of satisfying customers. Eliminate as many trappings of rank as possible. Many organizations have eliminated executive dining rooms, executive offices, and reserved parking spaces. Time clocks for hourly employees have sometimes been eliminated as well. Managers don't punch a clock, so why should others have to? Eliminating time clocks communicates, "We trust you to know what you have to do and to be here on time to do it."

Executives and managers should answer their own phones and place their own calls. Set aside parking places closest to the front door for customers or for the Service Employee of the Month, not for executives. Have everyone eat in the same cafeteria and give most offices similar furnishings and decor. Such equalizing efforts help send the message that it's not executives who are important, but rather *customers*.

Many organizations *say* they've eliminated discriminating, status-based practices and that everyone focuses on customers, but often it's mostly lip service. Not so at Honda. In an article about how Japanese car companies and management styles are working in their U.S. plants, Louis Kraar describes what happens when everyone's focus is on customers and the job at hand. See if this could happen in *your* organization:

A Honda employee proposed a standardized form for quality-control inspections, but ran into resistance from a Japanese manager who preferred his own form. The Japanese manager rankled and demanded to know the employee's name and job title. Kraar reports that the employee said, "I'm the person who wants to fix this, so my title doesn't matter." The Japanese manager shrugged and agreed.

---

24. Provide orientation and training for new employees

Service-oriented companies recognize the importance of a formal, structured orientation for new hires. I'm not talking about a 30-minute, or even half-day, session, most of which is devoted to filling out employment forms, W-4s, benefits enrollment forms, and so on. That's all part of it, but I'm talking about continuing the process started during the hiring process of indoctrinating new employees into the culture of the company and continuing to emphasize that the number-one message, especially for customer-contact people, is service.

Since customer relations mirrors employee relations, service-oriented organizations know that employees who feel welcomed, respected, important, needed, and cared for are much more likely to make the customers feel the same.

Training in service-oriented organizations emphasizes confidence and self-esteem first. These companies believe that organizations are only as good as their people. They realize that for change or growth to occur in the organization, it must occur in individual employees first. And, the higher employees' self-esteem, the better service and performance they'll provide. Professional speaker and trainer Lou Heckler says it best: "Traditional organizations want to make their people better employees; service-oriented companies want to make their employees better people."

Robert Desatnick, former vice president of human resources for McDonald's

Corporation and author of *Managing to Keep the Customer*, says he's discovered that "to achieve service excellence, personal enrichment training is usually more effective than trying to teach people to have a good attitude."

Service-oriented organizations also recognize the importance of interpersonal or social skills, but they see these as hiring concerns, not training issues. These organizations realize that once people with the right background (technical and interpersonal skills) are hired, employees must see themselves as competent, important, trusted, worthwhile *people* first. If organizations were to offer *only* programs to build self-esteem and do *no* skills or knowledge training, most would improve service levels dramatically. And their employees would also be more open and receptive to other training.

Of course, orientation and initial training should include industry, company, and product knowledge along with job-specific skills. It should also help develop confidence, self-esteem, creativity, and independent thinking. And it should improve decision-making, communication, problem-solving, and conflict-resolution skills. This is a far better training strategy than teaching people only tips and techniques or "what to do if" rules without emphasizing any underlying skills.

Employees should leave their basic orientation and training knowing exactly what it takes to get excellent, average, or poor ratings; how to get rewards and promotions; how their job fits into the big picture; how to do the job correctly; and how to get help if they have questions or encounter problems.

Rather than emphasizing "what to do if" training or rules and procedures, training should include other skills. For instance, the skills most needed to improve service to customers are also those that enable employees to both provide and get good service within their own organizations. These skills include handling change, listening, giving feedback, being able and willing to learn new skills, resolving conflict, and keeping bosses informed.

Why is such training necessary? Gina DeLapa, editor of *High-Impact Communication & Training*, writes, "Too often telemarketers fail because they know only what's in their script and virtually nothing about the company they represent." In such cases, it's hard to feel like and project an attitude of "I can help you because I'm in the know."

Many service leaders spread orientation and training over several weeks to enable people to grasp things without being overwhelmed. This approach also enables people to bring back questions and problems as they begin to learn the culture and their jobs.

I prefer an overall approach that has three phases. The first phase is a general orientation to the organization. This orientation covers who you are and what you do; your history, traditions, and values; how you're organized and where you're located; who your customers are; how you do business;

your goals and mission; your products and services; and your industry and your competition.

The second phase is an orientation to a particular division, department, and work unit. It includes how communications flow, how problems are handled, how decisions are made, what behavior is rewarded, and what behavior is punished. This phase should emphasize quality and teamwork.

The third phase is orientation to specific job, including a review of job descriptions, standards, and responsibilities. It also shows how the job fits into the rest of the organization; why it's important; and how that job's work, outputs, and errors affect other people and units. During this phase, specific product or job skill training can begin.

The Walt Disney Company believes in making sure employees are well-trained and well-informed. The first day for any new Disney employee, from groundskeepers to executives, anywhere in the company, includes a class called "Traditions I." This class provides the foundation on which the company has built its reputation for quality and magic. The class presents Walt Disney's philosophies by drawing from his characters, movies, and theme parks over the years to the present and beyond. Following that, Disney also provides extensive training for jobs as simple as groundskeeper or ticket-taker.

Other service leaders also believe it makes sense to provide adequate orientation and training on company history and values, job-specific information, how jobs relate to the rest of the organization, performance standards, and more. Sony, for example, offers 8 weeks of training; IBM takes 16 weeks. Staff at the GE Answer Center receives 5 weeks of initial training before talking to customers.

Here are some additional suggestions for employee orientation:

1. Plan the orientation. Decide what to cover, who'll do it, on what days, at what times. *Put orientation plans in writing.* Don't let people just wing it. It's too easy to forget things.

Several years ago, I designed a detailed orientation program for a subsidiary of the Coca-Cola Company. Some experienced managers thought it was silly at first to have such a detailed checklist, but after using it, they said, "That list was really helpful. There's so much involved in this job, it's hard to remember to tell someone everything, especially those things I'm used to doing out of habit. This list really helped me to not forget anything."

---

2. Get the highest-ranking executive manager you can to kick off the orientation and deliver a strong message about service to communicate management's commitment.

3. Provide information about the company; its history; and its products, markets, and competitors.

4. Give people a tour of the facility—all of it, not just where they'll be working. If there's a plant or distribution center, take them—or send them— there. If this isn't feasible, at least show them a well-done video of all the facilities.

5. Familiarize employees with your products or services. Give them more than a cursory, "Here's what we make (or do)." This part of orientation may take weeks or months, but its' worth it.

6. Introduce new employees to key people.

7. Give new employees time alone with other new hires. Schedule time for this mingling or arrange for it at lunch to give the new people a chance to share common feelings and anxieties.

8. Use a mentor system. There are two ways to do this. One is to pair up employees with experienced people, primarily to learn the job. Better yet, invite people with similar backgrounds or interests to volunteer to be part of a buddy system. Their role isn't to "train" the new hires but to help them learn the culture—"how to get things done around here."

Keep paperwork and forms to a minimum. My experience with orientation at several companies was that I was given lots of information and asked to make decisions on medical plans, insurance, pensions, credit unions, and other benefits without having a chance to think about it or discuss it with my family. I wanted to know about the company, learn my way around, and get a feel for things; instead, I stayed in a room with several other people all day and signed papers. The message was not, "Welcome, we care about you, we want you to feel welcome and needed here." The message was, "We're a big company and we need to process you, so hurry up and fill out these papers."

25. Provide ongoing training for all employees

Recognize that training must be for everyone—regardless of rank or responsibility—and it must be continuous. Unless everyone participates, training is seen by lower-level employees as something done *to* them rather than for them. They often resent it. Offering training only to certain groups of employees increases the risk of running today's business with yesterday's skills, technology, attitudes, and beliefs.

Service-oriented companies like Johnson & Johnson, Hewlett-Packard, Motorola, General Electric, and IBM make training continuous and ongoing for all employees, including executives. Most employees attend at least one program a year to reinforce and maintain their skills. The continuous training is part of the culture. The organizations recognize that trends, technologies, and management methods change and that they also need to keep up with changes in industry, products, and competition.

For example, Ford Motor Company CEO Don Peterson says, "I'm personally involved in taking courses. All 2,000 of our top managers from around the world have taken courses at our Executive Management Center." At Procter & Gamble, training is ongoing and the Annual Education program aims to give all P&G employees a meaningful training experience once each year. Not all of P&G's training occurs in classrooms; managers take an active part in training their people on a continual basis. John Pepper, the president of P&G, who also takes courses, believes that "training is too important to be left only to the training department."

Service leaders in the Citibank study typically made sizable investments in formal, ongoing training—often as much as 1 or 2 percent of gross sales. In 1988, the CEO of Corning Glass, James R. Houghton, announced that Corning would increase training so that by 1991 at least 5 percent of employee time would be spent in training sessions.

Panasonic's head of human resources, Steven L. Fishner, talks about management's role in developing people. Fishner says he strives to make managers responsible for improving the performance of their subordinates: "I tell managers, 'It's *your* job to train your people, not mine! I support you by teaching skills to your people, but you have to help them use these skills on the job via coaching.'"

There are three major reasons to provide ongoing training for all employees: (1) to bring about and maintain a shift in people's behavior and attitudes, (2) to provide continuous improvement in skills, and (3) to provide cross training. These topics are discussed in detail below.

Training can help shift beliefs.   If you are about to undertake a major transformation in your organization to change the way people see themselves, their mission, and their role in meeting and exceeding customer needs, training will be essential. To improve your service levels, your people must have different skills, knowledge, and attitudes.

All employees are new employees in the new organization you're creating. Training can help many of them to examine their beliefs, practices, and skills and to begin to develop new ones. Even long-termers can benefit from increased self-esteem, confidence, and creativity. Changing employee attitudes and beliefs takes time, especially with experienced people who are used to having and doing things a certain way. Training can help reinforce your service mission.

William F. Haupt, General Motors' manager of executive development, asserts that "corporate repositioning cannot be accomplished without extensive retraining and reeducation of the entire corporate family." Particularly for executives, he sees training and education as a "continuous task of retraining and reeducating our organizations and ourselves."

Training provides continuous skill improvement. Quad/Graphics is one of the largest and most profitable printers in the country. The company employs over 2,000 people and prints over 200 magazines, catalogs, and other publications, such as *Inc.* magazine, *Time, U.S. News and World Report,* and *Newsweek.* Quad/Graphics believes strongly in ongoing training. In fact, a recent annual report described the company's commitment to education as follows: "The circle of life at Quad/Graphics revolves around education. An employee's first duty is to learn his or her job, then to know it, improve it, and lastly to teach it to the next person who comes after."

Service-oriented companies recognize that managers need training, too. Managers may *want* to reinforce certain behaviors in their employees, but they may not know how. One executive put it this way: "We cannot assume the exemplary employee will automatically be a crackerjack supervisor on instincts alone because he or she is promoted."

Training is also needed by those in upper-management levels. Organizational Dynamics Inc. (ODI), a Burlington, Massachusetts, management training and consulting company, surveyed *Fortune* 500 executives and found that the majority believed senior managers should "stay out front" on quality-related issues. The survey also revealed that senior managers receive the *least* training in quality improvement. The implication here is "do as I say, not as I do." But senior managers must lead by example, not by dictum.

General Motor's Haupt talks about the "need to prepare our executives to navigate as far into the future as we can see. We don't expect to arrive at any sheltered harbors." He talks about building leadership skills in areas such as creating and communicating a vision and purpose, building a sense of urgency, empowering peers and subordinate managers, building trust, and modeling personal leadership and accountability.

Many organizations go beyond having executives and other employees just *take* courses. Procter & Gamble executives teach courses as well. So does the president of Quad/Graphics, Harry Quadrucci.

General Electric, Xerox, and other companies have also found that employees make the best trainers. The old adage that "The best way to learn something is to teach it" is true. The process of learning the material well enough to teach it benefits the employees who teach it. Teaching also builds self-esteem.

Home Depot supports managers and employees teaching in a big way. Founders Marcus and Blank still teach classes for new management trainees and require that members of their senior management team do the same. The axiom at Home Depot is: "No one gets into management without getting into training." One of Home Depot's regional managers put it this way: "Classes taught by fellow employees are more real world, because they know the questions that the customers are asking. Sometimes, we'll ask one of the least-informed salespeople to teach the class and give them three weeks to prepare. We want everyone knowledgeable about the products."

Companies such as Johnsonville Foods have taken the idea of continuous education even further. At this Wisconsin sausage-making company, everyone takes part in continuous learning. All employees take a course in economics to help them understand the financial side of their business. Employees are also encouraged to study anything, even if it's not directly job-related, at the company's expense. One employee's explanation of the way Johnsonville Foods views the education issue: "Anything you learn means you're using your head more. You're engaged. And if you're engaged, then the chances are you'll make better sausage."

Cross-training provides depth and flexibility.   Many organizations realize the value of having employees know more than just their job or work area. At Quad/Graphics, newly hired customer service reps typically spend up to 6 months working in virtually every department before assuming their service duties.

Providing cross-training at all levels has several benefits:

- ☐ If key employees are out, customers don't suffer because no one knows how to fill an order, run a certain machine, or find the necessary paperwork.
- ☐ The more functions people can perform, the more they know about your organization. The more "in the know" employees feel, the more they are able and willing to help customers.
- ☐ Cross-training enables employees to pitch in at the front lines, or elsewhere, during peak times, thus keeping service levels constant and avoiding delays or backlogs.
- ☐ Cross-training makes employees feel important. It communicates to employees that they are a valued and valuable part of an organization. People notice when you spend the time and money to improve their skills.
- ☐ Cross-training can be part of your career development plan for employees.
- ☐ Cross-training can be (and should be) positioned as a reward—something prestigious that employees are selected for, not sent to.

Unfortunately, many organizations refuse to let employees take any courses that don't relate directly to their current job responsibilities.

In one of our programs, a bank executive assistant told me she was interested in taking a company-sponsored course on project management. Her boss refused to approve the course because it wasn't related to what she does. I asked her why she wanted to take the course, and she said, "A friend of mine took it, and it sounded interesting. I think I'd like it, and anything I can learn will benefit me in *my* job." Her boss refused!

The balance of this section on ongoing training offers some additional specific things you can do to be sure that training plays an important part in making your organization service-oriented.

Make an investment in training.   In a report called "Gaining the Competitive Edge," the American Society for Training and Development said that if American business is to regain its edge in world markets, companies should start investing at least 2 percent of their payroll to train and develop their employees.

Instead of cutting training budgets when times are tough or when competition gets rough, increase them. In many cases, the worst thing you can do during difficult times is to cut back on training, because that's when people skills must be at their best.

Make sure employees are fully trained before being turned loose without direct supervision.   Avoid "head work" training in which trainees learn information but never have a chance to practice using the knowledge or applying their skills.

Even role plays in a training-room environment are often not enough to teach people how to handle real-world situations. Being able to recite or write the steps for doing something is one thing; doing that thing well under pressure is another. The latter comes only with practice, and many organizations provide elaborate simulations to enable employees to get such practice. For example, a restaurant client of ours has a week-long training program for employees when it opens a new restaurant. After the employees learn their jobs and before the doors are opened to customers, they have several dry runs. Field supervisors, trainers, company executives, and others act as customers. All conditions are exactly as they'll be when the doors are really opened for business. The "customers" order real food, make real demands (often more demanding than normal), get real bills, and pay with real money or credit cards. Each department gets to experience what it'll be like under fire. Afterward, they debrief and then work on areas that require improvement. Then they try it again.

Provide interaction, assertiveness, and conflict-resolution skills for people who have frequent customer contact.   These are not innate skills. They must be taught—and practiced.

Offer stress management for frontline employees.   Frontline employees may need help coping with pressure from job demands, constant customer contact, and dealings with hostile or negative customers.

Provide in-depth training.   For many skills and attitudes, the traditional 1-, 2-, or 3-day training program with no follow-up is a waste of time, particularly when an organization is striving to change people's attitudes and beliefs or to improve employee confidence and self-esteem.

Reward employees for improving their knowledge or skills.   Define the courses or experiences or the improved capabilities that contribute to improved service. Reward these with permanent pay increases, incentive pay, recognition, pins or badges, or other means.

26. If you are the CEO, your role and actions must change

Creating and maintaining a service-oriented environment requires that the vision, values, norms, and beliefs of the organization be constantly focused on service to the customer at all times. This is primarily a top-down affair. Robert G. Oatley, executive vice president for special projects at American Airlines, says, "Commitment [to becoming customer-focused] must start with the CEO. We're lucky because Bob Crandall [the CEO] supports it."

Without the direction and commitment of top management, organizational change can be slow or nonexistent. Those in top management positions should provide service role models, and it is important for management at *all* levels to take an active and visible role in serving customers at the front lines. Actions do speak louder than words. Of course, improved service can happen without the CEO's support, commitment, and presence, but it takes much, much longer that way.

Frederick E. Webster, Jr., executive director of the Marketing Science Institute, has observed:

> The CEO has to be the principal advocate and spokesperson for customer orientation, and he or she has to maintain that position consistently. There has to be a pervasive attitude throughout the corporation, whatever the issue—customer service, products, or the financial implications of customer complaints. The dominant consideration has to be what is in the customer's best interest.

In *Managing to Keep the Customer*, Robert Desatnick says:

> The role of the CEO is to *personally* provide the overall service direction, actually write or endorse the organization's service policy, define the customer service objectives, and direct the overall integration of the organization's service efforts. Once the overall

strategy and plans are formulated, the CEO provides the necessary funding, conducts quarterly service reviews, and evaluates service accomplishments against plans.

One of the key findings of the Citibank study is that "senior executives . . . personally establish and manage service excellence as a top priority corporate goal." The report concluded that although top management commitment alone isn't enough to achieve service excellence, the responses from senior managers reflect their beliefs that their active and visible role is a "prerequisite for a company to become a preeminent service organization."

Specifically, the senior managers in these companies actively participate in managing service by frequently reviewing service performance reports; getting involved in decisions that affect service; knowing how customers feel about their experience with the company by reading correspondence, comment cards, and complaints; and taking an active, visible role in communicating service policies and practices throughout the organization. This often includes writing notes on customer correspondence so managers know that senior executives read these letters and see them as important.

In his newsletter *On Achieving Excellence*, Tom Peters asserts that "the new role of the chief executive and top team is to create and live energetically an inspiring vision, to ensure that hustle is the norm throughout the firm, and to vigilantly nip in the bud bureaucracy as it rears its ugly head." In *some* ways, this leadership role is nothing new. Most CEOs have known for ages that their leadership is important. What's different is that if you are a CEO today, that role requires different things of you than it did in the past. You can no longer confine yourself solely to board meetings, finances, physical growth, and corporate public relations. That worked before, but this is a different game. There are different rules, and sometimes there are no rules. There were no rules for playing the fast-food home-delivery game before Domino's came on the scene, and no rules for overnight package delivery before the advent of Federal Express.

Today's game requires different skills, and maybe even different players. Many executives don't have the skills needed to play today's game. Many aren't willing or able to change their practices or develop new skills.

One of our clients asked us to conduct a workshop for a group of customer-contact people. During the program, we learned that one of the biggest problems these frontline people had was customers going over their heads. Many customers who didn't like a quote or a delivery date, or who didn't like the answer to an inquiry, went directly to the company president. The president was a very hands-on, get-in-the-middle-of-things manager who had started the company and built it into a diversified company with over 150 employees. He frequently resolved many of these customer issues personally. By doing so he was unwittingly teaching his customers that if they didn't like an answer from someone, all they had to do was ask for him. He often reversed his staff's decisions. His frontline people reported that many customers routinely bypassed them altogether and just called the president directly. The president needed to learn a new way of managing. What had worked when there were only a handful of employees no longer did.

So what can you do as a CEO to create or maintain a service orientation?

☐ Demonstrate *your* commitment to service.

☐ Create an environment that focuses on customers and takes care of employees.

☐ Spend time with customers.

☐ Spend time with employees. Communicate the vision.

☐ Develop or enhance the skills needed for today's game.

Demonstrate your commitment to service. For service improvement to occur, management must be totally and visibly committed to it—from the CEO on down. Senior managers must practice it, promote it, and do it—not just put "them" through it. You must be willing to look at what *you've* been doing, to allow people to criticize it, and to be willing to change it. You must demand that the same be done throughout the organization at every level. You must be willing to make stands and take actions that are radical, uncharacteristic, and uncomfortable. Your competitors are probably doing these things, or they will be soon. You must, too, if you want to survive.

Citicorp's Walter E. Wriston has this to say about how to create the right environment:

> The first issue is to define the idea and get a consensus among management on where you want to go and on how people will be treated. The second issue is that you have to create a real climate in which people are fairly treated. Then, you have to communicate that over and over again to the rest of the company.
>
> In the end, of course, it really doesn't make any difference how many times you say it. What the staff looks for is what you actually do.

The key word in this whole discussion is *demonstrate*. Senior executives must walk the walk, not just talk the talk. And actions *do* speak louder than words. You can't just *say* training's important and then not participate in it. Top management must both take and present training. You can't talk about the importance of listening to customers and then not spend any time on the front lines.

Nordstrom executives reportedly will not take the elevators in their stores during the busy lunch hours because it takes up space for customers. Jan Carlzon says he refuses flight attendants' offers of newspapers or magazines on Scandinavian Airlines System flights until he's sure his customers have what they want to read. He says that more than words, these actions communicate who's most important on that airplane.

Harvard professor John J. Gabarro has studied how managers established themselves and "took charge" when accepting new positions. He relates several examples of how executives communicated their values without words. In one company, a division was behind on its shipments—again. The president called the executives of the division together and suggested that anyone who was "really concerned" about the shipment situation stay that day until shipments were caught up. It took until 2 A.M. Someone remarked, "There is no question of our being late on shipments again."

The reporting relationship of top service positions in your organization's hierarchy also sends a message to employees about how important service is. The manager of the General Electric Answer Center reports to an executive vice president. At Digital Equipment Corporation (DEC), the manager of quality and customer satisfaction reports to the executive committee and has its blessing to do whatever is needed to improve service, product quality, and customer satisfaction.

Use dramatic gestures that get people's attention and continually reinforce your commitment to service. The chairman of Management Science America Inc. (MSA), John Imlay Jr., is known for a touch of the dramatic. He once appeared on stage at a company meeting dressed in a tuxedo, top hat, and cape, leading a Bengal tiger. At another meeting, where he was introducing some new computer software that would "kill" old-style large mainframe computers by enabling them to perform more like personal computers, Imlay led a mock funeral procession for a mainframe, complete with a New Orleans jazz band, mourners dressed in black, and a casket bearing a mainframe computer. In a similarly dramatic gesture, at a company awards dinner with a circus theme, Quad/Graphics president Harry Quadrucci came in dressed as a ringmaster riding an elephant.

Here are some other ways you can demonstrate your commitment to service:

☐ Make a public commitment about the amount of time you'll spend each month with customers. Require your managers to do the same, and hold them to it.

☐ Put your name and private office phone number on customer comment cards. Invite customers to call you directly.

☐ Put your home phone number on your business card. Invite customers to call you any time they have a problem.

☐ Visit locations that have service problems.

☐ Call for, and act on, changes to your organization's structure, systems, products, location, policies, or anything else that will enable the organization to be more customer-focused.

☐ Approve budget items that will improve the service focus.

☐ Look for, encourage, support, and reward employees at all levels who demonstrate customer focus.

☐ Refuse to let managers drop out of training programs at the last minute because of an "emergency." Yes, crises do occur, but allowing such dropouts sends a message to other employees that training isn't really that important.

☐ Rotate managers into frontline positions. Have the production managers and sales manager switch jobs for a few weeks or months. Have the warehouse or distribution manager switch with the customer service manager. Living in the other person's shoes for a while may be uncomfortable, but the switch can lead to valuable insights and help break down artificial barriers that get in the way of serving customers.

Create an environment that focuses on customers and takes care of employees. You, your executives, and your managers must set the tone for your organization. It's like planting a garden: you usually have to do a lot of work before you actually plant the seeds. Without careful preparation, chances are that little will grow and prosper.

Author John Naisbitt has commented on "the shift from managers who traditionally were supposed to have all the answers and tell everyone what to do, to managers whose role it is to create a nourishing environment for personal growth. Increasingly we will think of managers as teachers, mentors, [and] developers of human potential." He goes on to say that in the years ahead, the challenge will be to retrain managers, not workers.

General Motors' William F. Haupt also believes that for change to occur within organizations, "We must have the direct ownership and involvement of key executives in the learning process. The key may well be to develop leaders who know how to create a learning climate."

Begin immediately to create a receptive environment with your senior managers that will increase the likelihood that a service-oriented culture will germinate when it is planted, rather than die in a hostile environment. Establish a set of values for your organization that defines the way you want to do business with your customers. Many executives see this set of values as being so important that they take personal responsibility for developing and implementing the values.

Avoid making trade-offs between short-term profitability and service. Also, if service policies or practices change, personally communicate the changes throughout the organization and continually reinforce the organization's commitment to service.

Part of creating a service-oriented environment involves reminding employees about what's expected, reassuring them about the new direction and practices, and keeping the service spirit alive. Stories about your service heroes and their actions is a great way to accomplish these things.

In Ray Wild's *How to Manage,* former 3M CEO Lewis M. Lehr describes how he intentionally circulated stories about maverick innovators to encourage new dreamers within the company. Lehr tells of researchers who had to bootleg time and equipment to develop and test new products. A typical example involved a researcher experimenting with creating nonwoven materials who was told to quit after 6 months of trials didn't produce a product. The researcher persisted anyway, and today nonwovens are a key part of the manufacturing processes of many 3M divisions.

The point that Lehr makes is this: "We keep these stories alive, and tell them often, so that anyone with innovative instincts today who feels discouraged, frustrated, and ineffective in the corporate environment will know that he or she is not the first one to wonder about management's attitude toward innovation." The larger issue for innovation—and service—is that top management must take the responsibility to see that these stories continue to live in the organization. Most service-oriented companies also have their service heroes, and stories about them continue to live in these organizations.

Spend time with customers.   Presidents, vice presidents, and branch managers must come out of their offices and Plexiglas cubbyholes and *talk* to customers—ask them what they like, what they don't like, and what else they'd like. This means that the operations or manufacturing vice president should go out to visit customers—not to make sales calls but to meet them personally and to talk about *their* business and their needs.

Our bank is apparently unfamiliar with this approach. The branch we use appointed a "Customer Service Officer" who sent out a "Dear Customer" letter to all the bank's customers. She introduced herself via letter and invited me (and several thousand other customers) to call her if she could be of assistance. I've never heard from her since. I've been a customer of at least one bank in whatever city I was living in for over 20 years now. I've never had a phone call from a bank, nor has anyone in a bank ever personally asked me, "How are we doing? How can we serve you better?"

Spend time with employees. Communicate the vision.   Executives in top service-oriented organizations make a point to establish a personal relationship with key service people at all levels to "get the view from the trenches" and to communicate their own service goals down through the organization. In other words, they get out with the troops and with mid-level managers who are responsible for service delivery.

William B. Walton, one of the founders of Holiday Inn, believed in the importance of keeping in touch with people on his staff and letting them know he was interested in what they were doing. In his book, *The New Bottom Line: People and Loyalty in Business*, Walton explains that he visited every hotel. He would start at the top floor and make his way from floor to floor, pausing to greet housekeepers and other workers he saw. He'd call each person by name (which he read from their name tags), chat for a few minutes, and remind them all how important they were. He says he continued this practice even when the chain grew, because "the worst occupational hazard for top management is losing touch with people."

Treat *employees* as customers and ask them how the organization can support them better, make their jobs easier, and provide what they need. Develop a 2- to 3-minute motivational speech that describes your organization's mission, its importance, and people's role in it. Talk about how important customers are. Give this talk as many times as you can to as many employee groups as possible.

And keep in mind that, in changing situations, managers often feel like they're overcommunicating, only to find out later that people are uninformed or misinformed. In a change situation, people need more information. They need clarity. They need to know that you're in charge and that you know where you're going. They need to know what to expect, which is somtimes difficult to convey because even top management may not know.

When executives don't communicate with employees, it can be harmful to their organizations.

Several years ago I was conducting several training programs for the national sales force of a hospital consulting company. The vice president of sales didn't attend our executive briefing or preview session, so he really didn't understand the philosophy of the program. He was not there for the kickoff session and never sat in on any of the sessions. On the last day, he joined us for lunch and asked if he could say a few words to the group. He gave an impassioned, 20-minute speech that contradicted everything the group had learned in the previous 3 days about building relationships with clients. His people left confused and demotivated: Were they to do what they had just learned or what they had heard their vice president say? The bigger issue is, why was there a contradiction at all?

My rule of thumb in a situation of major change is to double communication efforts. Many organizations do just the opposite. Fearing they'll let out information before it's finalized, they communicate *less*. This often leads to rumor, suspicion, anger, loss of credibility, and resentment.

Develop or enhance the skills needed for today's game. Some of this change and some of the suggested approaches may be difficult, risky, and uncomfortable for you or your managers. If you or your managers and executives come from highly technical backgrounds and are used to dealing mostly with board members, other executives, finances, long-range strategies, mergers, and acquisitions—or if you have a difficult time going out to press the flesh in your own organization—you may find things like attending rallies and giving speeches about your new mission to be particularly difficult. However, you must do these things anyway. You cannot shift the focus of your organization from behind your desk or by memo, mandate, or meeting.

You and your managers may need support, coaching, and possibly training during the transition process. If you're not a flamboyant person or a dynamic speaker, get some coaching on your image, presence, and delivery. Add a little pizzazz to your presentations.

You may want to hire someone to help you write your speeches. Just make sure they're built around *your* ideas. I know of one CEO who just read what someone else wrote for him. As a result, he used terms that weren't his style, and what he read promoted a direction different from where his organization was actually trying to go.

27. Change the roles of management and supervisory personnel so their job is to support the front line

In traditional organizations, the job of managers and supervisors is to plan, organize, delegate, control, and evaluate the work of their subordinates. These beliefs about what managers should do come from our history of hierarchical, patriarchal models, such as military and political organizations. Yet every successful politician knows that the key to a winning campaign is the grass-roots effort—the foot soldiers closest to the voters.

The game is also different today for managers and supervisors. And, like CEOs, their roles must change in a service-oriented organization. In his newsletter, *On Achieving Excellence*, Tom Peters writes, "Supervisors, for a century or more, were schedulers, disciplinarians, and the first line of management's 'defense' in its adversarial dealings with the union. . . . Now we hear of the new supervisor as 'facilitator, teacher, mentor, developer of people.' "

A human resources manager at a General Motors plant talks about the changing role of supervisors: "The job calls for different skills today. Before, if you were good in the military, you'd be good at GM. Now it's about how you get along with people. Motivation used to be an outer sort of thing—threat and force. Today, it's inner—personal satisfaction."

The emerging role of supervisors in service-oriented organizations is that *they* "work for" the front line, instead of the other way around. Their sole responsibility is to support the people who are serving the customer. Jan Carlzon puts it this way: "Seizing golden opportunities to serve the customer is the responsibility of the front line. Enabling them to do so is the responsibility of middle managers." That means providing frontline employees with the training, resources, information, encouragement, coaching, and freedom from bureaucratic bungling they need to best meet their customers' needs.

In *The Service Edge*, Ron Zemke describes how James Barksdale, a manager at Federal Express, sees it. Barksdale tells about a Federal Express employee who, without getting management's authorization, approved shipping some emergency rescue equipment in the middle of the night to try to save a life: "[M]y job is to see to it that we hire, train, and pay people to make that kind of decision right there on the front line. If that person calls me at home in the middle of the night to okay doing something important, I've failed as a manager."

If you're a manager or supervisor, you must also look beyond your departmental concerns and look for relationships between your mission and your organization's objectives. You must recognize that *you* must help create the vision of what your organization will look like. As a manager, you should have the broad organizational perspective necessary for this.

You must also help your employees do likewise. You must help each employee and each department see how they fit into the bigger picture of customer satisfaction.

Given the traditional organization's structure, this is difficult for many managers and supervisors at first. Some never do make the transition, and they may have to be invited to leave.

It's also difficult for employees. Many frontline people have been in rigid environments with little or no decision-making authority or skills provided. They *will* make some mistakes as they take on more responsibility, but management must believe that the payoffs will far outweigh the mistakes.

Here are some things supervisors and managers can do to provide support for the frontline:

1 Eliminate outdated policies and any other obstacles that can get in the way of meeting or exceeding customer expectations.
2 Create service circles, which are similar to quality circles. (See page 213 for more information on service circles.)
3 Make sure people have the equipment and resources they need. If they need better ways of capturing customer complaint data, provide data entry and reporting. If they need information faster, provide on-line computer terminals.
4 Hire service-oriented people.

5 Provide training. Make sure people are thoroughly familiar with the organization's products, services, and policies.

6 Reinforce training back on the job.

7 Provide positive, constructive feedback when people are not performing.

8 Be a positive role model. Demonstrate the beliefs and behaviors expected from your employees.

9 Be consistent and predictable. This is critical for first-line supervisors and their managers. If employees know they can depend on those who are supporting them to be reliable and consistent, they're much more likely to treat customers the same way. Remember, customer relations mirror employee relations.

10 Reward performance. Celebrate successes.

11 Upgrade their own skills. These new supportive supervisory roles will require new skills, or at least an upgrading some of present skills. Supervisors and managers may want to improve their ability to interview and hire, train, coach, give feedback, share decision making, give frequent praise, celebrate wins, trust team members, and so on.

28. Let employees bend the rules to satisfy customers

As I see it, rules are usually quite limiting and restrictive, rather than being helpful. They often say, "This is the only way to do it." *Guidelines*, however, are broader, and they provide *general* direction. They define limits and give people latitude within those limits. Establish guidelines for what people can and can't do, and give people the authority to bend the rules (without breaking them) in their efforts to satisfy customers. Also give them authority to go beyond what customers expect or ask for, especially with better customers and with those who have problems or complaints. A small investment in a current situation can pay huge dividends down the road.

Trust employees, especially at the front line, to do what's best for customers and the organization. Give them the authority to make decisions on the spot to do what's right for customers. That also means training them to think on their feet.

My parents live in Pennsylvania. The winters can get cold and blustery, so my dad likes to wear hats in the winter. A few years ago he and my mom saw an especially nice hat in a store window. The salesperson showed him the hats but didn't have my dad's size. My dad asked if the hat in the window was his size. The clerk told him, "I can't disturb the window display." My dad insisted, and the clerk finally agreed to at least check the size. It was the right size. It took another few minutes to convince the clerk to let my dad try it on—just to see if he liked it. He did. The clerk continued to argue that he couldn't take (or sell) anything out of the window. My dad suggested he could put a different size hat back in the window. The clerk refused: "I'm not allowed to take anything out of the window."

Here's a customer who wanted the product, but the rules said employees couldn't take anything out of the window displays. The clerk—and whoever made the rules—apparently didn't understand that window displays exist to appeal to customers so they'll come in and buy the merchandise and thereby have their needs met. My dad needed a hat, he liked the one in the window, it was the right size, and the price was right. But the clerk wouldn't give it to him. The clerk could have easily replaced the display hat with a different size; surely, the mannequin wouldn't have minded! But he wouldn't bend the rules to satisfy a customer.

Actually, a situation such as this isn't the clerk's fault. The blame should be placed with his company and his manager. Whether it's what they intended or not, the message this clerk got from them was that his job was not to satisfy customers—or even sell hats. It was to follow the rules. He apparently believed that it was more important to not take merchandise out of the window than to help a customer; and that if he broke the rules, there would be negative consequences.

29. Communicate with customers

Many organizations aren't aware of how their actions affect customers.

For most people, the *Good Housekeeping* seal stands for quality and reliability in the American marketplace. *Good Housekeeping* has worked hard to make it so. However, see the rejection slip my partner received from *Good Housekeeping* for an article she submitted. Although the content of the letter is nice, the other message it sends is, "We can't be bothered with you contributors. We'll just send you a copy of a copy of a copy of a form letter." The letter doesn't fit with the standard image of *Good Housekeeping*—the image *Good Housekeeping* strives to project and protect. But *Good Housekeeping* should remember that potential article contributors are customers, too.

Consider carefully what you're communicating to customers; it may not be what you intend. For example, think about when you go to a doctor's or dentist's office for the first time. There's usually a closed window with someone behind it who seems too busy with other things to pay much attention to you. The person hands you a clipboard and asks you to fill out a three-page medical history. Some of the questions often require information, dates, and doctors' phone numbers you don't have with you. You return the clipboard and then wait 15 minutes or more with several other people who've also been waiting that

GOOD HOUSEKEEPING

959 eighth avenue / new york, n.y. 10019 / john mack carter, editor

Dear Contributor:

Thank you for your recent article proposal. Unfortunately, we will not be able to use it at this time.

You should know, however, that every submission to Good Housekeeping is read by one or more editors. Many excellent ideas are turned down because they conflict with projects already underway or because they do not meet the particular editorial needs of Good Housekeeping.

We wish you the very best of luck in placing your material elsewhere.

Sincerely,

Joan Thursh
Articles Editor

long. Does this situation communicate, "I know you're ill or hurting and I'm concerned about that"—or does it communicate, "This is an impersonal operation run by someone who makes poor judgments about how long it takes to treat people"? Does it cause you to wonder if the doctor's judgment is any better in making diagnosis?

Most of us have had someone call us on the phone and read a "canned" presentation, or we've seen locally produced commercials on late-night television in which car dealers or athletes read from a teleprompter. The "message" customers hear is more than the words, and it's often not what the company doing the advertising intends to convey.

Several years ago, Eastern Airlines had a promotional package called the Weekender Club. Eastern listed an 800 number to call for information about joining. What I heard when I called was a bored young lady reading a script about various wonderful, exciting trips. It was not what she intended—and I know it was not what Eastern intended—but the message I heard was, "God, this is boring. This is the 30th call today. Here's another bozo calling to ask the same stupid questions. I'll just read this to him and hope he doesn't ask any questions." What I also "heard" was that Eastern didn't care enough about either this program or that employee to help her get excited about what she was doing. And the script she had to read didn't help, for it was full of words most people don't use in normal, casual conversation.

If you must use scripts for new people, encourage them not to *read* the scripts verbatim. Instead, have them *say* the information in the script in their own words. When people read, their cadence changes and their pronunciation changes. Listeners can tell when they are being read to—or at. The same is true for radio and TV commercials. It's easy to tell when someone is reading a script. Remember, the medium is the message, meaning that *how* you communicate often says more than *what* you say. Reading telephone (or other) scripts communicates, "I don't care. I'm just going through the motions."

Our research shows that even something as commonplace as a business letter conveys much more than the message contained in the words. Your correspondence is an interaction—a moment of truth—and people make many unconscious evaluations about you, your organization, your products, and your services based on the way your correspondence looks and reads. The letter shown on page 191 is one an associate of ours received from a car dealer he visited. Based only on this free-form, unprofessional letter, what impression do you have of that dealership and the cars it sells?

Even when correspondence *is* original, personalized, and neatly typed on letterhead, if you use outdated letter styles, write in the formal way you learned in school, or use old spelling or punctuation forms, many readers may subconsciously decide that your products or services may also be old-fashioned, outdated, and out of step. Similarly, when people receive correspondence from you with errors, misspellings, incorrect word usage, or other problems, they may decide that if your letters are sloppy, inept, or inattentive to details, your product or service may also be sloppy, inept, or inattentive to details.

When you're writing to a customer, be very sure to spell the person's name and the organizational name correctly. Many people tell me they find such misspellings especially irritating after they've contacted the organization. They say, "I wonder about the quality of their products and services if they can't do something as simple as copy my name correctly from my letterhead or business card." This kind of error communicates to many that the organization doesn't really care about customers or their concerns.

Examine the letters from General Mills and Golden Flake and compare the responses of the two food companies to my letters saying I couldn't find their product in my area and asking them to tell me which stores carry them. Of the two letters, the letter from Golden Flake (page 193) sounds more like the writer is really interested in helping me find the company's products, and it even names the stores near me that carry them. It also sounds like the people at Golden Flakes are proud of their products and their quality control and are interested in my satisfaction.

The letter from General Mills (page 192) essentially says, "I don't know and I don't care. Talk to the store manager." The General Mills customer service rep could have called the distributor in my area to learn who the retailers are, or at least given *me* the distributor's name, but she did neither. And she hardly even mentioned her company's products. The tone of the letter struck me as cold and impersonal. And the letter spelled my name wrong; it should be Jeff*rey*, not Jeff*ery*.

This idea of putting forth a service-oriented, customer-focused image applies to all your written documents. If you sell tangible products, take a look at your operating instructions, owner's manuals, procedure manuals, and other printed materials. Look at them from the *customer's* point of view: Are they written with so many technical or legal terms that customers have no idea what they say? Can customers find the information they want quickly? Can they understand it once they find it? Insurance policies, legal documents, computer manuals, and government documents are often the worse offenders. It's as though the manuals and documents are written for the convenience and protection of the *company*, not for the use and information of the customer. Thankfully, some enlightened companies are now writing important documents in plain English that their *customers* can understand.

Before printing them, test your instructions or manuals on several groups of typical users. Give them the assembly instructions and the component parts, or the manual and software, and let them have at it—by themselves. They'll tell you if your manuals are user-friendly and understandable. If you deal with computers and the manual you provide to users is called a "documentation" manual, chances are it's developer- or programmer-friendly, not user-friendly. Get a noncomputer person, preferable a user, to help you rewrite it. The same can be done with insurance policies, instruction manuals, and other technical documents. Get *users* to read them and help make them understandable. (These

Dear Tracy,

Thank you for visiting our dealership. It was a pleasure showing you one of our fine cars. We appreciate your interest and would welcome the opportunity to see you again.

We do hope that you will decide to become the owner of a Dyer & Dyer Original.

Sincerely,

Larry Richardson

Dyer & Dyer, Inc.
Peachtree Road at Roswell Highway / Atlanta, Georgia 30341 / (404) 451-0002

General Mills Consumer Services

P.O. Box 1113, Minneapolis, MN 55440

November 4, 1988

Jeffery Disend
2137 Mt. Vernon Road
Atlanta, GA   30338

Dear Mr. Disend:

Thank you for contacting us regarding the availability of Nature Valley granola bars. We appreciate your interest in our products.

Our records indicate the product is currently available to the wholesalers supplying stores in your area. However, distribution may be limited. If your supermarket doesn't currently carry the product, you may wish to ask the store manager if it could be ordered from the supplier.

I wish I could have given you a store name where to purchase the product. As a manufacturer, we do not sell directly to the retailers and, therefore, have delivery records only on wholesale suppliers.

As a thank you for your interest, I am enclosing coupons toward your next purchases of General Mills consumer food products of your choice.

                              Sincerely,

                              Cheri A. Kovacic

                              Consumer Service Representative

CAK:mp

General Offices at One General Mills Boulevard

GOLDEN FLAKE SNACK FOODS, INC.

July 20, 1988

Mr. Jeff Disend
2137 Mount Vernon Rd.
Atlanta, GA 30338

Dear Mr. Disend:

I can't tell you how pleased we were to receive your letter and hear the nice comments. We are always happy to hear from folks who enjoy our snacks, especially our Tortilla Strips.

I have spoken to our sales office in your area, and they have informed me that you should be able to find the Tortilla Strips in Big Star, Kroger or Brunos. They did experience a shortage recently, but that situation should be corrected by now. Let me know if you experience any more difficulties finding our products.

The number one objective of Golden Flake is to provide our customers with high quality snacks that they can enjoy at a fair and reasonable price. Our staff of Quality Control Technicians constantly sample our products, checking them for such things as overall appearance, salt content, moisture content and flavor.

Your comments certainly prove that our efforts are paying dividends. I assure you that we will continue to strive for excellence in quality and economy.

As a token of our appreciation for your support of our products, I have enclosed some complimentary coupons so that you can have an opportunity to enjoy some of our other fine snacks.

Sincerely,

Mark A. Hilley

Mark A. Hilley
Quality Control Manager

MAH:lrb

ideas also apply to *internal* documents and correspondence going to other departments, managers, or executives.)

Also pay attention to how people answer the phones—internally and for customers. The people answering the phones may not be communicating what the organization intends them to.

Several years ago, Kay was leaving a telephone message with a client's secretary. Kay said, "My name is Kay duPont. That's spelled small *d-u*, capital *P-o-n-t*." The woman said, "Are you sure?" "Yes I'm sure. I've been spelling it that way all my life." "Well, it doesn't matter anyway." [unspoken: "It's just a telephone message going to my boss."]

It does matter.

We've called businesses and heard phones answered by a number: "6122." This is a very poor way to be greeted. People who answer the phones should let customers know they've reached a viable enterprise with real people and a real name, not a series of numbers.

Some secretaries and receptionists answer with acronyms or abbreviations that only insiders could know: "CCRO" or "Recomp." If I'm a customer calling for the first time, I don't know what those shorthand names mean.

I had a client at the School of Business at a major university. Each time I called, the receptionist said something that sounded like "Biz Ossie in OBA." I thought I had a wrong number. I said, "Whom have I reached?" She repeated, "Biz Ossie in OBA." I told her I didn't understand and asked her to say it again, slowly. By this time, the irritated tone in her voice communicated that she thought I was pretty stupid. The third time she said, "This is Business Policy and OBA." Even when I understood the words, I still didn't know what it was or if I had the right number. Eventually I learned that I had reached the office for the departments of Business Policy and Organizational Behavior and Administration (OBA).

Sometimes the people who answer the phones are busy when calls come in. Instruct them to request (not order) callers to state their business before putting the callers on hold: "May I put you on hold?" not "Hold please!" Avoid telephone switching. If the person who answers the phone is not absolutely sure who a caller should talk to, the call should not be transferred. The answerer should tell the caller that the person who can help the caller will call him back. Make sure the people who answer the phones make good on such promises.

If you answer the phone and you do have to transfer a call, if the party the caller is trying to reach isn't there or is on the phone, tell the caller. Don't just connect the caller to the first voice that answers the phone. It may be a temp who hasn't the foggiest idea how to help the customer, or it may be someone who was just walking by the ringing phone. Being connected to someone who can't help is likely to irritate an already upset customer more.

Encourage everyone to use the full name of your organization and to pronounce it so callers can understand it. Some organizations have long or unusual names, and the company receptionist says the name so fast that callers can't make it out. What callers hear may sound like "Sprfhsbdle and Dnrpsltibfks Company," and all they're sure of are the words "and" and "Company."

And people who communicate with customers should smile. Yet, it's trite and sounds corny, but 93 percent of the message we get from others is nonverbal, and 38 percent of it is conveyed by tone of voice. On the phone, customers *hear* you and the tone you project, even if they never *see* you.

If you do see customers face-to-face and you wear a sour or even a neutral look, customers may perceive that you're unhappy with them, with your job, or with the company. They may subconsciously conclude, "If he (or she) is that upset with this company or the job, maybe I shouldn't buy here."

Some people's faces just naturally look more unhappy, even in a neutral position. People with such natural expressions may not *feel* particularly happy or unhappy, but they may *look* like they're sad or angry. It really doesn't matter how they feel; what matters is what customers perceive. A smile makes customers feel that they are welcome and that employees *like* what they're doing. A smile may seem like such a small, insignificant gesture, but it can make a big difference to customers.

There are several other dimensions to communicating with customers. People like to do business with organizations they know and trust. It is a good idea to periodically send customers reprints of favorable publicity *about* your organization, products, or services. If your organization or some of your people receive awards or recognition in your industry, let your customers know. Also send copies of articles written *by* people in your organization. This also helps improve your credibility.

Let customers know how *they* benefit from doing business with you. Many organizations assume that customers and potential customers know what the organizations do and know about all their products and services. This is rarely true. Remind customers of the services you offer, and of any "extras" you offer (such as free delivery, next-day service, money-back guarantees). Let them know about new products, new features, and new services.

Communicating to customers is especially important in industries that are often perceived as poor service providers, such as bill collection, utilities, tax collection, postal service, auto repairs, and so on. If you're in an industry or an organization not known for service, communicating to customers about your service, reliability, value, and other benefits is important.

Michael LeBoeuf, author of *How to Win Customers and Keep Them for Life*, recommends building on your perceived strengths. He says that if feedback from your customers tells you they see you as reliable or responsive, mention or allude to these attributes in your advertising, marketing, and other communications. Remind them that "We deliver what we promise" or "We're there when you need us."

Stay in touch regularly. Customers don't like to hear from you only when you want to sell them something. Seeing your name or getting something useful from you keeps your organization in the customer's mind without constantly "selling."

Help customers run their businesses. Pass along ideas and information that can help them improve, even if the ideas don't involve anything you do. Tell them about some new technology or equipment, send books or articles about their industry, refer them to experts that may be able to help them with some problem, and so on. Of course, mention *your* products or services, if they can help.

Say "thank you." Many organizations forget this simple courtesy, and customers don't like to be taken for granted. Tell your customers you appreciate their business. Make follow-up phone calls. Send letters, handwritten notes, or gifts. Every contact you make gives you another opportunity to talk to your customers, see how they're doing, learn if there are any new needs or problems, and keep them satisfied. The real-life samples reprinted here show that it doesn't take much to show appreciation and stay in contact with customers

Another important part of your communications is your integrity, credibility, and believability with internal and external customers. Here are some suggestions for communicating with your customers:

☐ Make and keep agreements.

☐ Don't make agreements or promises you don't intend to or can't keep just to appease someone or "get them off your back."

☐ Pin down agreements. If someone says, "I'll do it next week," get an agreement on exactly what day—even what time—you can expect "it" to be done. Get consent to call the person on it if he or she doesn't come through as promised.

☐ Expect others to honor their agreements. If they don't, call them on their promises assertively but tactfully. A good way to do this is to use the agreement-status-goal-commitment formula:

Review the *agreement:* "You agreed to have that report to me by Monday afternoon."

Describe the *status:* "It's now Wednesday and I don't have it."

THANK YOU

. . . Just wanted to drop you a note to let you know that I enjoyed helping you with your recent clothing purchase at J. Riggings.

Since I am looking forward to serving you again in the future, I will keep you informed about new merchandise arrivals and give you advance notice of our periodic sales.

Thanks again for letting me help you.

Josh Borden Asst. Mgr.

J. RIGGINGS

State your *goal:* "I'd like to have it by the end of the day today."
Ask for *commitment:* "Will you do that?"

☐ Give early warning. If you can't fulfill an agreement, let others involved know at the earliest possible time *before* the agreed-upon time of fulfillment.

☐ Making excuses after the fact, no matter how valid, hurts your credibility.

30. Actively solicit comments and complaints from customers

Why solicit customer comments and complaints?   Many organizations view customer complaints as a drain on resources, but USOCA (U.S. Office of Consumer Affairs) research on customer satisfaction reveals that complaints can be an extremely valuable marketing asset because they offer opportunities to rectify customer's problems. Companies that capitalize on these opportunities generally earn customer loyalty.

Properly handling customer complaints has many advantages:

1 It helps keep customers who might otherwise switch to competitors.

2 It negates the negative effects of word of mouth. Studies show that unhappy customers tell twice as many people about their negative experiences as satisfied customers tell about their positive experiences.

3 It enables you to identify and eliminate the causes of problems. For example, if you get a lot of complaints about product quality, responsiveness, or billing errors, you can examine these areas and try to improve them.

Fidelity USA

82 Devonshire Street, Boston, MA 02109

September 17, 1988

.'s

Ms. Kay D. Disend
2137 Mount Vernon Road   nge
Atlanta, Georgia 30338   mall

Dear Ms. Disend:

.A

0

    It's not too often I have the opportunity to write our most-valued   uest
customers and simply say "thank you for investing with us."   at

    But I would like you to know how much all of us here at Fidelity
Investments appreciate your business and look forward to serving you   aining
in the future.   d

ᴜs

    As an investor who has a sizeable account balance with us -- yᴏ·
continued satisfaction is extremely important to Fidelity, and ᵗ
personally.   ᴊ best that Fidelity
                                                              ᴀy!

    That's why I'm writing to you today, Ms. Disᴇᵣ
a way to make your relationship with Fidelity ᴄ ᵃmong the select group of investors
rewarding in the months and years ahead.   ᵃ Fidelity USA Account.

    It's a way to help ensure thᴀ
for you, at all times -- ever   Sincerely,

    A way to maintᵃ·
you alleviate sᴄ
accounts anᵈ   Edward C. Johnson 3d
                                       President

        ECJ/dd

        P.S. Many Fidelity customers have found their USA Account to be so
             useful in managing their personal finances that they've even
             established a separate Account for their trust or business
             activities.

(1),(2) Neither any investment company identified (e.g. any mutual fund/money market fund) nor Fidelity
Distributors Corporation, nor Fidelity Brokerage Services, Inc. is a bank and fund shares are not backed or
guaranteed by any bank or insured by the FDIC.

Fidelity Brokerage Services, Inc.
Fidelity Distributors Corporation, General Distribution Agent.

4 It can decrease the number and severity of costly third-party claims, litigation, and redress actions.

5 It provides valuable information for new-product development, product redesign, and packaging.

6 It can generate profits. In the seven industries TARP (Technical Assistance Research Programs Institute) studied (package goods, banking, utilities, consumer durable goods, electronic products, retailing, and automotive service), *every* industry showed at least some return on investment for a complaint-handling department. Some showed more than a 100 percent return on investment. In other words, the complaint-handling operation actually *made* money.

7 It calls attention to your strong points. If you get good marks on quality or dependability, capitalize on that trait. Chrysler Corporation has done that for years with its advertising campaign and warranty: "We back them better because we build them better."

8 It helps focus the organization's attention on doing things right and satisfying customers from the outset. If *employees* know that customers can easily call someone at corporate headquarters on a toll-free line to complain or report problems, they're more likely to be service-conscious from the beginning of every transaction and interaction. And, putting customer compliments and complaints in your newsletter and on bulletin boards helps focus attention on customer comments inside the organization. It sends the message that you pay attention to what customers say.

We know that one in four customers may be dissatisfied at any given time. And of those, as many as 70 percent won't tell you. Most just take their business elsewhere. As the USOCA report says, "The irony here is that the problems of the noncomplainants are generally the easiest to resolve. If only given the chance, business could have retained the patronage of many of these customers. Therefore, this often large pool of noncomplainants represents a significant lost marketing opportunity."

Getting customers to complain pays off. A study in the telecommunications industry found that only 31 percent of the people who complained said they'd do business again with the company involved. The figure jumps to 75 percent for people whose complaints were satisfactorily resolved.

Studies in other industries have shown that as many as 90 percent of customers will return if their complaints are satisfactorily resolved. Even those whose complaints were *not* resolved to their satisfaction reported a repurchase intention, indicating that there's still a huge marketing advantage to addressing complaints, even if complaints are not satisfactorily resolved.

Other research studies in financial services, automotive service, consumer products, and large-ticket durable goods companies also confirm that customers who do not complain are the least likely to return, customers who do complain but are not satisfied with the response are slightly more likely to return, and the majority of customers who complain and are satisfied with the response remain as customers. And in every study, even customers whose complaints were *not* resolved to their satisfaction were more likely to repurchase than those who never bothered to complain.

Customer-focused organizations don't avoid complaints, they encourage them. And they make it easy for customers to complain. Remember, one of the major reasons customer don't complain is because they don't know who to complain to or how to reach someone to complain to. Customer-focused organizations make complaints part of their corporate service strategy. They know that customers who complain give them a chance to solve their problems.

Beware the dangers of encouraging customer complaints.   Separate studies conducted for a chain of national automotive repair shops and a major car rental company showed that both companies took a long time to respond to customer complaints, so customers perceived them as being unresponsive. These companies also created unrealistically high expectations regarding the remedial action they would take.

The two companies mentioned are not alone in this problem. According to the USOCA report, "Some companies handle complaints so poorly that they would be better off not soliciting complaints." USOCA's studies showed that many organizations take too long to act on complaints or else raise customer expectations and then can't deliver at all. USOCA's conclusion is that "before a company adopts an aggressive complaint solicitation strategy, corporate complaint handling polices should be thoroughly reviewed and upgraded where necessary. For complaint handling to be effective as a marketing strategy, companies must be willing to make a serious commitment to resolving customer problems."

Make sure your complaint-handling system is designed to work *for* you, not *against* you. Train frontline people the proper way to handle inquiries, questions, problems, and complaints. Teach them how to deal with the customer as a *person*. Ensure rapid responses to customer problems.

Keep in mind, though, that responsiveness, quickness, and fairness are based on customers' *perceptions* of these qualities. Simply *saying* your organization is responsive may not be enough.

Polaroid uses the date on a customer's letter as the entry date into the complaint-handling system, instead of using the date Polaroid receives the letter. Since response time is a critical component in the customer's perception, this simple move shifts the response time from the company's point of view to the customer's point of view.

Make sure you have the systems, people, and procedures for handling customer complaints and comments.   Identify the areas that have, or are most likely to cause, the most problems. Get input from your frontline people on these.

An organization should have specific standards for handling and resolving complaints; for example, "handle all complaints by the end of the day," or "resolve 100 percent of all complaints to customer's satisfaction."

Make it easy for customers to register complaints or offer comments. Use toll-free numbers and comment cards. Make managers accessible to customers. Make the process easy, too. Very few people will take the time to complete long written forms. The closer a complaint can be made to the time and point of delivery of the transaction, the better. If people have to wait until they get home, look up an address or phone number, and send a letter to some distant location, they often end up not complaining. And they get more upset about problems the longer they think about them.

It is crucial to have the right people handling complaints. Of course, all frontline employees should have the right temperament for dealing with people. If your organization is such that certain people or departments spend most of their time handling problems, complaints, requests, or inquiries, employee selection is an even more critical issue. You probably need thick-skinned, sensitive, compassionate people. Spend the extra time and money to identify them and pay them. It's a very small investment for keeping the business of customers who might leave. Figure out what it's costing your business to lose customers compared to paying 10 to 15 percent above scale for top customer-contact people.

People who are most likely to handle complaints should be fully and continually trained. Training should focus on

☐ Self-esteem and confidence. When people spend much of their time answering problems or complaints, their egos can get bruised a lot. Help them keep their spirits and self-confidence up.

☐ Communication skills. Such skills include listening, getting information, handling upset customers, understanding difficult people, resolving disagreements, and diffusing anger.

☐ Product/technical knowledge. Many problems and complaints stem from misunderstandings. A customer may misread a product's warranty or instructions (or not read them at all), may expect the product to do something it won't, and so on. Frontline people need to know the capabilities and limitations of their products and services. Procter & Gamble organizes its consumer services department by product categories, and each group becomes thoroughly familiar with its products. The employees visit plants to see how specific products are made, watch the products being tested, and actually use the products themselves.

☐ Internal workings of the organization. Frontline people need to know who does what. The more they know about which people to contact to resolve particular problems, the better.

Establish rules and guidelines. Decide on what issues frontline people *must* stand fast—especially if health, safety, or legal issues are involved—and where they have some leeway. Determine also how far people can go under normal circumstances, what they can do in out-of-the-ordinary situations, what alternatives they can suggest to customers, and who responds to customers under various circumstances.

As much as possible, frontline employees should be given broad leeway in resolving problems and making amends with customers. TARP studies in several industries reveal that up to 80 percent of customers who had their complaints settled satisfactorily will purchase other products or services from the offending company. On the other hand, only about 30 percent of customers who were *dissatisfied* with the outcome of their complaints said they'd purchase other products or services from the company. Remember, the more satisfied customers are with the way a problem is handled, the more likely they are to remain customers. And satisfying existing customers is less costly than finding new customers.

A quick response to customer complaints is key. Don't make customers wait weeks to get an answer or to get a problem resolved. Establish effective, efficient ways to investigate problems, take action, and respond to customers. According to the USOCA studies, time spent investigating problems and complaints is the major cause of delayed responses. Figure out how to speed up the investigation phase, even if it means hiring more staff people.

The last—but still very important—part of handling customer complaints is follow-up. The *way* problems are handled affects customers' willingness to return. In your organization, contact customers who registered complaints, got some special service, wrote a letter, or contacted you in some way. Thank them for contacting you. Find out if they were satisfied with your organization's action or response. If not, why not? What would it take to satisfy them?

Use the information you collect.   Just taking care of the customer's problem or complaint isn't enough. You must also use information concerning complaints to prevent future problems and to improve your products or services.

Here are some suggestions:

☐ Decide what information is necessary to collect.

☐ Provide a form or a computer terminal with fields to help collect and sort information about complaints.

☐ Decide how to classify complaints. Does the complaint have to do with delivery? Billing? Inaccurate or incomplete orders? Late orders? Product quality or operation? Customer–employee interaction? Certain locations? Special requests? Other problems?

☐ Also decide how much detail you want people to capture for each category.

☐ Provide data to the departments or work units involved. Do this as soon as possible so they can use it to correct problems or redesign products. Also provide data to the frontline employees involved.

TARP research has shown that the most common complaints to businesses center around the quality of the product or service and around billing disputes. These issues are fixable, but it means changing some things inside the organization. There has to be an efficient way to get information about a problem to the people who can fix it.

Let customers know you want to hear from them. Customers often don't complain because they believe (1) it's not worth their time or effort, (2) it won't do any good—no one wants to listen, and (3) they don't know how or where to complain. Customers have very low expectations that anything will be done about problems if they do make the effort to complain.

If you're serious about soliciting customer complaints and comments, the prescription is pretty simple:

1. Let them know you're sincere about hearing from them—the good news and the bad. For example, customers at Barlow & Eaton Jewelry stores are invited by president Michael M. Poole to tell him what they think on the form shown.

2. Tell customers repeatedly how to reach you. This advice is easy to follow for small businesses like hair salons or plumbers, or small companies in which customers deal directly with owners or in which the owner or manager is easy to find. A trip to the Yellow Pages is often all the customer needs. But if an organization has multiple locations or its products are delivered to customers by dealers or distributors, it's harder for customers to find out whom to contact. And with mergers and acquisitions, it's difficult for many customers to know who owns the company and where the main office is. Only the most upset or most elated customer will spend the time and energy to find out. Result: Most customers just don't bother.

3. Make it easy for customers to reach you. For example, at one time, British Airways set up booths in major airports where dissatisfied customers could lodge their complaints. A customer could go inside a booth; explain his or her situation, problem, or complaint; and be videotaped.

Put your name, address, and telephone number on every piece of product literature. Also put it right on the product, if possible. Use a toll-free number.

Provide a help line, service desk, or answer center. Companies like General Electric, Polaroid, Moen, Procter & Gamble, and others provide well-publicized toll-free numbers so customers can get information, ask questions, report problems, get repair service, lodge complaints, give compliments, and make suggestions.

The USOCA recommends that business and government agencies put an address and phone number on all product or service literature and put toll-free

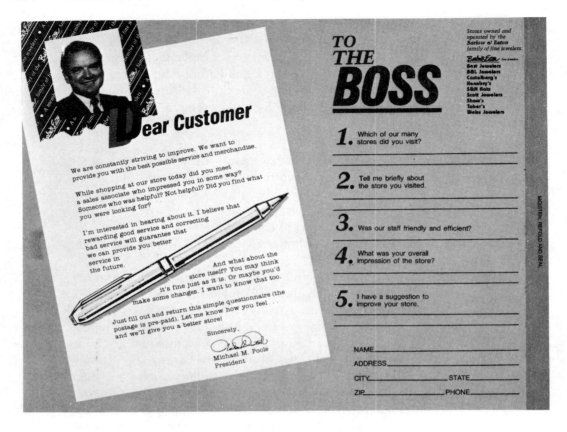

numbers directly on products, where possible. Doing so helps break consumers' perceived barriers to complaining. Toll-free numbers, especially, address the three previously mentioned primary reasons why people don't complain: (1) Toll-free numbers are easy, and most people would rather call than write; (2) with highly visible, well-publicized toll-free numbers, customers are more likely to feel that a company is interested in and cares about their problems because they can pick up the phone and talk to someone at the company who's trained in dealing with customers; (3) even if a customer never uses the toll-free number, knowing that your organization cares enough to have a toll-free line and publicize it may be enough to change that customer's perceptions about the company's willingness and responsiveness.

My wife and I love going to outdoor symphony concerts. We usually take some cheese or pasta salad and a bottle of wine in a small Styrofoam cooler. Most coolers are not tall enough to hold a bottle of wine, but several years ago I found one that was. It also had a long carrying strap so I could carry the cooler over my shoulder. After many concert seasons, the cooler wore out and had to be replaced. I looked in every store I could think of that sells coolers, but I couldn't find this particular cooler.

Finally, I thought I'd contact the manufacturer directly. I looked on the bottom of my old cooler for the company's name, and there it was: "LIFOAM, Baltimore, MD 21211." I got the number from directory assistance and called LIFOAM. The company still makes that cooler and was happy to send me one.

The name and address on the product made it easy for customers to contact LIFOAM, although I suggested that the company also put its phone number on the cooler.

Require top managers to spend time at the front lines working, listening, and talking to customers. Anyone who spends some time answering the phones or dealing with correspondence from customers will learn a lot about the organization this way.

One final note: Make a special effort to reach those customers who are least likely to complain, such as senior citizens and the poor.

31. Continually seek to learn what your customers want and expect—and what they get

Things change. Customers change, customer preferences change, and your organization's ability to deliver may change. A new competitor may spring up, or an old competitor may launch a new product or service that customers like better. And so on. Things never stay the same, so you can't afford to be out of touch for very long.

Northern Telecom Inc. (NTI) uses a series of three surveys with its customers. The first survey, sent 30 days after NTI equipment has been installed, asks for customer reactions to delivery, installation, and training. About 6 months later, another survey asks customers for feedback on how the product is performing and on NTI's maintenance and repair services. Then once a year, customers receive a questionnaire asking for additional information about how NTI products are performing, what additional features customers would like, and how satisfied they are with NTI overall.

Although customers are your best source of information, they'll rarely volunteer the kind of information you need. You have to ask them specific questions such as the following:

What's most important to you?

What do you expect from a product or service like ours?

Are these expectations being met?

If not, where are the shortfalls?

How does our product or service compare to the competition's?

What do you like most? Least?

What's the most common or most bothersome problem you face when dealing with us? How would you fix it if you were in charge here?

What if we could . . . . (or, what if the product could . . . .)

How can we make it or do it better?

What would you like us to do differently from or in addition to what we're doing now?

If you could change anything about our product or service, what would it be?

Your next best source of information is your employees, especially those on the front lines. The adage that people closest to a situation know what's needed applies here, too. Ask employees for their ideas on improving service. Ask about the most troublesome or most frequent problem they face in serving customers and how they'd fix it if they were in charge.

Make sure your employees are alert to customer comments such as, "I wish you made this in green," or "This won't fit in our machines. If only it had a notch right here, we could use it." Long lines, repeated problems with a particular part, form, or procedure, and overheard conversations of customers grumbling to each other are signals that you're not as user-friendly as you think. Rather than chalking such things up to picky customers, employees need to learn to recognize them as symptoms of problems that can be addressed and cured.

Encourage employees to pass along comments and ideas—no matter how silly they may seem—to the right people in your organization. And be sure to acknowledge and reward employees for doing so; otherwise, the flow of ideas may slow or stop.

Another source of information is your *potential* customers. Find out what they like about their current suppliers or providers and what it would take for them to do business with you.

And don't forget your former customers. Make it a practice to contact them regularly. Find out what they liked when they were customers and what they didn't like. Ask why they stopped buying and what it would take to get them back. Who knows, you may be able to help a former customer solve some problem he or she is facing. Maybe just the fact that you contacted the former customer, showed some interest, or corrected some earlier problem or misunderstanding may be enough to win that former customer back.

Regardless of whom you talk to and which questions you ask, the hard part is being open to the answers you hear. Tom Peters calls this receptiveness "naive listening." I call it neutral listening—listening without becoming defensive or giving all the "reasons" why things aren't the way customers would like them to be. You must also be willing to act on what people tell you. If you ask for input and never use it, you'll stop getting it.

Use as many methods as you can to gather information. Toll-free numbers, comment cards, surveys and questionnaires, focus groups, interviews, and mystery shoppers are commonly used methods, but don't overlook other less formal methods. Firsthand experience and observation by executives and managers is important also. Call your own organization. How is your call handled? How are you treated? What image is your organization communicating to customers?

Senior executives at Digital Equipment Corporation (DEC) often spend time in their own warehouses to actually experience what's involved in opening, unpacking, and installing DEC equipment. The executives get to experience firsthand what their customers experience with DEC products. Along similar lines, experienced mail-order organizations always send packages to themselves to see how the packages arrive.

Executives at Wal-Mart spend 1 week a year in Wal-Mart stores. Disney executives must spend 1 week each year in the Disney parks. Other companies also require executives and managers to go out to listen to customers.

Talk to customers when you're in your own stores, offices, restaurants, or whatever. Ask, "What do you think of this product/service/procedure?" or "What do you think we could do to improve things around here?"

Many organizations also use mystery shoppers to help measure performance. Such shoppers can help spot strengths and weaknesses in your systems, procedures, policies, rules, and training. Some organizations even create specific situations, requests, orders, or problems to test the responsiveness of the organization to customer needs.

If much of your organization's contact with customers takes place over the phone, use mystery *callers* instead of mystery shoppers. Such callers can rate the way employees handle their calls according to your standards of speed, courtesy, creativity, resolution time, and so on.

Several cautions about using shopper services:

- [ ] Make sure shoppers know what they're looking for. They should know your standards—what you expect from your units, systems, and people. Otherwise, they will just be wandering around aimlessly in search of good service, and they won't "know it when they see it."

- [ ] Use shoppers to test your systems, policies, responsiveness, waiting times, and so on, not to spy on your people. Use of shoppers is not a substitute for hands-on management.

- [ ] Do not have shoppers reprimand or intervene if employees provide poor service. Shoppers should only document these events in their reports. Any counseling or disciplinary action should come from the involved employee's supervisor, not from a shopper.

- [ ] Shop the shoppers. Be sure they're doing what they're supposed to do and reporting accurately. Most shopping services have their own auditing procedures; make sure you know what these are before you set the shoppers loose on your organization.

32. Learn what your competition is doing

Traditional, inwardly focused companies believe their only competition comes from organizations that do essentially what they do—that provide basically the same product or service they do. Customer-centered, outwardly focused companies realize that there's more to competition than that simplistic approach.

The meaning of competition is changing. In *Managing Innovation,* John Rydz says, "Today, competition means anything that diverts your customers' attention, and ultimately their money, from your product." Rydz divides competition into two types: direct and indirect. Although his distinctions are helpful, I think a third distinction and a slight change in terminology are needed. To me it's more useful to think about competition as being direct, indirect, or hidden.

Direct competition, according to Rydz, comes from a product or service that provides customers with essentially the same thing others are providing. For example, most swimming pool supply companies, office supplies companies, banks, and airlines offer roughly the same products or services as others in their business. This is the traditional view of competition.

Rydz says some forms of direct competition are often overlooked, but I think it's more accurate to call these forms *indirect* competition. I define *indirect competition* as competition coming from innovations or technology in other, usually noncompetitive, industries. For example, Rydz describes how a company called Emaloid launched a sizable effort in the 1960s to develop innovative uses for carbon paper. By developing products such as pressure-sensitive and no-smudge carbonless paper, Emaloid hoped to gain an advantage over its direct competitors: other carbon paper companies. However, Emaloid's direct competition wasn't as important as its *indirect* competition: the innovations Xerox and other companies made in the copier business virtually killed the market for carbon paper.

In another example, Rydz describes how businesses in the banking equipment industry also suffered major losses from technology outside their own industry. Banking equipment companies were competing to develop larger, mechanized vertical filing cabinets that made filing and retrieving documents easier than it had been using the old manual method with horizontal file drawers. However, the banking equipment companies' *real* competitors were companies that specialized in transferring information to microfilm, microfiche, and computer disks.

Finally, Rydz says indirect competition comes from an unexpected arena. I think this type of competition should be called hidden competition. For example,

Rydz explains that during the 1970s, the sales of Singer sewing machines declined steadily. At first Singer thought the declining sales were due to bad weather. The next year poor sales were attributed to the oil crisis, and the following year to cheap foreign labor. After doing a market study, Singer discovered that its competition wasn't from any of those factors. Rather, the competition was everything that competed for women's free time. A record number of women had joined the work force outside the home, and women were also increasingly involved in jogging, political activities, gourmet cooking, and going back to school. More homes had cable television. Women had less time to sew and more money to buy clothes rather than make them. They simply had less interest in making clothes.

Another example of hidden competition occurs in relation to the heating oil business in the northeastern United States. Although the oil business faces direct competition from coal, electricity, and natural gas, a major hidden competitor is also the population shift to the Sunbelt. Similarly, the alcoholic beverage and tobacco companies are facing hidden competition from health and fitness awareness.

Identify your direct, indirect, and hidden competitors. Then decide how to compete with or react to them. If you have indirect or hidden competitors, it may mean shifting your focus, dropping certain products, relocating, or changing tactics.

Find out as much as you can about competitive organizations. Some suggestions for doing this are listed below:

☐ Buy one share of stock in each competitive company. This gets you the company's annual report and other information about the organization that you might not have or get in some other way.

☐ Encourage all employees to look for, and be aware of, competitive activity—new locations, products, distributors, price changes, and so on. Employees hear lots of things about competitors. They need to pick up on the information, assess its importance, and pass it along. Especially encourage your salespeople and other frontline, customer-contact people to (tactfully) ask customers about the competition: "What do they offer that you really like?"

☐ Have frontline people attend trade shows so they can see who the competitors are; what the competitors are offering; and what competitors' products, prices, quality, and people are like. Getting this perspective gives employees a better idea what they're up against and what they have to do to compete.

☐ Have frontline people "shop" the competition. This helps you gauge how well you're doing in comparison and helps spot the competition's strengths and weaknesses—and your own. Ask people to look for specific things, such as response time, cleanliness, accuracy, and so on. You decide what they should be looking for. I suggest studying those areas where you suspect the competition is much stronger than you are and weaker than you are. Confirm the differences so you can capitalize on those that are in your favor. Be sure to provide ways for employees to channel the information they learn about competitors to the people in your organization who need it most.

☐ Have shoppers service-shop your competitors. Use the same "shopper's checklist" you use for shoppers who shop your own organization. Have shoppers ask for the same normal and out-of-the-ordinary items or services and see how both organizations respond.

33. Learn what other organizations are doing to improve service

No one person or organization has all the answers to becoming and remaining service-oriented, so find out what others are doing. Identify a number of organizations in your industry, and outside of it, that you see as service leaders. Find out what they do, how they do it, and what results they get. Create a task force to do this. Get lots of people involved. Send out teams of people to various organizations. Develop a checklist of things for them to observe, ask about, and report back on. The idea isn't to steal ideas or to bring back copies of forms or documents to replicate in your organization; instead, look for general approaches, philosophies, and strategies that work (or don't), and adapt the best ideas to your unique culture.

34. Develop internal (employee) support systems

A support system is a set of well-defined actilvities, procedures, and methods to help keep the service transformation process moving. It should provide formal and informal ways for people to vent problems and frustrations, remind people of the importance of the transformation and their role in it, and acknowledge people's contributions and accomplishments. A support system helps eliminate structures, policies, and practices that get in the way of providing excellent service. (Some of these elements of support systems are described in greater detail in separate sections.)

A support system is also an intangible network within the organization that is based on pride, respect, and teamwork. For example, frontline people need to know that the rest of the organization is there to support and assist them in serving customers. When people know they can depend on the systems, equipment, procedures, and people behind the scenes to deliver, keep commitments, and handle problems, they can act more confidently and with less stress.

If your frontline people have to contend with difficult and time-consuming procedures, runarounds trying to get information, missed deadlines, unresponsive coworkers, and other difficulties, they may be more concerned about their own internal problems and difficulties than with serving customers.

To keep your organization customer-focused, support systems must address two major areas:

1 *External*: How you support your products or services to customers and how you are organized to continuously meet customer needs.

2 *Internal*: How your organization supports your employees in delivering products and services to customers and how you maintain a customer-oriented point of view.

In this section, I'll present some ideas for developing internal support systems. We'll look at external support systems in the next section.

A friend of ours, Howard Spitalny, has been an executive in retailing for many years. Howard is an outgoing, likable, friendly sort who's great with people. He spends a lot of time on the sales floor talking with customers. He understands what they like (what they'll buy) and what they don't.

A few years ago, Howard's company moved its corporate offices to a new building. Howard's new office needed some light because two of the fluorescent bulbs in his office were burned out. He asked the company's maintenance engineer for two bulbs. The engineer said he couldn't give them to him. Howard had to submit a written requisition. It took 4 days for him to get the bulbs he needed.

The point is this: The whole organization should support the people who are supporting the customers. Does your organization put employees through hoops to get something as basic as light bulbs so they can do their work? If so, it's likely your employees also put your customers through hoops to do business with you. Customer relations mirror employee relations.

You may need to make sure that your organizational structure, systems, policies, procedures, and physical facilities make it easy for employees to serve customers. Employees who believe in and want to achieve your service vision will get frustrated if paperwork, outdated rules, politics, or other obstacles hamper them in delivering the kind of service they'd like to provide.

Provide people with the equipment and resources they need. If they need better ways of capturing customer-complaint data, provide data entry and reporting. If they need in-the-moment access to customer records, provide on-line computer terminals. If your product line or prices change rapidly, make sure frontline people are kept up to date on current models and prices. If people in the field call the head office for information or decisions, make sure they have easy access to and quick response from the necessary people.

Bureaucracy, red tape, needless rules, and the like are like weeds in a summer garden—they're insidious. Pulling them out once isn't enough. They will come back! Your organization must be constantly vigilant, tending to weeds as they spring up rather than waiting until the garden is overgrown and the weeds choke out the flowers.

Appoint a person or create a group whose function is to help ensure that service-oriented policies and practices are implemented, that obstacles to transformation and implementation are eliminated, and that other customer-focused initiatives are supported. This person or group should have the authority to make things happen—to make decisions, not just recommendations. Only the CEO should have veto power over this person or group.

This person or group should not be set up with decision-making authority in order to remove power from anyone else or to relieve every individual's responsibility for finding better ways to serve customers and eliminating policies or practices that get in the way of doing that. This is an ad hoc position or group, necessary only during the initial transition. By the time the majority of the transformation has occurred, this ad hoc capacity should no longer be needed since everyone will have the authority and take the responsibility to do these service-directed things. However, this position or group may be necessary for a longer period in some organizations to keep the process moving and to send a message to the organization about the company's sincerity and commitment to the ongoing process.

Develop a service improvement recommendation (SIR) form. This can be a simple, one-page form that any employee can complete to call attention to a procedure, problem, policy, or anything else that gets in the way of doing his or her job or providing the best service possible. An SIR should also include recommendations for correcting the problems or improving service. SIRs should go directly to the manager of the work unit responsible for the problem or improvement, or to a group as described above. All SIRs should be acknowledged, even if certain ones are not acted on. Any decisions and actions resulting from SIRs should be shared with senior managers.

Especially during your period of transition, create a special service-oriented or customer-oriented newsletter. Use this to help people begin thinking about their own missions, policies, and practices, and to start delivering the "customer first" message.

Create task forces to review, report on, and make recommendations on any areas that affect service: order-entry procedures, product quality, delivery time, paperwork, waiting time and so on. If you have more than a dozen form letters that go to customers, examine the reasons for having so many. You may be able to clarify instructions, simplify a form, change a procedure, or take some other action to correct a problem instead of sending form letters.

Urge work units to examine their own policies and practices and identify ways to serve customers better. Hold problem-solving sessions where frontline employees share difficult problems or complaints they hear and come up with effective ways to handle these situations.

I called Southern Bell to report that one of our phone lines wasn't working. I got a recorded message that asked me to enter the number of the line having the problem. I did. A recorded voice repeated the number I had just entered and said someone would check into it. I had a question and wanted to talk to a person, so I stayed on the line. When the operator answered she asked me my name, address, and the telephone number having the problem. I said, "I just entered all that information." She said, "I understand, but it doesn't always go through. I don't have any information about your problem showing my screen."

The operators—the people closest to this situation—knew there was a problem getting information from the message system to their computer screens. This was either a very stubborn problem, or else it may never have been communicated to those who could fix it.

Establish service circles. People closest to the job and its problems are often in the best position to improve things and solve the problems. There are many ways to organize these circles. They can consist of intact groups of only frontline employees; or mixed groups of front line people, their supervisors, and their managers; or even cross-departmental groups. Groups should meet regularly to identify problems in delivering service and to identify ways to improve what's already working. Groups can be facilitated by a trained supervisor or an neutral "outsider," such as someone from human resources or an outside consultant.

As with quality circles, one of the keys to the success of service circles is management's support and commitment. If the organization only gives the circles lip service, ignores service recommendations, or takes too long to respond, service circles will die. Members will say, "What's the use?"

Employees should have ways to get help, seek redress, or resolve problems outside the normal channels. For example, senior executives at MassMutual Life Insurance are available to any employee on any matter. An employee must first have discussed the problem with his or her supervisor. If employees are not satisfied at that level and have exhausted the normal channels, they're free to have a confidential meeting with the top person in their division. Although only a relatively small number of MassMutual's 4,400 employees feel the need to actually take advantage of this opportunity, the company says the important thing is that it's available.

MassMutual also has several professional development boards representing each of their major product lines and corporate units. The boards, comprised of people from all levels, act as a sounding board, work on special projects, do problem solving, and make recommendations to management pertaining to their product lines and companywide issues.

Send newsletters, articles about service—and about customers—to employee's homes. Involve their families. Remember, they are people with families, talents, and other interests, as well as employees.

Talk about customers. Include information about customers in your in-house newsletter, annual report, bulletins, advertising, and other publications. Include success stories, what your employees did, the people involved, and testimonials from customers. Publish and distribute complimentary and critical comments, as well as correspondence from customers. Some companies get copies of their customers' literature (newsletters, annual reports, product announcements, etc.) and encourage their employees to read them.

Quill, a national mail-order office supply company, even gets photos of its customers—not its customers' buildings, but its customers' *people*—and puts them on a wall. Quill people call it the Customer Wall of Fame, and they report that the pictures "help us stay focused on our #1 goal—satisfied customers!" While I've been in many offices that display pictures of employees—founders, past presidents, officers, groups of employees, employee of the month, and others—I've never seen a wall covered with pictures of customers! Quill's Customer Wall of Fame sends a message about who's more important in the organization—long-dead presidents or today's customers!

One of the functions of an internal support system is to continuously remind employees of the organization's mission and the importance of customers. Stories and legends are an important part of this.

Delta Airlines employees tell a story about a passenger getting stuck in the lavatory of a plane. Several people tried to get him out, to no avail. Finally, a Delta employee used a galley knife to pry the door open. The trapped passenger asked who his rescuer was. It was Ronald Allen, Delta's CEO. As Allen came down the aisle, the entire plane burst into applause.

John Sharpe, executive vice president of operations for The Four Seasons hotels, loves to tell the story about the concierge who gave a guest his shoelaces. A hotel guest was late for a black-tie function in the hotel. While dressing, he realized his shoes had no laces. He asked the concierge where he could buy a pair of laces in a hurry. Without hesitating, the employee removed his own black laces and handed them to the guest.

Support can be in the form of posters, pins, key chains, buttons, note pads, and other things that can continually remind employees of their service mission. Support can also be in the form of fun and celebrations for promotions; birthdays, anniversaries, engagements, weddings, and births; retirements and relocations; service or longevity; new hires; major events; major milestones and accomplishments; and big wins.

Some companies create games or contests to reinforce training or emphasize the "customer first" message. Many of these games are noncompetitive; individuals, work units, departments, or divisions compete with themselves, not against other people or units. They strive to beat their own service records and improve their own performance.

A great example of this type of support is a board game created by Sonesta International Hotels vice president Jacqueline Sonnabend. The game presents situations similar to those employees face on the job. Players explain what they'd do in given situations, and their responses are judged by managers. Players win (or lose) play money based on their responses; for example, a player who:

Creates a positive relationship with a guest wins $5
Solves a problem wins $10
Goes beyond the scope of his or her job wins $20
Does or says anything negative loses $10

There are no "right" answers, and employees are encouraged to be creative in their responses.

An interesting twist is that 20 percent of the cards contain situations from other areas, so all employees get to experience some of the problems their coworkers face. The game reinforces the importance of service and encourages employees to find new ways to satisfy customers.

And does it work? Sonnabend says employees learn and have fun as well, and their guest surveys and comment cards indicate that hotel employees seem to be more willing to go out of their way to help.

You can create your own "game" to allow people to test themselves in tough situations. Create a series of realistic, difficult moments of truth, preferably with no right or wrong answers. Ask people to describe (or demonstrate) how they'd handle each situation.

Also give *customers* ways to have input into your internal support system by giving them ways to reward employees for good service and reminding them about poor service. Of course, customer comment cards, surveys, and correspondence can do this, but many companies also establish formal programs. Restaurants and hotels often institute programs in which guests are asked to write the name of any employee who does something exceptionally well or poorly on a form (see example). In some programs, employees earn points (or tokens) for their customer-oriented deeds and lose points for poor service. Employees can redeem points for cash and or prizes.

There are also programs in which the interaction is simply between a customer and a specific employee. Managers often don't even know when such an interaction takes place.

Northwest Airlines has combined the best of both types of program in its

---

Sheraton Savannah Resort

EMPLOYEE OF THE MONTH

Dear Guest,

Sheraton's "Employee of the Month" program is designed to acknowledge exceptional service by our employees.

Please help us by filling out this card when you have received outstanding service from any employee during your stay with us.

The employee who obtains the most cards from our guests in a month is awarded the "Employee of the Month" title. A second employee from the back areas of the Sheraton is selected by the management. Their names and photographs are displayed monthly in the Sheraton lobby.

Please fill in cards whenever you wish and deposit them in the special box at the check-out counter in the lobby.

Thank you for your cooperation.

Name of Employee: _____

Department: _____ Date_____

Comments:_____

_____

Name of Guest: _____ Room Number:_____

_____

"Phantom Customer" program. This program rewards desired behavior and subtly reminds employees about areas needing improvement. Northwest asks about 300 of its frequent flyers to be "Phantom Customers." Phantom Customers are given blue cards that say, "Congratulations! You met my great expectations today," and red cards that say, "Sorry. You did not meet my great expectations." Phantom Customers are encouraged to give a red or blue card to ticket agents or baggage handlers (not flight attendants) at any time. Employees can cash in blue cards for passes (worth about $150); red cards don't have to be turned in.

Giving customers a way to comment directly on the service they're getting serves as a tangible reminder to employees that customers really do have the last word about service. And it sends a strong message to employees that customers *do* have an easy way to make themselves heard about the service they're getting—both the good news and the bad.

35. Develop external (customer) support systems

In addition to having support systems for people inside the organization to enable them to adequately serve customers, there should also be a support system for customers. Many of the ideas discussed above apply here as well. Focus groups, task forces, sounding boards, toll-free numbers, help desks, service reminders in correspondence, and celebrations for success can all be used with customers as well as employees. Perhaps most important is to ensure that your organizational structure, systems, policies, paperwork, facilities, and other factors all make it easier, not harder, for customers to do business with you.

Here's how *not* to do it:

Several years ago our office manager, Brenda Bradley, bought a dozen printer ribbons at a Micro Mart store. Every one of them was faulty. They didn't give good print impressions, and about half of them jammed. I was going near a Micro Mart in a different part of town on my way to an appointment, so I agreed to exchange the faulty batch for some new ones.

At the store, the clerk told me I couldn't exchange the ribbons there because they came from another store. He told me I had to take them back where I got them.

The manager finally agreed to exchange the ribbons. I needed twelve, but he only had two. He said he'd order the remainder and they would be in the next day. Four days later, Brenda called to ask if the ribbons were in. The manager was rude to her, and he told her the ribbons weren't in and he didn't know when they'd be there.

Eight days after that, Brenda called again. The ribbons still weren't in. The person she spoke to didn't know when they'd be in Brenda was told, "They must have been back ordered, but I really don't know *if* they've been ordered or why it's taking so long." Brenda asked to talk to the manager. He was at lunch, and the clerk said, "You can call him in about an hour to discuss this with him."

If your product is faulty—or the customer *thinks* it is—don't inconvenience the customer any more than you already have. Fix it. Don't make the customer feel like he or she is the one with a problem. If your company's inventory or bookkeeping system can't accomodate exchanges and refunds in different branches, fix the system instead of telling the customer, in effect, "That's not my problem." This is "we don't care" service.

Honor your agreements. If the products aren't going to be in, don't tell customers they will be just to get customers out of your hair.

And don't make your customers call you repeatedly to get their problems resolved. That employee should have told Brenda, "I'll have the manager call *you* as soon as he gets back from lunch." The manager should have researched the problem, determined the status of the ribbons, and had the information ready for Brenda when he called. If he couldn't get the ribbons, he should have told her that so we could get them elsewhere.

This ribbon story is a perfect example of what I call Indifferent Service, which will be explained in detail shortly.

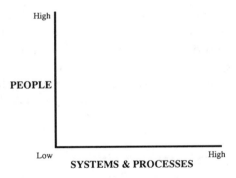

Sometimes it's helpful to break complex ideas into simpler terms. Of course, there's always the danger of oversimplifying or making generalizations that overlook important differences. However, knowing these risks, let's look at two dimensions that affect the kind of service customers get. These two dimensions are shown in the diagram.

I call one dimension *Systems and Processes*. This dimension refers to all the mechanisms an organization uses to accomplish its work and serve customers. It includes the organization's rules, procedures, forms, decision-making and complaint-handling processes, etc. Customers evaluate an organization's systems and processes in terms of their efficiency, responsiveness, convenience, flexibility, and similar traits. An organization can rate anywhere between low and high on these characteristics.

The other dimension is *People*. This dimension refers to the ability, training, attentiveness, willingness, friendliness, and similar traits of the people in an organization. Customers also rate organizations somewhere between low and high on these characteristics.

Any organization—even units within an organization—can be low or high on either dimension. If we put the two dimensions together, we can describe four kinds of service an organization is likely to provide: Airhead Service, Indifferent Service, By-the-Book Service, and Superior Service (see illustration).

As I mentioned earlier, the kind of service Brenda experienced at Micro Mart was Indifferent Service. Let's look at some ways you can make sure that *your* organization provides Superior Service.

Appoint a person or department as an internal customer advocate. That person's role is to be the customer's voice and to present the customer's point of view inside the company. The person's job level should be high enough—say, senior manager—to enable him or her to pull some weight and not get shouted down. The customer advocate's job is to determine, by whatever means are appropriate, what customers really want, like, and don't like; and how customers see the firm, its products, and its services. The person must be in on every policy and budget decision that can affect service. This position is different from a position in a traditional consumer affairs or customer service department. Traditionally, these departments deal with customers *after* the sale has been made or service delivered, or when there's a problem. This new position is intended to prevent problems by looking at things from the customer's point of view *before* the sale.

Ideally, everyone in your organization should be an internal customer advocate, but that may take awhile. It's worthwhile to appoint a specific customer advocate at first.

For external support systems, (as with your internal support systems), set up whatever people or groups are needed to ensure that service-oriented policies and practices are implemented and that obstacles to providing exceptional service are eliminated. A few support suggestions:

☐ Make sure your system will provide the inventory to the front line so employees don't have to make excuses or feel embarrassed.

☐ Make sure your repair people can get to customers in 48 hours (or whatever) if that's what you promise.

☐ Make sure customers don't get duplicate invoices or dunning letters because your system doesn't process their payments efficiently.

☐ If your business is dependent on computers, telephones, or special equipment (printing presses, fork lifts, etc.), make sure you're not out of business if these stop working.

☐ If you have peak times or seasons, be sure you've planned for these by having arranged for sufficient inventory, equipment, and storage space; hired and trained enough people; and provided adequate supervision.

36. Recognize and reward people for providing good service

Employees at all levels pay attention to what's rewarded. If customer focus and meeting customer needs is truly important to the organization, rewarding service performance throughout the entire organization is essential.

It's important that the reward system not be limited to those who have direct customer contact. Rewarding service performance throughout the entire organization helps cement and reinforce the idea that service is not just the responsibility of the front line.

Rewards should be tied to customer perceptions of service, which are tied to expectations. Therefore, you need to know what customers *expect* in order to

Four Kinds of Service

High

PEOPLE

Airhead Service

People are:	Systems & Processes are:
• Friendly	• Haphazard
• Well-meaning	• Disjointed
• Energetic	• Confusing
• Concerned	• Slow-moving (at times)
• Poorly trained	• Fast-moving (at times)
• Inept	• Inconsistent
• Uncertain	• Constantly changing

Communicates to customers:
• *"We try hard to please, but really don't know what we're doing."*

• *"We're doing our best, but we shoot ourselves in the foot a lot."*

Superior Service

People are:	Systems & Processes are:
• Caring	• Responsive
• Friendly	• Efficient
• Attentive	• Flexible
• Well trained	• Prompt
• Knowledgeable	• Consistent
• Energetic	• Convenient
• Confident	• Simplfied
• Never satisfied	• Uncomplicated

Communicates to customers:
• *"We're concerned."*

• *"We're here to help and we know what we're doing."*

• *"What else can we do for you?"*

Indifferent Service

People are:	Systems & Processes are:
• Disinterested	• Unresponsive
• Impersonal	• Slow-moving
• Distant	• Complicated
• Inattentive	• Confusing
• Insensitive	• Inconsistent
• Untrained	• Disjointed
• Unmotivated	• Inconvenient

Communicates to customers:
• *"I just work here."*

• *"Don't bother me. I've got more important things to do."*

• *"If you want to go somewhere else, fine. It's no sweat off my nose."*

By-the-Book Service

People are:	Systems & Processes are:
• Insensitive	• Efficient
• Apathetic	• Precise
• Impersonal	• Unwavering
• Aloof	• Consistent
• Disinterested	• Rigid
• Unresponsive	• Uniform
• Walking rulebooks	• Sacred

Communicates to customers:
• *"I've got to follow these rules."*

• *"Excuse me, but you're just one of many customers. If we make an exception for you, we'll have to do it for everyone."*

• *"That's not our policy."*

• *"If you don't like it, you can talk to my supervisor."*

Low   High

SYSTEMS & PROCESSES

reward employees fairly and to provide feedback to them on their performance. Otherwise, you end up rewarding performance that may be good from the *organization's* perspective but may be unsatisfactory from the *customer's* perspective.

Rewards can be primarily tangible (plaques, pins, premiums, and pay), mostly intangible (recognition or increased status or title), or a combination of both (articles about employees in company publications). Robert Desatnick reminds us that rewards can also be emotional and psychological. He tells of youthful McDonald's employees who quit to work elsewhere and then want to come back. When store managers ask why they want to leave higher-paying jobs to come back to McDonald's, they hear things like, "I felt I was needed here," "I made a difference," and "We worked as a team."

Rewards can be used as incentives to entice people to meet and exceed service or performance goals, take initiative, stimulate activity, or improve performance in weak areas. Find ways to acknowledge and recognize wins, even small ones, in the areas that are important to making a shift in your company. For some it might be quality, innovation, or productivity. For others it might be response time, customer complaints, profitability, or market share.

Rewards can be for individuals, teams, or both. The reward system at Scandinavian Airlines System includes both the person and the team by giving the person some symbol of recognition or appreciation, such as a watch, and doing something symbolic to recognize the group, like throwing a party.

Group reward activities can be small or large. In large international organizations, people are sometimes flown in for special events, or awards ceremonies occur simultaneously at all their worldwide locations.

Rewards can be formal and planned, or they can be spontaneous. BayBanks in Massachusetts has a formal program that honors its "Legend Makers." Each quarter, five outstanding branch employees are selected from nominations by peers, customers, and managers. Nominations are based on specific service experiences. A monthly newsletter tells all bank employees who the Legend Makers are, and recognition dinners and other events are held quarterly and are attended by bank senior executives, including the chairman. Legend Makers become "corporate emissaries" and, with their managers, visit organizations known for superior service, such as Claridges Hotel (London), Disney World, L. L. Bean, and Federal Express. According to Henry C. Riley, director of community banking, these visits are made to "discuss strategies, policies, and practices that have enhanced their customer service, thus broadening our knowledge of what service excellence means." Now in its third year, the program has been expanded to recognize legendary sales performance as well as outstanding service.

Ryder Systems has a program called "People Make the Difference." It was one of the Ryder programs recognized by the International Customer Service Association in honoring Ryder with the association's 1987 Award of Excellence.

A more spontaneous program can be found at Federal Express, which has adapted a U.S. Navy program called Bravo-Zulu. In the Navy, Bravo-Zulu stands for excellence, and it is recognized by two large flags flown on ship masts. Federal Express managers can award Bravo-Zulu awards to employees at any time by giving them a small set of flags and a cash bonus of up to $100.

Rewards for service excellence can be conferred on employees by fellow employees, managers, "shoppers," or customers. Criteria for service awards can be established by employees, managers, or both. Of course, the real criteria are set by customers.

Employees often know better than managers do who is going all out for customers. In some companies, there are awards programs run solely by frontline employees. Employees decide the award criteria and accept nominations from anyone in the organization. Then the employees decide which fellow employees receive the awards.

In organizations in which managers decide who gets recognition, praise, and thanks for providing outstanding service, the decisions are often highly subjective. There are often no criteria for distinguishing between good and excellent service. As a result, heroic or exceptional service often doesn't get the recognition it deserves, and many employees perceive award recipients as "teacher's pets."

In their role of supporting the front line, managers have the opportunity for and the responsibility of rewarding performance, celebrating wins, and providing encouragement. Managers can and should lavish praise on their teams.

Mystery shoppers can also immediately reward employees for excellent service. They can give cash, certificates, tokens, "Way to go!" cards, or other items. Shop'N Chek, Inc., is a national marketing company that employs over 16,000 people to shop its clients' businesses. President Carol D. Cherry says some companies do ask them to distribute on-the-spot cash bonuses to employees who provide outstanding service. One bank we know of has shoppers evaluate service performance by assigning points values in relation to how good or poor the service is. Each quarter, the individual employees and branches with the highest scores get cash and other prizes.

Give customers a way to "reward" employees. This is a "catch them doing something right" approach that gets customers involved in addition to supervisors. In some organizations, employees can also reward each other this way.

Episcopal Hospital in Philadelphia instituted a CIA (Caught in the Act) program to reward employees who go out of their way for each other and for customers. Any employee can nominate another employee for anything that's above the call of duty. Patients are also encouraged to call a special hospital telephone number to nominate employees who made their stay more comfortable. Vicky Anderson, Episcopal's director of public relations, whose department runs the program, says that most of the nominations come from patients. Nominated employees receive a framed certificate from the hospital president and coupons for free beverages and dessert in the cafeteria. Each quarter employees with the most nominations also receive a $50 check.

Below are some additional ways you can recognize and reward people for service performance. You can adapt these ideas to fit your organization. Rewards can take the following forms:

- ☐ A section of your organization's newsletter devoted to service excellence. Feature stories about employees who excel in satisfying customers.
- ☐ Company-paid dinners at nice restaurants.
- ☐ Private breakfast or lunch with the CEO.
- ☐ Plaques or certificates recognizing service accomplishments.
- ☐ A weekend for two at a resort, a classy hotel, Disneyland, etc.
- ☐ A new, higher-status title.
- ☐ Additional responsibilities. For example, have experienced employees do training and pay them slightly more for this privilege.
- ☐ Recognition dinners, lunches, or breakfasts.
- ☐ Employee of the month or employee of the year awards. Establish criteria such as attendance, productivity, or customer comments. Criteria definition and employee selection should be done by employees, not management.
- ☐ Special name tags, pins, or "merit badges" that tell customers and employees when employees have completed certain courses, acquired additional skills, or taken on additional responsibilities.
- ☐ Different levels of recognition for service accomplishments (similar to Bay-Banks' "Legend Makers" designation). Establish criteria for club membership and for each club level and offer attractive rewards for achieving these. Nordstrom's Pacesetter Club members get new business cards identifying them as Pacesetters, a night out on the town for two, and an additional 13 percent employee discount for a year.
- ☐ Awards for best department or unit of the month or year.
- ☐ Picnics, outings, or sporting events.
- ☐ Field trips.
- ☐ Green stamps for exceptional service.
- ☐ A Giraffe or Turtle award for those employees who stick their necks out for their customers.
- ☐ ABCD Awards for service "Above and Beyond the Call of Duty."
- ☐ Incentives and extra recognition for employees who work less-desirable shifts, have no tardiness or absenteeism, work holidays or weekends, or in some way do more than is expected.

☐ Opportunities for good performers to work elsewhere for a while. Elsewhere could be in a different location or job, or even in a training capacity. Such a change must be positioned as a reward, not a punishment, and must be something people *want* to do.

☐ Contests, especially when they involve teams and symbolic awards rather than money. Southern Bell has several contests between its four states. For example, the state winner for best annual profit growth gets a gold running-shoe award.

☐ Drawings. Complimentary letters from customers can qualify employees to enter. Drawings can be held quarterly or annually for cash TVs, stereos, vacations, and other prizes.

☐ Extra time off with pay (a day or half-day) for star performers.

☐ Bus fare or paid parking fees for some period (maybe a month).

☐ Free or reduced-price cafeteria lunches for individual employees or teams.

☐ Pins, hats, jackets, key chains, notebooks, memo pads, or T-shirts for individual or team efforts.

☐ Health club memberships or discounts.

☐ Personal commendation letters from the CEO or other top executives. (Put a copy in the employee's personnel file.)

☐ Letters and comments from customers extolling employee actions publicized or displayed.

As you can see, the alternatives are limitless. They're limited only by your imagination. You probably noticed that there are several types of rewards that haven't been mentioned yet: pay increases, bonuses, and promotions. I think these can send such a strong message about how the organization values service that I've addressed these in more detail in Ideas 37 and 38, below.

37. Base management compensation and bonuses on customer-satisfaction ratings

In most organizations, service plays a minor role in promotions, pay raises, incentive, or bonus pay. The Service 1st Corporation found that only 5 percent of senior management compensation depends on customer satisfaction.

If service is important, you must reward managers for their service results just as they're rewarded for profitability, market share, sales volume, production, or other key areas. This reward basis sends a signal to managers that *service is important*, and it encourages them to reward service performance in the people they supervise.

Establish clear standards for service for every position. Make the standards measurable and incorporate them into the performance-review system. If service is not part of every manager's job, from the top down, managers won't give it much attention. Managers must be held accountable for setting and reaching service-related goals. Tie compensation and bonuses to service performance, as measured by customer-satisfaction ratings, customer surveys, shopper-survey ratings, number of customer compliments or complaints, or whatever else is appropriate.

At Herman Miller, quarterly bonuses for managers and nonmanagers for contributing to surpassing goals are largely determined by customer-satisfaction surveys. According to John Berry, director of corporate communications, "We need to measure performance as our customer sees us and not focus so much on internal measures. We want every employee-owner to understand they are working for the customer."

At Xerox Corporation, 100 percent of management bonuses are determined by surveys that measure each customer's satisfaction levels, intention to do business with Xerox again, and willingness to recommend Xerox products to others.

If service is really important, track it and use it as basis for compensation and bonus pay. You can decide if service results will constitute 10 percent, 25 percent, 50 percent, or some other portion of base pay or bonuses. The higher you make the percentage, the more you communicate how important service is.

38. Base promotions and pay raises for frontline employees on customer service ratings

Your pay and promotion practices send a strong message to other employees. If service is important, compensation and bonuses for nonmanagement personnel should also reflect customer-satisfaction ratings. Decide what percentage should be dependent on service results and then establish fair, measurable, relevant criteria for measuring such results.

In traditional, top-down organizations, the "rewards" for promotions are often such things as higher salaries, bigger offices, cars, titles, bonuses, expense accounts, and the like. Getting promoted in these companies usually means moving "up" the pyramid. It also usually has little to do with customer satisfaction, and it often means moving people further away from customer contact. American Airlines vice president Robert G. Oatley says, "Provide promotions and pay increases to people who support the changes and consistently provide good service. People notice who gets promoted."

If service is important, make it part of the promotion process. Do people in your organization routinely get promoted primarily because they're good at the technical aspects of their jobs, they're cost-cutters, they have connections, or they have been there a long time? If people are promoted or given raises just because they've survived another year, that sends a message about what the company values—and it's not a message about the importance of service. Be sure your promotion practices send the message you want to get across.

Do your promotion criteria include service? Are your criteria more than vague generalities? They should be fair, measurable, objective criteria, such as customer-satisfaction ratings, number of compliment or complaint letters, response time, or repeat customers.

When someone is promoted, make sure your internal announcements and external press releases mention the person's service accomplishments. This also sends a message to employees and customers that service is valued, noticed, and rewarded.

Of course, tying pay and promotions to service results is certainly not limited to customer-contact people. If your organization is truly service-oriented, apply these criteria and rewards to everyone by also measuring the satisfaction of *internal* customers. For example, you might base 40 to 50 percent of a trainer's performance review and pay increase on participant-satisfaction ratings and the rest on on-the-job results of participants who've been through training.

39. Find or create pockets of service excellence

No matter how committed you are to being customer-centered, it's possible that not everyone will share your vision. It's unlikely you can turn everyone on to the service idea at once, so go with what you've got.

If you can't do this by virtue of your title or position with those who work with you, do it informally, one-on-one. Begin by asking people for their ideas on how you can improve service in some certain area. Gradually expand it to other areas and more people. Put something in writing and ask those who contributed to give you their feedback. Then share it with others, all the time asking for their ideas. The more people you can get involved with service, the greater will be the commitment to it. When the time is right, propose the service plan to your boss or implement it yourself. Ask those who helped you to assist in the implementation.

Use both formal and informal channels to promote your ideas and enroll others in support of service. Use meetings, rallies, special events, newsletters, and other "formal" channels to communicate with others in your organization, but don't underestimate the power of word of mouth and informal communications to spread the word. Casual conversations held over lunches and breakfasts with influential people are powerful tools for communicating ideas and getting feedback.

Find allies inside and outside your organization who believe as you do. People can help you crystallize and move toward your service vision. Find a division, a department, a unit, or even a person who is willing and able to commit to improving service. Establish and build relationships with other departments, especially those that don't normally have much customer contact. Start small. Work with them and encourage them. Document their successes and wins.

Acknowledge and reward small wins. It may be particularly helpful to enroll people or departments who do not normally have much customer contact.

Remember, nothing succeeds like success. So toot your own horn when you succeed. Send results to your boss, to your peers, and to others in the organization. Talk about the results people are having. Awareness will begin to spread like rings in water.

40. Teach people recovery skills

Recovery refers to how an individual or an organization handles mistakes. Mistakes and foul-ups will happen; no one's perfect, not even in the organizations that are the service leaders. The key is what you do when you fail to deliver, when you *don't* meet your customer's expectations—when you don't deliver as promised; when you just get it wrong; or when the customer just *thinks* you messed up, let them down, or got it wrong.

We've all heard the remark, "The customer is never wrong," and we all know that's just not true. We know because, as customers, we've been wrong ourselves. And you know from your experience in handling customers that sometimes they *are* wrong. They make mistakes.

So don't tell employees that the customer is never wrong, because they don't believe it anyway. Instead, teach your employees they should never make a customer *feel* like he or she is wrong. No one likes to be wrong, to admit they made a mistake. It's embarrassing to lose face or perhaps to look stupid—especially for someone who has made a big deal about something, only to find out the missing merchandise *is* in the warehouse after all or the invoice *is* correct after all or whatever.

Right or wrong, when a customer has problems, the customer often blames the person he or she has contact with in your organization. The issue is rarely with that contact person as an individual, but rather with that person as a representative of the organization. Unfortunately, customers and employees usually have difficulty making the distinction.

Chart 6 lists some specific recovery techniques to use in situations when you or someone in your organization messes up.

Several years ago, we'd been talking with Margaret Jeffiers about Kay doing seminars for the East Kentucky Power Cooperative in Winchester, near Lexington. Before deciding to have Kay

CHART 6   RECOVERY SKILLS

What to Do	How to Do It
Accept the responsibility.	Thank the customer for telling you about the problem and tell him or her you'll take care of it, even if it's not your job, area, or fault. Use "I" language: say "I'm sorry," instead of "We're sorry."
Acknowledge the problem or situation *and* the customer's feelings.	Say something like "That must be frustrating" or "I can see how upsetting it is to not get what you ordered."
Show empathy.	Be sincere. Let the customer be right. Don't argue. Treat the situation or problem seriously, even if it seems minor to you. Use "Mr." or "Ms." unless you know the person *very* well, even if the person tells you his or her first name. Assure the customer you want to help resolve the problem. Don't blame others or make excuses; upset customers don't care much about your internal problems or your policies.
Listen	Hear customers out. Don't assume you know what they're going to say just because you've heard the same problem before. Make eye contact. Stop doing other things. Let customers vent if they need to. Don't interrupt. Listen with your brain, not your ears.
Get all the details.	Write the details down. Ask questions to get all necessary information. Ask the customer to repeat any names, numbers, or terms you're not sure of. Don't guess. *Prove* you understand both the facts and feelings in the situation by restating them to the customer.
Ask what the customer wants.	Don't assume you know what customers want. Be open to their ideas. If an idea won't work, ask for other suggestions.
Explore alternatives.	Suggest alternatives. Explain what you *can* do, not what you can't do. Don't commit to things you or your organization can't or won't do.
Agree on the action to be taken.	Review what you've agreed to do. Give the customer a specific day and time to expect some action. Ask if your actions will satisfy the customer. Keep the customer informed of progress.

CHART 6   *continued*

What to Do	How to Do It
Make amends when possible.	Try to "make it right." Bend the rules a little, if appropriate. Offer a consolation: a rebate, replacement, or discount. Apologize, even if you know you're right. Apologize for the mix-up, inconvenience, or trouble.
Help the customer save face.	If the customer has made an error, be tactful and avoid embarrassing the customer or making him or her feel stupid.
Do a little more than promised.	Do something in 2 days instead of 3. Throw in something extra. *Under*-promise and *over*-deliver.
Give early notice if you can't keep your agreement.	Notify the customer immediately. Make other plans and get the customer's agreement on any new plans.
Follow up on whatever recovery action is taken.	Take personal responsibility to ensure the situation gets resolved, even if other people or departments are involved. Call the customer to see if the situation has been corrected or fixed. Ask if the customer is satisfied. Invite the customer to come back or do business with you again.
Avoid future occurrences.	Establish and follow procedures for reporting and analyzing problems, failures, and complaints so you can find causes and prevent future occurrences.

do the seminars, Margaret wanted to hear Kay speak. I told her Kay was conducting public seminars in Lexington and Louisville. I invited Margaret to attend one as our guest. She said she'd go to the one in Lexington and talk to Kay afterward.

I told Margaret the date, hotel, and starting time (9:00 A.M.) for Kay's program. At 9:30 that day, Margaret called me in Atlanta to say she had been to both Holiday Inns in Lexington and couldn't find the program, so she had driven to Louisville, about 50 miles away. Kay *was* in Lexington that day, and I still don't know how the mix-up occurred. However, I apologized profusely for the trouble Margaret had had finding the program and the extra drive she had made to Louisville and back. After talking to Kay later in the day, I tried to reach Margaret to arrange for her to have dinner with Kay that night, but I couldn't contact her.

My biggest concern was that Margaret went out of her way for nothing. I called her the next day and said, "I'm sorry about the mix-up. I know you took a day off work and drove a long way for nothing. And you never did get to hear Kay's program. I can't undo that, but Kay and I would like you to have a nice dinner—our treat—to make up for it." We sent her a gift certificate for a dinner for two at her favorite restaurant.

---

41. Once things are under way, maintain the momentum

Becoming a customer-focused organization is one thing; *staying* one is another. Momentum is often difficult to maintain.

Do you remember ever getting really excited about a project at home or work? A hobby? A new sport or adult "toy"? For a while, when it was new, it may have almost consumed you. You may have spent lots of time working at it or thinking about it. Then, after a while, you may have spent less and less time on it, until eventually it was just a memory. You may even still have the files or books on it sitting in a corner or have the equipment or tools in a closet somewhere. This kind of short-lived interest in something happens to most of us. It's a natural human phenomenon. Think about how difficult is it to stay on a diet the longer it goes on. There are always powerful forces around to pull the dieter back to old eating habits.

This loss of momentum can happen in your organization, too. Perhaps you'll get all excited about service in your organization and tell others about this book and all the wonderful things you're going to do to improve service. But quite likely, they won't all be as excited as you are. Many will be like the people Ceo encountered in Lipett (remember the story of the Terces in Idea 14?). They'll say things like, "That'll never work here," "*They* will never let you do that."

Others may catch your excitement and jump on the bandwagon—for a while. Then, over the weeks and months, they may begin to lose the enthusiasm. They'll get caught up in their day-to-day activities and responsibilities. That's when your organization's dedication to service will be truly tested.

Once you get your service levels where you want them, they must be maintained. Such maintenance requires constant attention; otherwise, all your efforts will be seen as just another program that ends after the training sessions have been delivered. The results will be short-lived. People will heave a collective sigh of relief and say, "Now that that's over, let's get back to business as usual." Your challenge is to keep them from doing that, which is not an easy task. The forces that pull us back to traditional beliefs and practices are strong—like the forces that pull dieters off their diets.

Being an outward-focused, customer-centered organization is a *process*, not a program or an event. It must be ongoing. That's why your support systems are so critical. They provide mechanisms for continuously reminding employees at every level of the importance of service and meeting customer needs. They help keep the focus on customers.

Things change. The people in your organizations change, markets change, and technology changes—and your organization must be able to respond to the changes. You must have ways to review systematically the vision, policies, procedures, skill levels, and commitment of your people. You must be able and willing to respond and make changes.

A common practice in many service-oriented organizations is to view their current efforts or programs as changeable—not static—solutions. Incentive programs are revised regularly, some annually, to keep them fresh and appealing. Training programs are continually upgraded. New team-building activities are always in the works. Basic procedures and practices are continually refined to solve problems in a better way or provide better services.

The exact ongoing updated process will vary from organization to organization. The key is to have a well-defined mechanism in place for periodic review of the service program and efforts. Conduct reviews at set times, such as every 6 months or once a year. Some of the things to consider:

☐ Have our customers changed?

☐ What do customers want *today*?

☐ Does our vision still serve us?

☐ Is our strategy still on target?

☐ In what ways are we not meeting our customers' needs as well as we can?

☐ How do our customers perceive us today?

Based on the results of these reviews and on hard data about sales, market share, and profits, people at every level of the organization must continuously define and implement the next steps they must take toward service improvement.

The next few pages discuss some additional things you and your organization can do to maintain the service momentum.

Believe that every individual can make a difference.

A number of years ago, scientists were studying monkeys on a small island in Asia. Monkeys are social creatures: they mate and live in extended families that are part of tribes. Some tribes can number in the thousands. The tribe these scientists were studying had several thousand monkeys.

Most monkeys are also vegetarians, eating mostly leaves, fruits, plant roots, and nuts. The scientists started putting sweet potatoes in feed stations. The monkeys liked the sweet potatoes, but they apparently didn't like the gritty sand on them.

One day, one monkey took a sweet potato to the water and washed the sand off before eating it. The next time this monkey had a sweet potato it did the same thing—took it to the water and washed it. None of the other monkeys had ever done this before.

Within a few days, another monkey started doing the same thing. You know the saying: "Monkey see, monkey do." Gradually more and more monkeys started imitating this washing behavior. Soon there were 50, then 75, then 95 monkeys washing. But thousands of other monkeys didn't; they still just ate the sandy sweet potatoes.

Then a very strange thing happened. When enough monkeys—perhaps 100—had adopted this strange new washing behavior, *all* the rest of the monkeys in the tribe adopted it almost at once. It was as if someone had waved a magic wand. From a tiny group to the entire tribe, their behavior changed practically overnight, and the culture of that tribe was changed forever!

And when enough human beings all think, believe, and act in same way, organizations change, just as that tribe of monkeys did. The problem is that with people, we never know who the 100th or *n*th monkey is—the one who creates the critical mass that transforms the organization. It could be you. It could be someone you talk to, support, or coach. But without the first 99, there is no 100th monkey. The culture won't change.

Too many people say, "I'm just a vice president [regional manager, department head, customer service rep, or whatever]. What can I do?" Mary Kay Ash turned a storefront business into a worldwide sales and marketing company we know as Mary Kay Cosmetics. Tom Monaghan and his brother took the idea of home pizza delivery to the bank when they started Domino's Pizza. Fred Smith had an idea in college about overnight package delivery to any point in the United States. We know his idea today as Federal Express, delivery.

There are lots more like Mary Kay Ash, Tom Monaghan, and Fred Smith. Some are well-known, but most are not. The key is this: You must believe you can make a difference in your organization, even if it's a small difference. And even if you can't change the entire organization, you can at least make a difference in your unit or department. Maybe you'll encourage—or be—the 100th monkey.

Take the approach that every moment of truth makes a difference.   Just don't confuse making a difference with getting credit or recognition for it. One of the major differences between Japanese and American organizations is that in the Japanese culture, the individual is subordinate to the group. Individuals largely get their identity, recognition, and rewards through their families, organizations, work teams, and other groups. In the United States, it's just the opposite. Our culture places the greatest importance on individual accomplishment.

Shift your focus. Think of yourself as part of something bigger than just you; learn to bask more in the accomplishments of your team, work unit, or organization; and place less emphasis on your personal accomplishments. You *will* make a difference.

Continue to create pockets of service excellence and find allies.   Involve others; you can't do it alone. People who are involved in the *development* of plans, programs, and strategies are more committed to them when they are implemented. This approach can work much better than the "customer service by edict" approach that many organizations try to use.

Keep a constant flow of task forces.   Create a task force, give it an assignment, and disband it when the assignment has been completed. Create other task forces to address other issues. Staff them with people from different levels and functional areas. Create teams to generate service, quality, productivity, and product ideas.

Find or create service champions.   These are people whose responsibility is to continually remind others about the outward customer focus. Their job is to raise the customer-service flag whenever needed.

Champions can be located in any level or location of an organization. They must be unequivocally supported by top management, because, like the champions of old, they may be knocked off their horses a few times. In the midst of change, they'll likely meet with hostility, resistance, fear, and possibly sabotage as they try to slay the dragons of customer insensitivity, inwardly focused practices, and bureaucratic procedures.

A champion is a special person. It takes someone who is thick-skinned and visible; has respect and credibility within an organization; is articulate and charismatic; enjoys turmoil, problems, and change; and has the ear of top management.

The knights of old would seek out young squires who aspired to be knights. The champions would teach the squires about knightly duties, actions, skills. Modern-day champions must do the same thing. They must seek out those in their organizations who aspire to change things, adopt new beliefs, implement customer-focused policies and practices, and give up the old ways. The champion must befriend these people, acknowledge them, support them, and be their ally and voice in the higher councils.

Keep your boss informed.   Depending on your level in the organization and the personalities involved, your boss may be an ally or an antagonist as you strive to improve service in your unit or organization.

If your boss is an ally, terrific! If not, you have a bigger challenge. First, make sure your work meets or exceeds expectations. In other words, keep up your own good work. Then devote as much time and energy to improving service as you can. Keep your boss informed about your normal work, and, if you can, keep him or her posted on the results of your other efforts as well. Most of all, make your boss look good. You may need to let him or her take some of the credit for the results you've worked hard for. Don't worry. In most cases, those in important positions know who the brains and backbone really are. The more you can network and get others committed to serving customers, the better your chances of getting the credit you deserve, even if it comes from informal channels.

Make corrections as needed.   Part of maintaining the momentum involves making changes and corrections as needed. Remember, being customer-focused and service-oriented is a continuous process, not a one-time event.

Remaining customer-focused demands that you regularly and systematically review your policies, procedures, and practices and make adjustments as needed. Unfortunately, the job is never done.

Continue training.   Training should be an ongoing activity for everyone. No one in the organization can ever be too knowledgeable or too skilled. People must periodically be retrained or given further education to upgrade their skills. Training also provides an excellent opportunity to remind people of the values, mission, and service orientation of the organization.

Support others in their efforts to make changes and to improve service in their units, departments, or organizations.   Lend assistance and give credit to others.

Keep communicating.   People need constant reminders about the importance of serving customers and about the organization's mission. Employees need to be continually reminded that little things matter, that they *are* the organization to customers, and so on. (*Every* issue of the Disney newsletter contains something about service and the importance of guests [customers].)

Stick with the service mission.   It may get lonely or frustrating. There may be times when you ask, "Is it really worth it?" Keep at it. Measure progress by months and quarters, not weeks. This will be especially difficult—and necessary—when people say things like, "It'll never work," "It costs too much," "We tried that before," and all the other comments that can discourage you. But your determination and persistence may be all that's needed to make a difference. You may be the 99th monkey. If you quit, transformation may be delayed—or it may never occur.

42. Help people manage change

Shifting the focus of an organization demands many changes. Some are tangible and obvious; others are intangible and more subtle. Some people may leave, and others may have different responsibilities. Procedures may change. Comfortable, familiar routines and practices may change. All in all, it makes for a pretty volatile situation. The faster and more profound the change, the more people will need help coping with it.

People resist change for many reasons: They fear a loss of control; they're uncomfortable doing new things in different ways; they don't want to look or feel awkward or stupid; old habits and beliefs provide security; and so on. The nature of the change and how it's introduced also contribute to the level of acceptance or resistance. And different people often react to the same change differently. Their reactions may take many forms. Some may be openly resistant, while others remain quiet.

You must expect that any attempt to change your organization's mission, philosophies, practices, or beliefs will cause some reactions. Some may be positive; however, more than likely, many will be negative. You must realize that this negativism will occur and be able to recognize the symptoms, identify the causes, and manage it as best you can. The best approach is prevention. Early and continuous communication and involvement of people in planning changes will lessen resistance and hasten acceptance of the service improvement goal.

There are books, seminars, and experts who specialize in dealing with change, which you should seek out if you feel the need. For the most part, it's only necessary that you realize the effect of change and the importance of being prepared for it and managing it.

43. Measure results

The Citibank study discovered that "managers with ongoing [customer] tracking data seem most successful in building a customer sensitive orientation in their companies." In other words, you need to keep score. There are both tangible and intangible results you can measure. Of course, you have measurable results such as turnover and associated costs, cost of doing business, profits, performance ratings, return on investment, number of customer complaints, customer retention rates, and others. These indicators are relatively easy to measure.

You'll also have intangible results, such as people who are more confident, self-starting, energized, able to make decisions quicker (often with less information), and more committed to their jobs and the company. There may also be an increase in the degree to which your organization is making a difference to your community or society as a whole. These intangibles are harder to measure and relate to the bottom line, but they are still important.

Many of the executives interviewed for the Citibank study said that financial results do not tell the whole story of service performance, or at least not quickly enough. By the time the quarterly or annual financial results are in, service may have been in trouble for quite sometime. The effects might not even show up on the balance sheet until the *next* reporting period. Even if the bottom line reflects some trouble, too few organizations recognize service performance as a contributing factor.

In *In Search of Excellence*, Peters and Waterman emphasized that the excellent companies value more than just the bottom line. As one executive told them: "Profit is like health. You need it, and the more the better. But it's not why you exist." And the winners identifed in the Clifford and Cavanagh study introduced in Part One were as concerned about making a difference as making a fortune.

While most executives, managers, and employees see the merits of measuring performance and service, many don't know what to measure or how. Many organizations have never even attempted to identify *service* performance measures or to set standards for them. However, many other organizations have identified and continue to refine their measures and standards, so it is far from impossible.

Here's the best method I've found for measuring results:

1 Decide what to measure. Management can decide this unilaterally or get employees involved. I prefer to get the front line involved.

2 Establish a base line. You need to know your starting point. If you don't already have current data for each measure available, track actual performance for each measure for several days or weeks.

3 Keep overall company goals in mind and then set standards for minimal acceptable performance.

4 Have individual performers or teams set interim goals for improving performance. Such goals enable the work unit, and eventually the entire organization, to gradually raise their standards.

5 Track results. Continually gather data on each performance measure. Look for trends. The key here is to determine whether your performance is getting better, getting worse, or staying the same.

This process works for practically any position or specific function, even if the function—for example, complaint handling—is performed by various people with various job titles.

Certainly the process is easier for some positions than for others. The more tangible and concrete a job's tasks and outputs are, the easier the measuring process is. As noted earlier, the service components of many jobs are generally *intangible*. Nevertheless, with a little diligence, they can be defined and measured. It may take someone from outside your organization (such as a consultant) to help define what to measure, either because no one in the organization is sufficiently objective or because no one has the time to address the concern.

There's no right or wrong way to measure results. What's important for one organization may not be for another. So you have to decide what to measure.

Some specific examples of what to measure are provided below. I've separated the measures into several categories:

Organizational performance

Employee performance

Customer satisfaction with routine service

Customer satisfaction with handling of problems and complaints

Bottom-line indicators

Internal indicators

The categories aren't as important as what you're measuring. Use categories and measures that apply to *your* organization. The important thing is that you measure those things that are important to your customers and important to the smooth and profitable functioning of your organization.

1. Organizational performance

Total orders shipped/services performed

Number and percentage of orders/services completed ahead of schedule

Number and percentage of orders/services completed on time

Number and percentage of orders/service completed late, and by how much time late

Number and percentage of errors, by type (entry codes, delivery problems, pricing problems, wrong item, etc.)

Number and percentage of accurate orders/services (enables you to reward people doing it well)

Order/transaction time (from first contact to completion)

Number of complaints (by phone, letter, comment cards, surveys, or in person)

Percentage of complaining, complimenting, and inquiring customer contacts

Number and percentage of *transactions* that customers complain about or compliment you on

Reason and frequency of complaints (stock-outs, wrong item, lateness, product didn't perform as expected, etc.)

Number and percentage of complaints to executives

Number and percentage of complaints to third-party agencies (Better Business Bureau, regulatory agencies, consumer affairs or consumer protection offices, attorneys general, or others)

Number of compliments

Number of inquiries

Number and percentage of misdirected calls, letters, complaints

Average time customers are on hold

Number and percentage of calls/complaints containing inaccurate or incomplete data, as you define it (You might define "complete" as containing name, address, and phone numbers; account or other identifying numbers; dates of purchase, complaint, warranty, etc.; progress record consisting of dates of contact, correspondence, meetings, people involved, offers made, current status, or other notations you require; final disposition; classification of product or complaint type; any supporting documents. You might define "accurate" as meaning that all information is valid, all data has been entered correctly, and actions have been taken as promised or according to policy guidelines.)

2. Employee performance

Number of contacts per person

Time spent per call or transaction

Number and percentage of processing errors

Number of times customers are transferred before reaching someone who can help them

3. Customer satisfaction with routine service

Average customer waiting time (in person or on the phone)

Quality and/or performance of product or service itself

The ordering process (how easy—or difficult—do customers think it is to place an order)

Delivery time (faster, slower, or about what customers expected?)

Dependability (did you do what was promised on delivery, installation, training, follow-up service, etc.?)

Responsiveness (how quickly and effectively you responded to customer needs, problems, and requests)

Efficiency (were orders/transactions handled quickly and competently or badly bungled?)

Attitude (how friendly, willing to help, and courteous were employees with whom customers dealt?)

Waiting time for performance (do customers feel they had to wait too long?)

Value (do customers feel they got more, less, or about what they expected for the money they spent? How do customers compare you to competitors on these areas?)

Number and percentage who intend to buy from or do business with you again

Reasons why certain customers won't buy again

Overall satisfaction

4. Customer satisfaction with handling of problems and complaints

Average response time (from time call is received until someone begins to work on it)

Average response time for complaints to executives

Problem resolution time from time of problem/complaint until it's resolved (sometimes called MTTR: mean time to repair)

Average resolution time for calls to executives

Number and percentage of callbacks (repeat visits for same problem in specified time period)

Number of problems/complaints resolved to customer's satisfaction

Number and percentage of these customers who say they'll buy from or do business with you again

Number and percentage of problems/complaints for which the solution is acceptable to the customer but is not the solution that the customer desired

Number and percentage of these customers who say they'll buy from or do business with you again

Number and percentage of problems/complaints for which solution is unacceptable to customer

Number and percentage of these customers who say they'll buy from or do business with you again

Regardless of the resolution, the number and percentage of customers who are satisfied or unsatisfied with the *way* their problem or complaint was handled

5. Bottom-line indicators

Sales

Earnings

Market share

Growth versus total market

Total number of customers

Number and percentage of new customers

Dollar value of new customers

Cost to acquire one new customer

Dollar amount of incremental business from current customers

Number and percentage of customers lost

Dollar value of lost customers

Reasons customers left

Reasons noncustomers don't buy from or do business with you

Dollar amount spent for returns, adjustments, and settlements

Dollar amount of settlements for third-party complaints

Average cost to handle a problem/complaint (including personnel time, telephone, correspondence, settlement, and other factors)

6. Internal indicators

Number of customer-contact employees

Ratio of customer-contact employees to customers

Ratio of customer-contact employees to other employees

Percent of total budget allocated to creating and developing service (as compared to product development, manufacturing, technology, sales, marketing, or other areas)

Turnover rates for customer-contact employees and their supervisors

Turnover costs (including lost productivity, recruiting, training, learning time, etc.)

Another important measure is an internal audit—a self-check. It's a critical look at the policies and practices of your own organization. It's also difficult to do because it involves asking why you're doing a lot of things that you've always been doing. Many people can't be objective about their own organziations, their departments, or their own jobs. They often perceive questions about their operations as personal and threatening.

You can adapt the topics and questions in Appendix A to include in your internal service audit.

44. Share results with everyone in the organization

Too often when organizations gather information from customers, the results go only to senior managers or to the market research department. Whatever results you decide to track, keep everyone informed—about the good news and the bad. People want to know how they're doing. Publish and circulate results of teams or groups. Provide data to appropriate divisions or departments as soon as possible so they can use it to correct problems, redesign products, and determine how effective they are at satisfying those customers who have complained. Publish successes, wins, major accomplishments, or improvements of individuals. Meet privately with individuals who are having problems or need major improvements.

One manager who participated in the Citibank study said, "After a team completes an [on-site] audit, a verbal report is made to the manager in charge. Afterward a written report is circulated to everybody, and I mean everybody, and the local manager must reply within 30 days. If for any reason we think satisfactory corrections may not have been made, the auditors may return to the location in 60 to 90 days."

It's also important to share results with customers. Tell customers what you intend to do with the ideas, suggestions, problems, and complaints they give you. Sharing results with customers is a good idea for several reasons.

1 It increases the chances of getting more information in the future. When customers believe organizations are paying attention, they're more willing to share their opinions in the future.

2 It's unexpected. Very few organizations do this. You can easily exceed your customer's expectations if you do it.

3 It shows your commitment, especially when you commit to some action and then follow through. It shows you're not just giving lip service to good service.

When sharing results, use more than just numbers, charts, and graphs. Tape focus-group sessions. Invite executives to observe or participate in focus groups. Audiotape complaining and complimentary telephone calls. Edit the videotapes and/or audiotapes to get a succinct, fast-paced picture of the good news and the bad. Use the tapes to augment your statistics and bring them to life. Send copies of the tapes to executives or managers who don't believe there's a problem. Show them some horror stories. Also send copies to those who have been working hard to improve service. Show them some success stories.

45. Avoid the common pitfalls

The road to exceptional service won't always be smooth. It's only fair to warn you of some of the problems others have encountered. As they say, forewarned is forearmed.

There is no magic pill, no quick fix.   Noted management expert Peter Drucker has observed, "One of the degenerative tendencies in the human race is the belief in the quick fix. This isn't just true in this country, though it may be more pronounced here. Simple solutions to complex problems, that's the universally seductive formula." And Tom Peters has written, "The most common misunderstanding of the excellence [or service] philosophy is that managers expect there is some *magic* approach—and that this magic can instantly transform an organization from a loser into a winner. The "magic" is simply a clear vision of quality [service] exercised and reflected in dozens and dozens of revolutionary actions every day."

There is no magic pill or quick fix—only long, hard work.

Becoming service-oriented takes time.   Changing beliefs and habits is a slow process. *Chronicles of Corporate Change* is the result of a lengthy study of AT&T divestiture and its aftereffects. Senior author Leonard A. Schlesinger reports that the continuing problem at the former Ma Bell has been its inability to "retool the mindsets" of employees to be competitive in the marketplace. What Schlesinger appears to be saying is that even several years after the AT&T breakup, many employees still thought they were "the only phone company in town" and they still acted like it.

And you can't rush the process. Some things just take as long as they take. Sometimes the fastest way to get commitment is to allow managers or work teams to move at their own pace along a well-defined course toward a common vision. Pushing too hard or too fast tends to increase resistance and may actually *slow* the process.

How long transformation takes depends on many things. It depends how strongly the current culture and habits are entrenched, how much of a shift is needed, how quickly the change is needed, the organization's previous experience with change processes, and other factors.

American Airlines' Robert G. Oatley says:

> Top management support and commitment for an extended period of time is essential if this process is to catch hold and grow over the years. It requires changes in attitudes, organizational systems, organizational structures, and norms of behavior. It should not be viewed as a quick fix. Constant commitment and patience is required. The process cannot be mandated; it could take as long as five to seven years to totally institutionalize it within a company.

It may be simple, but it's not easy.   Zemke and Albrecht warn: "Implementing the service management concept in a large organization seems straightforward in concept. In fact, it is so simple in concept that many managers are tempted to underestimate the magnitude of the task. Changing the culture of a group of people is anything but easy. It is seldom simple, and it is almost never quick."

Expect some resistance, and manage it.   Many managers recognize that continuously providing exceptional service requires a tolerance for, even an enjoyment of, sudden and dramatic change. Tom Peters writes about "thriving on chaos." That's all fine, but saying we need to embrace change doesn't make it happen. Especially since so many people in the work force were so heavily influenced by schools, religion, the military, and other highly structured organizations. In these organizations, there are strict rules; roles and responsibilities are clearly defined; there are right and wrong ways of thinking; and change is not welcomed. After 20 or more years of daily contact with these kinds of organizations, change comes slowly. We've learned to conform, not challenge. So people may resist change in your organization.

Sometimes managers contribute to the resistance. In writing about resistance to change in organizations, Paul R. Lawrence wrote for *Harvard Business Review*:

> [I]t takes *time* to put the change successfully into production use. Time is necessary even though there may be no resistance to the change itself. The operators must develop the skill needed to use new methods and new equipment efficiently; there

are always bugs to be taken out of a new method or piece of equipment, even with the best of engineering. When staff people begin to lose patience with the amount of time those steps take, the workers begin to feel they are being pushed; *this* amounts to a change in their customary work relationships and resistance will start building up where there was none before.

The situation is aggravated if the staff specialist mistakenly accuses the operators of resisting the idea of the change, for few things irritate people more than to be blamed for resisting change when actually they are doing their best to learn a difficult procedure.

Lawrence also cautions: "When resistance *does* appear, it should not be thought of as something to *overcome*. Instead, it can best be thought of as a useful red flag—a signal that something is going wrong. . . . Signs of resistance in a social organization are useful in the same way that pain is useful to the body as a signal that some bodily functions are getting out of adjustment."

If you do encounter resistance, find out why. Have new policies and practices been forced on people without their input? Are policies unclear? Are current practices inconsistent with the mission? Are you saying one thing but rewarding another? Do employees feel you're asking too much of them too soon? Do they have the knowledge and skills to do what you're asking? Find out why they're resisting.

Expect initial improvements and excitement to level off.   You'll no doubt see rapid improvements and high levels of employee interest at first, but it's possible that these will level off after a few weeks or months. Without constant attention, they may even slip a little, back toward the way things used to be. That's why it's so important to go all out to keep the momentum going.

Don't mandate change, manage it.   Mandating change won't make it happen. Saying things like "Take more risks!" or "Provide better service!" is futile, because they're too abstract. People don't know what these commands mean, and they certainly don't automatically know what to *do* to take more risks or give better service.

Unless people are committed to, and see the value in, shifting their beliefs and practices, even the best mission statements, policies, and good intentions won't make much difference. Without commitment, people will say one thing but do another or else quickly lapse back into old, comfortable habits.

The more involved employees at all levels are in shaping the overall vision, creating their own visions, establishing customer-focused practices, and eliminating internally focused practices, the more likely they are to support a new direction without having to have it forced on them.

Rather than receiving mandates, people need to see a new direction, be given the necessary skills to effect change, and see that management will actually support them, even if they make mistakes.

Becoming service-oriented is a process, not an event.   Transforming an organization is not something that occurs quickly. Exceptional service is not something to get fired up about for a few months or a year and then forget about. It's a commitment to a lifelong approach to making customers the focal point of the organization. After the initial transformation begins, the momentum must be maintained.

Avoid creating an attitude of BOHICA: "Bend over, here it comes again." That's when employees say, "It's just another program. This, too, will pass."

Also avoid tantalizing your organization by announcing a new customer service effort and then spending months planning, analyzing, and collecting research before doing anything concrete. This is like a coach giving a rousing half-time talk to the team, getting the players all excited about their ability to win, and then, at the peak of their frenzy, sending them charging out to the field—only to find the locker room door is locked. Delays in taking definitive action often result in demotivation, skepticism, rumors, feeling of betrayal, and BOHICA. Management loses credibility.

Don't overorganize.   Beware of the tendency to overorganize by creating new forms, procedures, policies, reports, and other bureaucratic mumbo jumbo in the name of service. Change is hard enough without complicating the process by overstructuring. If anything, the goal should be to simplify and remove layers of bureaucracy and paperwork, not add them.

Keep the focus on satisfying customers.   Many organizations confuse new products, equipment, or technology with better service. Scandinavian Airlines System's (SAS) Jan Carlzon told his organization, "We won't buy airplanes just to give our pilots new cockpits or our mechanics something new to fiddle with—we'll do it only when new aircraft will enhance our value to our business travelers and make us more competitive."

The focus must be on satisfying customers, not on equipment, technology, or anything else that is only a means to the end.

Make sure your organization's structure, systems, and policies support your service efforts.   Some organizations launch a new advertising campaign like "Customers First" or "Your Satisfaction is Our Only Business" without providing their people with the training, information, or resources they need to make the ads come true. Campaigns like those raise customer expectations. Customers expect your service to be better if you say it will be. If it's not—because the rest of the organization can't get it together—you're liable to get more complaints than compliments.

Avoid disjointed efforts.   Many organizations view improved service and product support as a lot of separate tasks to be handled by various people or departments. Everyone is urged to work harder and be more customer-conscious, but people still do their own thing. They just do more of it. There is no unifying mission or theme. Departmental and functional barriers don't come down easily, and many people will try to protect their turf.

Similarly, some organizations come up with lofty, desirable goals but have no system for achieving them. They may state a goal such as "Maximize customer satisfaction" or "Be the best in the field" or "Establish close relationships with customers," but they have no specific plans for achieving the goal.

Too often, these laudable goals actually conflict with the day-to-day reality of the business. Executives at one company told us they wanted to "establish better relationships with customers and become the customer's partner." The problem was that each account rep had several thousand accounts. It was impossible for reps to even *see* all their accounts in a year, let alone begin to establish relationships!

Don't rely on training as a cure-all.   Training is important, but by itself it won't do much to change service levels. You must take an organizational approach that *includes* training but doesn't depend on it as *the* answer. And, of course, "smile training" and "Be nice!" training is hardly the answer.

Avoid hype in lieu of transformation.   As mentioned earlier in the book, many organizations are lured into showboating, slogans, rallies, posters, films, or training classes *instead of* the more time-consuming, difficult, expensive process of shifting the organization's focus, policies, practices, and beliefs. It's easier and faster to use the first approach, and it gives the appearance that something is being done. When the excitement fades, however, and nothing else has been done, this approach serves only to damage management's credibility and its efforts to do anything else later.

You need more than hype and fanfare. Excitement and training activities are important, but just doing the show biz and nothing else won't work. People will quickly spot such an effort as being phony and manipulative—as hype. They'll see there is no real intention to change things.

Measure and reward the behavior you really want.   Many service leaders warn about promising one thing and measuring something else. At one time, SAS promised its customers fast and accurate cargo delivery, but the company was actually measuring whether the paperwork and package got separated en route. SAS discovered that a shipment could arrive later than promised and not be considered late as long as the paperwork was with it.

Recognize that some managers and supervisors may not be able or willing to survive in a different environment. Zemke and Albrecht observed, "Few managers will admit to being bureaucratic in their methods, and almost all of them will agree with the need for creative new approaches. But when the time comes to change their own ways of doing things, the difference between 'theory' and 'practice' emerges. People in organizations can become amazingly attached to their current habits and procedures."

Many managers are not used to seeing themselves in support roles, especially when the people they're supporting used to be considered subordinates. To many, "support" connotes catering to individual needs, not managing. In many organizations, support and service functions have traditionally been low-status jobs handled by low-status people. Some managers become confused or resentful about the new role they are being asked to fill. They can become defensive, hostile, and counterproductive.

Be wary of improving service in some areas while hurting it in others. Another problem to watch out for is letting your efforts to improve service in some areas actually hurt service in other areas.

I was at an office supply store buying some supplies for our office. I had only a few items. The cashier started to ring them up. He looked at the price tags, entered some numbers into the register's keypad, and then stood looking at his computer screen for a long time. I stood across the counter looking at him. Finally, he sensed that this had gone beyond the customary waiting time. He turned to me and said, "I'm sorry this is taking so long, but each item is logged into our computer and every time we sell something it does an inventory check. When inventory levels get below a certain point, the computer orders the items. The problem is, it makes customers wait." Thus, a system that's supposed to ensure proper inventory levels is actually hurting this store's service at the point of purchase.

Also be aware that performance may initially decrease when changes are implemented as people and processes adjust. It's important for supervisors and managers to expect this initial decrease and to not overcorrect when it occurs. Follow-up and support by supervisors is critical here.

Take small steps instead of quantum leaps. Strive for continued improvement over the long haul instead of rapid changes in a short time. Many managers demand to see major changes immediately. After that, they periodically get excited about service. For example, they may do a service audit only once a year and make many changes as a result, instead of managing service continuously throughout the year and making minor adjustments as needed. Or they have "shoppers" visit all their locations at once instead of continually shopping a number of locations throughout the year.

Service-oriented organizations strive for ways to continually make small improvements rather than trying to fix everything at once.

Avoid creating unrealistic customer expectations.　In your zest to be service-oriented (or competitive), beware of making promises you can't keep. The net effect is loss of customer respect and believability.

Don't place too much stock in one or two measurements.　Use many types of measurement. Making decisions based only on quarterly profits or only on customer-satisfaction ratings is dangerous. Get a balanced picture that includes both tangible and intangible measures from inside and outside the organization, potential and former customers, satisfied and dissatisfied cutomers, and comparisons to your competitors. Your products and services may be improving, but if your competitors are improving faster, you haven't gained anything.

Don't undercommunicate.　Most organizations involved in any kind of change fail to communicate accurately or often enough. Management often thinks it has communicated effectively and frequently, only to learn that people were uninformed or misinformed. Changing beliefs and behaviors takes repeated communication, in many forms. Rely heavily on personal appearances, speeches, meetings, rallies, bulletin boards, contests, letters to employee homes, and other methods to keep employees informed of results, problems, changes, and other matters that affect them. Many organizations are (rightly) accused of poor communications with employees. You will rarely be accused of overcommunicating.

Of course, all communications should be relevant and useful. Burying employees with useless information in the name of good communications is just as bad as not communicating at all.

PUTTING IDEAS INTO ACTION

By now you've had a chance to think about many of the things that keep organizations from providing excellent service and to see if some of these problems apply to your organization. You've also seen a lot of ideas for improving service in your organization. Now it's time to act on these. (If your organization is a government agency, a regulated industry, or a nonprofit organization, it would be helpful to read Part Six before getting into the concrete planning steps detailed on the next few pages. Likewise, if your organization is undergoing a reorganization, Part Seven offers some information and suggestions specific to your situation.)

You may be thinking, "There's so much to do! Where do I start?" It's actually quite simple: Figure out what you need to do, in what order, and do it. I know some people need more guidance than that, so I've suggested a process that will give you the structure and detail you need to put your ideas to work in your organization:

1 Review the notes you've made throughout the book and in the Action Ideas section.

2 Look at the Blueprint in Part Three. Figure out approximately where you are—that is, what phase your organization is in right now.

3 Develop a plan. You can't do everything at once, and some things will need to be done before others. Use my Action Plan, or devise one of your own.

Some tips for using the Action Plan will be helpful here. As you look back through your notes and the Action Ideas section, make a list of those things you want to do in column A. Don't worry about the order they're in; you can put them in order later.

List what you want to accomplish by describing the desired *results*. Think in terms of what you want to *have* at the end. You'll probably find yourself listing activities—things to *do*. That's OK. State them in terms of results and write them in column A. If something really *is* an activity only, write it in column C.

Then establish your priorities. Decide which results are essential, which are important, and which are just nice to have. Which have the highest payoff? Assign 1, 2, or 3 priority in column B.

Next, list those things you need to *do* to achieve the results you've listed. If you don't know all the things you'll need to do for each result yet, list what you do know. For third-priority items, you may choose not to list any actions until the items become higher priority.

At this point, some people like to determine the best order for tackling the activities they list in column D. This step isn't always necessary, but it can help you figure out what to *do* first, second, third, and so on. It can also help you identify activities that *must* be started or completed before other activities get under way.

Where possible, start with your priorities labeled "1," then go on to your "2's" and "3's." After determining priorities and sequence, some people like to rewrite their list before doing the next step so all their first-, second-, and third-priority items are together.

Next assign start dates and end dates in columns E and G. You can assign dates for each result you want to have or for specific activities. Some people like

Action Plan

A Desired Result	B Priority	C Actions Needed	D Sequence	E Start Date	F Resources Needed	G End Date

to list end dates only. However you do it, you'll probably have several activities going on simultaneously.

In column F, consider what resources you'll need to accomplish the results you've listed. List the people, equipment, outside expertise, management approvals, budget, and other resources you'll need.

Set a date to review your progress in each area. If you've achieved the results you wanted by that date, put a check mark, a big star, or "YES!" in column G. If you haven't yet achieved some of the results you wanted, relist the unfinished portion in column A and repeat the process: reassess its priority, examine your actions, set new dates, and consider new or different resources.

Caution: Don't get so bogged down with this planning process and all the details that you don't take any action. Include only the amount of detail *you* need to start improving service in your organization. And don't use the planning process as an excuse for not acting.

Be sure to read Part Five, which offers some additional examples of actual moments of truth in various organizations. The insights provided about these examples can be useful to many kinds of organizations seeking a service orientation.

PART FIVE

GOOD NEWS, BAD NEWS: MORE MOMENTS OF TRUTH

- [ ] BURLINGTON COAT FACTORY
- [ ] THE TORONTO FOUR SEASONS HOTEL
- [ ] T.G.I. FRIDAY'S RESTAURANT
- [ ] GUARDIAN ALARM SYSTEMS
- [ ] AMERICAN ELECTRIC SUPPLY, INC.
- [ ] DOCKTOR PET CENTER
- [ ] WALGREEN'S
- [ ] COMMANDER'S PALACE
- [ ] SEARS
- [ ] SOUTHERN BELL AND SOUTHERNNET
- [ ] LORAL ELECTRONICS SYSTEMS
- [ ] J.C. PENNEY
- [ ] THE SAN JUAN CONVENTION CENTER

This section contains descriptions of 13 moments of truth. As you know from your own experience, interactions with an organization can involve just one employee (or department) or many. And any interaction can be totally positive, totally negative, or—more often—some of both. I've included examples of each.

In some of these situations, the point is self-evident. In others, I think it's useful to briefly review *why* the service was poor, in order to learn from the mistakes presented—or *why* the service was excellent, in order to emulate the success. Although the examples themselves are instructive, I suggest that you look beyond the specific incidents involving a certain restaurant, mail-order company, department store, or other business and think about how the lessons from each situation can apply to your organization.

BURLINGTON COAT FACTORY

Several years ago my wife wanted an Ultrasuede coat. I called several stores to see who had them in stock. One of the stores I called was the Burlington Coat Factory. Here's the gist of my conversation with an employee over the phone:

JEFF: I want to buy an Ultrasuede coat for my wife. Do you carry them?

CLERK: Yes.

JEFF: Do you have any in stock now?

CLERK: No.

JEFF: Are you going to be getting any more in?

CLERK: They're bringing some stock out now. There might be some in there.

JEFF: How can I find out if you'll have any in the size I need?

CLERK: You can call me later.

JEFF: Surely someone there must know what's been ordered. Can I talk to the buyer?

CLERK: (*sighs*) OK. (*Puts me on hold. Several minutes later she comes back on*) Sir, are you still there?

JEFF: Yes.

CLERK: We're not going to be getting any more for several weeks.

JEFF: Will you call me when they come in?

CLERK: (*hesitates*) Uh, well . . . I guess so. You know, we're not the only store. Maybe some of the others have what you're looking for.

JEFF: OK, I'll check. Where are the other stores? I mean, what part of town are they in?

CLERK: I don't know.

JEFF: Can you give me the phone numbers of the other stores so I can call them?

CLERK: No. I don't know their numbers.

JEFF: (*exasperated*) Never mind. I'll get them from the phone book. (*hangs up*)

This employee certainly didn't try very hard to help a customer who wanted information and was willing to buy. She seemed completely uninterested in me as a customer or as a person. If customers are interested in what you sell or provide, don't make *them* call you back. Take the responsibility for getting the information and promise to call them back.

THE TORONTO FOUR SEASONS HOTEL

Roy Dyment is a bellman at the Four Seasons Hotel in Toronto. One day he was helping a departing guest into a taxi. The guest was on his way to the airport. The man's luggage made it, but somehow Roy forgot to put the man's briefcase in the cab. Roy felt personally responsible for the mix-up. He also figured the man would be worried about the missing briefcase, so he called the man's office in Washington, D.C., to tell him he had it.

The man was relieved to know his briefcase was safe, but he was also quite upset because he needed some papers inside for an important meeting. Roy had some time off and, at his own expense and unknown to hotel management, flew to Washington and returned the briefcase.

The Four Seasons Hotel named Roy the Employee of the Year, in part because of the initiative he showed in this situation. Roy's handling of the briefcase situation exemplifies the best kind of moment of truth, when an employee takes an interest in customers, accepts responsibility for service (and for mistakes), and thinks about *customer* needs above everything else.

T.G.I. FRIDAY'S RESTAURANT

Kay and I stopped at a T.G.I. Friday's restaurant late one Monday evening for a light snack. It was about 9:30, and the restaurant wasn't very crowded. I ordered a combination appetizer plate with fried cheese, zucchini strips, and mushrooms. Kay ordered a hamburger, medium well, which had fried potatoes as a side dish. Kay told the waitress she's allergic to onions, and specifically said, "So please don't put them anywhere near my plate." Kay also asked our waitress to bring some mayonnaise with her burger. We each ordered a glass of wine while waiting for our food.

When our waitress brought the combination plate, it didn't have any fried cheese on it. It had broccoli instead. I asked the waitress, "Isn't this supposed to have fried cheese?" She said she wasn't sure but would go check. She came back to report that they were out of fried cheese. She apologized but made no offer to replace the broccoli or do anything else. I finished everything on the plate except the broccoli, which I didn't like. When the waitress came to pick up the plate, the broccoli was the only thing on it. She said nothing about it, so I said, "I'd like to make a suggestion. If you're out of something a customer orders, I suggest you tell them before serving it. I really like the fried cheese, and I would have ordered something else if I had known you were out of it. Besides, the broccoli wasn't very good."

She said, "They didn't tell me they were out of cheese. They just put it up and I brought it out."

About that time, someone else brought Kay's burger. It was rare. We sent it back to be cooked some more. A few minutes after the burger came back, we had both finished our wine and wanted another glass to finish our food. Our waitress was nowhere to be found. After bringing the recooked burger, she never returned to our table to see if the burger was satisfactory now or if we needed anything else.

We also discovered that Kay's cup of mayonnaise had several pieces of what looked like somebody else's tortilla chips in it. There were also fried onions in with her potatoes. We decided this was enough! We wanted to tell the manager how disappointing our experience there was. Since we hadn't seen our waitress for about 10 minutes, I went to the hostess stand and asked her to send the manager to our table. No one appeared for several minutes.

Eventually, our waitress came over to apologize for not having any fried cheese and wanted to know if I wanted a glass of wine to make up for it. By then, Kay and I were both finished eating and no longer wanted more wine. I thanked the waitress for offering and asked to talk to the manager. She said Robin would be right over. No one came. At least 5 minutes later, Robin appeared at our table with an order of fried cheese! I was shocked. I had thought they were out of fried cheese!

I thanked Robin for the cheese and told her we had finished eating now, but we did want her to know how disappointing the evening was. We recounted to her what had happened, telling her of the substituted broccoli and the under-cooked burger. We also showed her the onions, as well as the tortillas in the mayo. Robin apologized and said, "What would you like me to do?" I asked her to take my appetizer plate off the bill. She agreed.

Our waitress returned shortly with our bill. Stamped on the bill in two different places in inch-high, bright-red letters were the words "PROMO ±".

In your organization, how could you make sure that such a situation would be handled with more customer focus and would result in more customer satisfaction? A few suggestions are provided below:

☐ Encourage *everyone* to accept responsibility for what goes out of the kitchen [your organization], not just the cooks [manufacturing, management, etc.].

☐ Train servers [frontline employees] to know what's supposed to be on dishes [what quality and service should look like].

☐ If anything doesn't look the way it should, employees should know to talk to the cooks [manufacturing] *before* leaving the kitchen [shipping the product].

☐ Encourage servers [front-liners] to think about what they're doing and not just pick up a plate assuming it was someone else's job to put the right items on the plate.

☐ Restaurants (and other businesses) do run out of things. When this happens, employees should tell customers and give them the option of changing their orders. The cooks know when they run out of items, and they should put up a sign in the kitchen to tell all servers when certain items are no longer available.

☐ Empower the servers [the front line] to make amends for screw-ups right on the spot. In the situation recounted above, it was fully 15 minutes after the fact (and after I was finished eating) when our waitress offered a complimentary glass of wine. She should have offered the wine, offered to take the appetizer plate off my bill, offered to comp half of the bill, or offered to do *something* the instant she saw I was dissatisfied.

☐ Respond to customers. If a customer asks to see the manager, unless the building is on fire the manager should drop what he or she is doing and go talk to the customers. At T.G.I. Friday's it took at least five minutes for Robin to appear, and she came with a plate of the supposedly nonexistent cheese. I appreciated the gesture, but right then I wanted to talk to her more than I wanted to wait for her to fry the cheese.

☐ People in an organization should be taught to go out of their way to show customers they care if the customers have a pleasant experience. Sure, people will screw up sometimes. But when they do, they should be encouraged and empowered to take the initiative to satisfy the customer. Asking, "What would you like me to do?" sounds like something the accounting department thought up as a way to minimize comp costs with complaining customers. "Maybe they'll ask for less than what it would cost us to comp the whole bill" goes the logic. Well, add again! Compare comping a $20 to $35 bill and ending up with customers who are more likely to come back again *and* tell others about how well they were treated to comping only $5 to $10 and having customers who leave feeling they were "had." The disappointed customers will also tell others about how they were treated. In our case, the total bill was only $16. And the money isn't the issue. The point is that upon hearing how unhappy we were, Robin should have *offered* to comp our dinner and heartily invited us to come back the next night to "let us show you how good we really can be." We've never been back to that restaurant.

☐ Think about what is being communicated to your customers. The big red "PROMO" letters stamped not once, but twice, across my bill struck me as arrogant. It was as though they had to have the last word. It said to me,

"Look here, we want you to know what we did for you. You asked us to comp your appetizer and we did. So there!"

GUARDIAN ALARM SYSTEMS

When we bought the building that our office is in, there was a security system. It was an older model, we'd had some problems with it, and alarm systems had improved greatly; so we had the system upgraded. Shortly thereafter we began having false alarms. We'd be awakened in the middle of the night, and we'd have to make sure the building was secure and then try to go back to bed. After every false alarm I called Guardian Alarm Systems. Someone would come out to look at the system and then would give me some reason for the false alarm. The reasons included: thunder, heavy trucks on the street, moisture in the air, a loose wire, and—my favorite—one of the little metal fasteners they use to tack wires up along the ceiling fell out and landed on a window contact point.

I finally wrote a scathing letter to the owner of the alarm company. I described all the problems and demanded that he correct them immediately or refund our money. I was looking forward to hearing from him so I could vent my anger and frustration.

The day after I sent the letter, the owner called. He said, "You have every reason to be upset. I would be too. I don't blame you for being angry." He didn't try to make excuses or give me "reasons" for the problems we'd encountered. He was not defensive, but very matter-of-fact and sincere. He said, "The reason I'm calling is to try to straighten out the situation and correct the problem."

As we talked, I realized that he was very prepared for his call. He had in front of him all the work orders for everything that had been done. He had the printouts that showed the exact dates and times of all our false alarms. He had talked to his sales and installation people, so he knew about the situation before he called. He was also prepared to address every point I'd brought out in my letter, paragraph by paragraph, and to offer a solution or course of action for each of the things I'd asked for.

At one point in our conversation, he said, "I want you to know the buck stops here. I own this company. I'm not interested in placing any blame; I just want to address all these issues and correct the situation to your satisfaction." I said, "Thank you. That's why I sent the letter. I knew you'd take care of it."

He said, "To tell you the truth, I don't know what's causing the problem," but then he went on to describe to me what he was going to do to find and correct it. He said, "If that doesn't work, here's what I'll do next and here's what I'll do after that." He laid out what sounded like a logical approach. Finally, he said, "If that doesn't fix it, or if you have any other problems, please call me directly," and he gave me his private number.

When he called I was prepared for a fight. I was prepared to escalate my demands for satisfaction and to take legal action. He eliminated the need for any of that. He was very calm, understanding, and prepared. He said, in effect, "You're right, we blew it, and here's what we're going to do to fix it."

This is an excellent example of recovery skills. The owner got all the facts and recognized how I was feeling about the situation. He placed no blame but was more concerned with fixing the problem. He accepted responsibility: "If that doesn't fix it, we'll try something else." The problem ended up being faulty wiring that occurred when the system was upgraded. Guardian rewired the building, and we haven't had any problems since.

AMERICAN ELECTRIC SUPPLY, INC.

We got an unsolicited catalog from American Electric Supply, Inc., a mail-order company in California that sells high-quality name-brand audiovisual and electronic equipment such as TVs, slide projectors, flip charts, stage lighting, transformers, tubes for TVs and other electric equipment, and safety cases for shipping video equipment. It's an impressive catalog—640 pages. It's an inch and a half thick. It came at a good time, because we were in the market to buy a light table and an easel stand. I'd already looked at several models of both items in Atlanta. I called American Electric to get more information. For example, I wanted to know how many bulbs were in the light table I was interested in. I also wanted to know what the shipping weight was for both items because I had to pay shipping. I wanted enough information to figure out if it was cheaper to buy these items locally or through the mail.

Each time I asked the salesperson a question, she put me on hold to get the answer. It seemed like hours on hold, but it was probably only a few minutes. When she returned, she only gave me answers that I could find myself in the catalog. I think all she did was look at the same catalog I had on my desk in front of me, because anything that wasn't printed on those pages, she didn't know and couldn't find out. Finally, I said, "I'll go ahead and buy the two items, provided I can return them for a refund if they don't meet my needs. Can I do that?" She said she wasn't sure. She put me on hold again to find out. She came back and said that I could return the items if they weren't what I wanted. Then I told her I wanted to charge the items to my company's credit card account, and she said they don't take credit cards.

If you're going to rely on mail-order catalogs and telephone business, here are a few helpful hints, based on this situation:

1 Make sure you're able to provide customers with the information they need. Make sure the people answering your phones are trained and can answer customers' questions without putting them on hold for every little thing.

2 If the people talking to customers don't have the information they need, make sure there's a way they can get it quickly. It's irritating enough to talk to people who can't answer simple questions about their own products. It's even more irritating if they don't know where to get the answers and have to keep customers on hold for long periods of time.

3 Make it easy for customers to buy. This is a credit-card society. We buy from a lot of mail-order companies, and this is the only one I can recall that doesn't take credit cards.

4 Many of the products American Electric sells are big-ticket items. Encourage customers to buy by giving them the security of knowing they can return anything if they don't like it or it doesn't meet their needs.

→ My impression of this company was based on the person I spoke with. Even though the company carried nationally known, reputable brands, I had no confidence in *this* company's ability to deliver them to me.

And the result of this call? American Electric made it so difficult to buy and gave me so little confidence that the company would back up what it sells, I decided not to buy from that source. American Electric lost several hundred dollars worth of business on this transaction, as well as our future business. Oh yes, it's been over 3 years since this happened. No one has ever called me from this company to apologize for being so inept or has tried again to get our business. And we've never received another American Electric catalog.

DOCKTOR PET CENTER

Kay loves to go into pet stores. If they'd let her, she'd hold every furry creature in the store. One day we were at a Docktor Pet Center in a shopping mall. As we walked in, I noticed two employees behind the checkout counter near the front door. One was working the register and had just finished ringing up a sale. Standing next to her, the other was bent over, totally engrossed in making a sign for a fish sale. She was using a large felt-tip marker to carefully color in the 4-inch-high letters.

A couple walked in the door just behind us. They were in their early 30s, nicely dressed, preppie looking. I sensed from looking at them and the way they walked into the store that they wanted to buy, not to browse as we were doing. The woman was about 5 feet ahead of her husband. She walked straight to the back of the store, where the dogs were, pointed to one and said, "That's the one I want!"

The employee working on the sign put down her marker pen and said to the other employee, "I'll be right back. I just heard a 'That's the one I want.'" The other associate looked at her with a puzzled look that communicated "You heard what?" and said, "Huh?" The sign-maker said it again and headed for the back of the store.

1 She was attentive to customers. She was listening to them, even though she was *doing* something else.

2 She heard an obvious buying signal and recognized it as such.

3 She dropped what she was doing to assist a customer. The other employee never heard the customer's comment, didn't recognize it as indicating a potential sale, and was not aware of what her associate was talking about, even when her associate repeated the customer's statement.

The point here is that whenever you're in close proximity to customers—as in retail shops, hotels, restaurants, airports, or showrooms—you must always listen to them with extreme, although not obvious, attentiveness. Listen for their buying signals, their suggestions of how you might help them, remarks about things they might be looking for, or even problems or complaints they're having.

How often have you said to someone else, "I wonder if they have so-and-so here?" or "I can't find the [fill in the blank]; I wonder where it is," and employees within earshot totally ignore you? What a great opportunity for an employee to *manage* a moment of truth and create a positive impression with a simple act, rather than allowing that moment to go unmanaged and create a neutral or negative impression.

WALGREEN'S

Sheila, an associate of ours who lived in Chicago, told us about an incident at a Walgreen's store. Sheila was in line at the front checkout counter, holding a handful of items (shampoo, deodorant, perfume, etc.). The manager noticed that there were several people in line and said that anyone who wasn't buying cigarettes could go to the cosmetics counter to check out. Sheila was the first customer to reach the cosmetics counter. The employee there was busy pricing merchandise and told Sheila, "I have to get all these things priced and put away before we close tonight. You can go over to the other register. They'll ring you out."

The other register still had people waiting in line. There were no customers at the cosmetics register. Sheila didn't want to wait in line, so she said to the employee, "I want these things, but there's nothing here I can't buy somewhere else. Do you want me to buy them here or not?" The clerk said, "I don't care."

No employee should ever be too busy to talk to or help customers, and especially to take their money when they're ready to buy. It's the employee's job to care. If employees don't care about customers, or if they inconvenience customers, or if they drive customers to buy from a competitor, they shouldn't be working where they are.

Sheila left the items on the counter and walked out. She later wrote a letter to the store manager and regional manager describing the incident. She got a letter back apologizing for her inconvenience and telling her that the employee had been severely disciplined.

COMMANDER'S PALACE

In contrast to "I don't care" service, here's a great example of "What else can we do for you?"

We were in New Orleans. Some friends suggested we go with them for Sunday brunch at Commander's Palace. Commander's Palace is one of New Orleans' traditions and is famous for its Sunday brunch. It's practically impossible to get in anytime without reservations, but it's especially popular for Sunday brunch. Typical of New Orleans, the restaurant is built around a lovely courtyard with tables, palm trees, and camellia bushes.

Our friend, Rick, had reserved a table in the courtyard, but it was raining so we had to eat inside. One wall of the room we were escorted to is a ceiling-to-floor window facing the courtyard. The room also has a huge tree in it that literally grows up through the restaurant. Unfortunately, the maitre d' seated us behind the tree so we couldn't see the courtyard. We noticed several empty tables along the window, next to the courtyard. Rick asked our waiter if we could move to one of the empty tables. He said he'd check.

Almost out of nowhere, the manager, Bob, appeared. Rick said, "We'd like to move to a table closer to the window." Bob immediately replied, in a very friendly, cheerful voice, "Well, let's go! You won't be happy here." As we were walking over to the table Bob said, "I believe you never say 'no' to a customer." After we were seated he said, "Now you'll be so easy to serve, because you'll be happy. If you'd sat over there, you wouldn't have enjoyed anything. The coffee would have been too cold, the service would have been too slow; but now you'll be happy." And he was absolutely right.

Compare this situation to times when the maitre d' tells you all the reasons why he *can't* move you to another table. Bob was cheerful and accommodating. He didn't make us feel guilty or stupid for asking to be moved.

Our friend Rick is a sports fan. Later in the meal, Rick asked our waiter, Scott, if he knew the score of the Saints game. Scott said he hadn't heard a score. That was perfectly understandable—Scott came to work early in the morning before the game started, and by 2:30, when Rick inquired, Scott was too busy to stop and listen to the game on the radio. No more than 5 minutes later, Scott came back and gave us the third quarter score. I don't know how he got it. He sure didn't go out to his car, because he was busy serving us the whole time. But he made the effort to find out the score for a customer. He didn't project an attitude, as most servers probably would have, of "Look, I have all these tables to take care of. I'm too busy to find scores to the ball game. You can get the score from the radio while you're driving home or on the news tonight."

SEARS

The southeastern United States had an unusually wet fall in 1989. There were hurricanes and tornadoes and times when it rained steadily—and hard—for days. During one spell of unusually heavy rain, our basement flooded, and soon the whole house smelled musty from the water.

In 2 days, we were to leave town for a month. I had dozens of errands to run and was in a hurry. I needed a wet vac to get the water out of the carpet in the rec room. I called six or eight hardware stores, but they were all sold out. I finally found some at Sears, and I told the salesman on the phone to hold one for me—I'd be there in a few hours.

When I got to Sears, the salesman I talked with on the phone was gone. He left no message for anyone else that I had called. The salesman who was there now, Jim, said they were sold out of the model I wanted. He had only a much smaller one and a larger one. I explained that I had called a few hours ago, given another salesman my name, and told him I'd be in. Jim pulled a stack of seven or eight pieces of paper out of his shirt pocket and started looking through them. "Nope, he didn't leave me anything on this."

Jim then walked to a cash register where there was another note taped to the register with the sizes and prices of the different wet vacs. He looked at it and said, "This says we're sold out of that one."

We walked over to the floor model of the larger unit and, as we were looking at it, another salesman happened to walk by and overheard our conversation. Jim said, "There aren't any more of these $99 wet vacs in the back are there?" The other fellow said, "Yes, a whole bunch of them." "Are you sure? My notes say we're sold out." "Yes, I was just back there. I saw a whole stack of them," the other salesman told Jim. Jim went to the back room to look and came out carrying the unit I wanted.

I handed him my MasterCard. He said, "We only take Sears and Discover cards." I said, "I have a Sears card, but I don't carry it with me." He said, "You'll have to go over to the credit department to get a temporary card before I can ring this up."

I walked over to the credit department, which is also the collections and gift wrapping department. There were four employees behind the counter. One employee was on the phone. Another one was showing gift boxes to a customer who spent 5 minutes trying to decide which size to use for a coat he had just bought. Another employee was sitting at a desk doing paperwork. She looked up several times and made eye contact with me, but she continued working. (I guess she doesn't deal with customers.) The fourth employee was in the back room.

Finally the gift wrap saga ended and Pat Moraitakis turned to me. I explained that I needed a temporary card. She asked whose name the account is in. I said, "Mine, I think." (When Kay and I got married, we each had credit cards for major retailers. We left some in her name, some in mine. We also have different last names, so it's hard to remember sometimes.)

Pat went to her desk and punched some numbers into a computer terminal, but she couldn't find my account. I told her Kay's last name. Pat entered more numbers into the computer and then made a phone call. Finally, about 5 minutes later, she said, "I can't issue you a temporary card. Your wife has a restricted account. She's the only one who can use it." I said, "That's ridiculous! Please let me talk to whoever you were talking to." Following an exasperated sigh that communicated, "Why bother, bozo? I told you 'No,' and they're only going to tell you the same thing," she dialed the number and handed me the phone over the counter.

The woman I talked with explained again that no one was authorized to use this account except Kay, but she checked again. When I told her my name, she told *me* my correct street address (so they must have *some* record of me in their system), but she found no account listed in my name. She put me on hold for another 4 or 5 minutes, and then she came back and again told me they couldn't issue a temporary card because Kay had a restricted account.

I tried to explain to her that we have no restricted accounts, we're not getting a divorce, and there must be some mixup. She asked if I could give her a phone number to reach Kay so she could get Kay's authorization for me to charge something on her account. Kay was with a client, conducting a training program, and couldn't be reached. The woman put me on hold again.

A different person, Debbie, came back on the phone and again told me that

Kay's account is restricted. I told her that I had charged items on a Sears account and also had Sears service people at my house and charged the repair work, and I had never had a problem. She, too, put me on hold. Several minutes later, Debbie came back and said there had been a mistake when entering the data for Kay's account and that it shouldn't have been designated as being restricted. I asked her to explain that to Pat so she could issue me a temporary card so I could buy the wet vac. Debbie talked to Pat, Pat gave me the temporary card (with no apologies for the error, the delay, or the inconvenience), and I walked back to the hardware department to pay for the wet vac.

Jim wrote up the ticket. He asked if I wanted him to send the carton over to the pickup department or if I'd take it now. I said, "As long as it has taken me so far, I don't want any more delays. I'll just carry it out to my car from here." He agreed and dialed a phone number to verify my credit. He hung up the phone, handed me back the temporary card, and said, "I can't accept this. This is a restricted account. Only Kay duPont can use this card."

I blew up! I yelled, "I've just spent 20 minutes going through all that with your credit department! They issued me this card! That means I'm authorized to buy this merchandise on this account!" He said, "I'm sorry. I can't accept that card. You'll have to go back to the credit department." By this time I was seeing red.

When I got back to the credit department, Pat was with a customer and had another one in line. The woman who was doing paperwork earlier was now standing at the counter helping customers, and she said "May I help you?" as though she'd never seen me before. When Pat finished with her other customers, I explained what had happened. She called Debbie back. Debbie wasn't there. Pat asked for someone else. She wasn't there either. She asked for another person. Not there. Apparently someone at the other end thought it amusing that Pat couldn't find anyone to talk to, because I heard Pat say sternly into the phone, "It isn't funny when I'm here and there's an upset customer standing here."

Pat hung up and made another call, and then made two more attempts to locate someone who could resolve this problem. When she finally reached someone, Pat explained the situation and was put on hold. Whoever she was talking to had no idea what had just transpired because, when they came back on the line, Pat had to explain the entire situation and explain that an error had been made in listing the account as restricted. She was put on hold again. A few minutes later, the person gave her an authorization number.

Pat hung up and said, "Let's go over to the hardware department. I'll go with you." When we got there, Jim was on the phone, completing a transaction for another customer. We waited a minute or two for him to finish. He turned to me and said, "Let me finish with this other customer." Pat interrupted and said, "All you have to do is ring this up and he can take his wet vac and leave." Jim did, reluctantly. In all it took me 50 minutes to make a 5-minute purchase!

Several hours later, I uncarted the wet vac and began to assemble it. There was a part missing. A large nut that holds the filter on was not to be found anywhere. After all I had gone through to get it, I couldn't use it because a part was missing! I was seeing red again.

I called the hardware department and a young lady answered. I told her I had bought a wet vac that afternoon and it was missing the filter nut. She asked the model number. I said, "The box with the model number on it is in the other room. It's a 16-gallon, 2-1/2-horsepower model that sells for $99. It's the only kind like it in the store." She put me on hold for several minutes. She came back and told me I could call the parts department in the morning. I said, "No I can't wait until morning. I paid to have all the parts, and I need to use it tonight." She put me on hold again. She came back and asked me more questions about the model I had and put me on hold again. She came back after a minute and said they had a filter nut there and I could come there to pick it up. I said, "I shouldn't have to come back to pick up a part that was supposed to be in the box in the first place and I don't have the time to drive back there." She put me on hold again. After another minute or so, she said they would send it to me. I asked how she was going to send it, hoping she'd say via courier. She said, "By UPS." She said it would take about 2 days. In 2 days, I was going to be out of town and still have soggy carpets. I insisted, "I need to get the part tonight." She put me on hold again. Another minute went by and she came back on. She said they could send me the part in the morning or else I could come in and pick it up. I asked to talk to the store manager. She put me on hold again.

After several minutes, Bob, the hardware department manager came on the line. I asked to talk to the store manager. He told me the manager wouldn't be in until morning and gave me the manager's name. I explained the trouble I had had earlier in the day and told him I needed to use the wet vac that night. He said, "There's nothing I can do. There's no way I can get it to you tonight." I said, "I can think of several. You could send an employee over with it right now, or you could ask an employee who lives in this direction to stop here on the way home tonight, or you could call a taxi or courier and have them deliver it to me." He said, "I'd deliver it myself, but I can't leave the store until closing. It's my night to close." I said, "Fine. I can wait. You can drop it off after you close the store." He then refused to do that. He said that he has no employees who live in my area (he didn't even know my name or where I lived at that point) and that he couldn't deliver the part after he closed. I said, "Fine. Then call a courier to pick up the part. You pay the courier to deliver the part to me." After a little convincing, he agreed to do so.

This incident illustrates several important points:

1. Make it easy, not difficult, for customers to buy. Find an easy way to accept payment. I don't carry retail cards because most businesses accept VISA or MasterCard. I don't carry gasoline cards any more either: too many different cards to carry. Besides, I like to have all my charges on one bill rather than ten different bills.

In the store, provide an easy way to accommodate people who don't have their cards with them. Sending the *customer* all over the store to get temporary credit cards is for the *store's* convenience. It's certainly inconvenient and time-consuming for customers.

2. Make sure your system supports service. Sears' left hand seemed not to know what the right hand was doing. One salesperson had no way to tell other salespeople that a customer was coming in for a wet vac; salespeople didn't even know if they had any in stock; when credit was issued, it was refused again; the department manager was unable (or unwilling) to rectify a problem; and behind-the-scenes employees seemed insensitive to another employee's difficulty in finding someone to help a customer with a problem. If an employee is not serving the customer, he or she had better be serving someone who is.

3. Help the customer, even if it means bending some rules. Sears' rules said that no one else can charge to a restricted account. Had I not *insisted* that Pat let me talk to the central credit department, I would not have had a wet vac. The employee doing paperwork seemed more concerned about what she was doing than helping me buy merchandise (even though merchandise sales are what pay her salary). The salesman followed the rules and refused to sell me the wet vac, even after I came back with a temporary credit card. The clerk I talked to at night either didn't know the rules or was unwilling to break them to satisfy a customer.

Had I not *needed* this wet vac to soak up the water in my house and had I been able to find one elsewhere in town, I would have left. As it turned out, the longer the incident went on, the more interested I became in how they would handle it. It was also interesting to notice the shift in Pat's behavior when she changed her view of the situation. At first she appeared to be just "doing her job." She was efficient and followed the rules, but she wasn't especially personable or helpful. Then I insisted she bend the rules ("Let *me* talk to your regional credit office"). Then when Jim refused to accept my temporary credit card, it seemed that Pat came over to my side. When she stood up and said, "Let's go over to the hardware department. I'll go with you," it was as though she had said, "Enough is enough! *I'm* going to straighten this out personally." I felt her become an ally. She took a personal interest, and her actions communicated, "I'm going to make this right for this customer myself."

SOUTHERN BELL AND SOUTHERNNET

Members of our office staff keep a log of their long-distance calls. About a year ago, I noticed several calls on our company phone bill that weren't accounted for. The next month, calls to the same cities showed up. The calls were to several numbers in Arizona, Vermont, and Utah. Some of the calls were made in the evening, on weekends, and on holidays. I knew the calls weren't ours. I even called the numbers to find out who they belonged to. One was a college dormitory, and one was a county airport. I checked with our office staff and ruled out our cleaning staff. We own our own building, so I knew others couldn't get in, especially since the alarm system now worked. After several months, I began to suspect that this might have started earlier than when I first discovered it. I found out that it had been occurring for about 5 months.

Our long-distance calls are handled by SouthernNet, and we have direct-access dialing, so for long-distance calls we just dial "1" and the 10-digit number. I called SouthernNet and explained the problem. I said, "We don't know anyone at those numbers, and we didn't make these calls. Some of the calls occurred when we weren't even here."

The person I talked with told me that if the calls were on our bill, they must have been made from our number. She also told me that with their computer system, the calls couldn't possibly be on our bill unless they were ours. She suggested I call Southern Bell. I did.

Southern Bell told me the situation couldn't possibly be their problem. They explained that this matter was between SouthernNet and me.

I had a problem, and both companies said, in effect, "It's not our problem; call *them*." I wrote a letter to the presidents of both Southern Bell and SouthernNet, explaining the problem. I said I didn't care whose problem it was or how they fixed it, but I wanted it taken care of. Two days later, I got a personal call from Gene Gabbard, president of SouthernNet. He thanked me for taking the time to write and bring it to his attention and said he'd assigned someone work on it. He said it may take a special team from both companies to resolve it.

Two days after that, a customer service representative from Southern Bell called. He said the lines appeared to be clear now. I took that to mean, "We've checked our part, and the problem doesn't lie with us." I said, "That's fine. I really don't care what you do as long as it corrects the problem."

As it turned out, the problem was caused by a "leave in," a line that was left in place and in operation when someone had discontinued service. This was like having our phone in a stranger's house, because many of their calls ended up on our bill.

LORAL ELECTRONICS SYSTEMS

An associate suggested that Loral Electronics Systems in New York might be interested in some of the services we provide and suggested that I contact Susan Silverman. Since I'm in Atlanta, a phone call seemed a good way to find out. I called Susan's company. The receptionist answered, "Loral." I said, "Susan Silverman, please." She said, "Do you know his extension?" I said, "No, I don't," so while I was on hold, on my nickel, she took about 2 minutes to look up the number.

It's not the caller's job to know the extensions of every person he or she calls in every organization, especially on the first call. Receptionists should have easy, fast access to employee telephone extensions and should be familiar with an organization's employees. Certainly they should at *least* know if "Susan" is male or female.

J.C. PENNEY

Kay and I were on a trip to Southern California in December several years ago. Although it's usually warm that time of year, we were unlucky enough to be there during a record-breaking cold spell. We had brought mostly summer-weight clothes, so we needed heavy jackets, sweaters, hats, and gloves.

We went to a J.C. Penney department store in a shopping mall to try to find these items. We asked an employee at one of the checkout counters where we could find the items we needed. Instead of pointing in the general direction, she said, "I'd show you myself, but I can't leave my register unattended." Then she proceeded to give us detailed instructions: "Do you see that pillar down there? Go down to there and turn left. Go up the escalator. At the top, turn right. You'll see the handbags and leather goods on one side and the hats and gloves on the other side. I hope you'll be able to find what you're looking for there. Oh, and if you can't find what you're looking for, come back and I'll help you." Her attention was so unusual for something as simple as giving directions, we both commented on it. What a positive moment of truth.

Later, as we were looking at sweaters in another department, we watched an interaction between another employee and a customer. The customer was holding a sweater, several dress shirts, and some other items. We only heard the last part of the conversation. It went like this:

CUSTOMER: My driver's license is in the car.

EMPLOYEE: Well, you'll just have to go get it. I can't ring these up without it.

CUSTOMER: What should I do with these in the meantime?

EMPLOYEE: I don't really care. I'm going on break now anyway. I was supposed to go fifteen minutes ago.

The employee walked out from behind the counter and walked away, leaving the customer standing there dumbfounded. After a few seconds, the customer left the items on the counter and walked out of the store. The customer never came back. What a different moment in truth!

Instill in your employees the idea that customers are never an interruption. Customers are the reason for an employee's work, and they deserve full attention. Filing, stocking, taking inventory, and lunch can wait.

THE SAN JUAN CONVENTION CENTER

Several years ago, Kay was conducting a seminar at the San Juan Convention Center, an enormous facility with many different ballrooms and meeting rooms. The main ballroom seats 1,500 for dinner and has a large stage that would be the envy of any Broadway theater. The convention center is so big that our meeting room was on a different level and in a separate wing from the main ballroom.

We expected about 300 people for the all-day seminar and had decided to tape this program to use in a cassette album we were producing. We brought a FREEDOMIKE (a portable, wireless microphone system) with us. This system would plug directly into the convention center's sound system and enable us to tape directly from Kay's lapel microphone to get a good-quality recording.

The program started at 9:00 A.M. Participants begin arriving around 8:15. We were there at 8:00 to get set up. I set up the microphone, but it wouldn't work. I tried everything I could think of, but I couldn't get it to work. One of the hotel staff was in the room checking the risers and setting up the projection screen. I asked him if he knew anything about these systems. He said that he didn't, but he told me there was an electrician on staff and he'd see if he could find him. I thought, "Fine, but he'll probably show up around 2:00." Several minutes later, Vincente Cartagena, the center's sound and light technician, was there. He had never seen a FREEDOMIKE before, but he looked at it. After a few minutes, he said it might need a new battery for the transmitter. He told me there was a pharmacy across the street that was open and he'd wait until I got back. I put in a new battery, it still didn't work.

Vincente said he'd take the unit to his office to see what he could do. I went with him. We took an elevator up two floors, walked through the main ballroom to the opposite end, climbed up on stage, and then went up two flights of narrow stairs behind the stage to his office high above the stage. His office looked like a small-scale electrical shop with stage lights, cords, speakers, plugs, and tools all over the place. Vincente sat down at his desk and began to take the microphone apart. After a while he said he couldn't find anything wrong.

Our microphone system has two major parts: an amplifier and a transmitter. Vincente had a sound system of his own in his office. To find the problem with ours, he hooked our amplifier up to his system, plugged it into a set of speakers in the office, and tested it. It worked, so we knew the problem was in our transmitter, not the amplifier. Vincente took the transmitter apart, found a loose wire, and fixed it.

Unfortunately, our transmitter wasn't compatible with his system, so we couldn't test it in his office. I had to take it back to our meeting room. Vincente said if that didn't work to bring it back and he'd try something else. I made the long walk back. By this time, it was past 8:30. The room was filling up. The microphone didn't work.

By the time I got back to Vincente's office it was 8:45. Vincente took the transmitter apart again and discovered a loose connection somewhere in the small microphone wire. Although he didn't have the parts or tools to fix it, he set up the mini sound system in his office again and spent several minutes trying different transmitters and amplifiers to find some that were compatible. He worked feverishly, taking several microphone jacks off his equipment, putting them on different amplifiers, and testing different transmitters until he came up with a patched-together system that worked. At least it worked in his office. This time we both trekked back to the meeting room to test it. It worked! With 3 minutes to spare! And throughout the day, Vincente came back at *every* break to make sure the system was still working.

Vincente Cartagena went way beyond what I expected. I've worked with enough hotels and convention centers to be pleasantly surprised to have someone respond quickly when we had a problem at 8:00. After the battery didn't work, most hotel and meeting staff people would have said, ''That's not my problem.'' Vincente didn't. After trying to fix it the first time, all but a few people would have said, ''I've tried, but there's something wrong with your unit. When you get home, take it to the dealer and get it fixed.'' Vincente didn't. He knew there was no tomorrow. It had to be working today. He kept trying, using his own parts, jacks and other components to get it to work.

We were so appreciative of Vincente's efforts that we sent a letter to his boss. We described exactly what Vincente did and how he went out of his way to help us.

You've probably had similar experiences with both exceptional and lousy service, or with people who've messed up and then recovered well or poorly. I'd like to hear about these moments of truth you have encountered. If you'd like to share them, please send a detailed account of one or several such experiences to Jeffrey Disend, c/o Chilton Book Company, 201 King of Prussia Road, Radnor, PA 19089. (Please include your name and address in case we would like to contact you.)

PART SIX

IMPROVING SERVICE IN NONPROFITS

☐ SERVICE IS IMPORTANT IN THE PUBLIC SECTOR

☐ SIMILARITIES BETWEEN PRIVATE AND PUBLIC SECTORS

☐ WHY SERVICE IS SO POOR IN THE PUBLIC SECTOR

☐ HOW TO IMPROVE SERVICE IN THE PUBLIC SECTOR

☐ EXAMPLES OF WHAT IS BEING DONE

After hearing the ideas in the last several chapters, executives, managers, and seminar participants frequently say something like, "Yes, that all makes sense. And I agree with you. Those are some good ideas. But they won't work for us. We're [choose one; we've heard all of these]:

A government agency
In a regulated industry
A nonprofit organization
A publicly held company
A privately held company
A small company
A big company
Just a part of a huge company
In the middle of a merger or takeover
Different."

To all these reasons, I say "Hogwash!" There isn't a company, institution, business, government agency, nonprofit organization, or other enterprise I can think of that can't be more customer-oriented and that can't use most of the ideas described in Part Four. Sure, every organization is different. But they're not so different that the beliefs and practices used by leading service organizations in the private sector won't work.

The companies represented in the Citibank and Lele studies introduced in Part One and the various "excellent" companies profiled by Peters and Waterman in *In Search of Excellence* are about as diverse as you could imagine in their products, services, cultures, size, and management styles. Despite these differences, the organizations we recognize as superior service providers have remarkable similar beliefs and practices—so much so that the authors of the Citibank study remarked that executives from many companies used practically the same words to describe their service policies and practices.

Yet managers and executives continue to insist, "You don't understand. We're different. Those things won't work here." Then they tell us all the reasons it won't work.

The key here is to remember that our behavior is determined by our beliefs. If managers and executives believe (for whatever reason) that they don't have "customers," that they can't motivate public sector employees, that employees must follow the regulations at all costs, that supervisors must check everything, that no one cares about quality service, that no one notices or appreciates what they do, then they're right—any attempt to improve service won't work in their organization. Fortunately, there are a few government agencies, regulated businesses, and nonprofits that have proved it *can* work and it *does* work.

In this discussion I'll highlight some common problems and describe what banks, utilities, colleges, hospitals, professional organizations, and government agencies have done to shift their beliefs and practices to become more customer-centered. I'll refer collectively to government agencies, regulated businesses, and nonprofits as "the public sector," even though some enterprises such as utilities, banks, hospitals, trade and professional organizations, social service agencies, and others may actually be privately held corporations. I also use the term "customer" to collectively refer to citizens, taxpayers, consumers, trade association members, public TV subscribers, and so on.

SERVICE IS IMPORTANT IN THE PUBLIC SECTOR

Service *is* important in the public sector, even if many working there don't believe it yet or don't want to admit it. The next several paragraphs cite some studies and examples concerning poor service in the public sector.

According to Technical Assistance Research Programs Institute (TARP) studies in specific industries, 39 percent of utility company customers are unhappy with how the companies respond to their problems. In financial services, TARP reported that 26 percent were unhappy with the way they were treated.

In 1988, a study by the General Accounting Office found that information given over the phone by Internal Revenue Service employees was wrong 36 percent of the time. And one study showed that on routine calls to the IRS, callers were put on hold for an average of 55 seconds. In calls for which the IRS phone representative had to do research (access a file or check rulings or regulations), the average time on hold was 77 seconds. While that may not *sound* like a long time, being on hold for a minute or more can be very irritating. How many people would put up with that kind of response from an accountant, attorney, or banker?

U.S. Attorney General Richard T. Thornburgh reported on results of a poll showing that "seven of ten Americans think illegal payoffs are common in the federal government" and that half of the people polled said "dishonesty is widespread in government."

The Southern Governors Association study found that thousands of people who are eligible for various government assistance programs are denied aid because of problems in completing their applications (such as incomplete applications and inaccurate or undocumented information). In many instances, the applicant's inability to read or understand the application or instructions resulted in loss of benefits the person might otherwise have been eligible for.

Population groups with high rates of illiteracy or with other language problems are often denied services—sometimes life-sustaining services—simply because they cannot fill out the required forms or produce birth certificates or other documents. Many of these people, born at home or in another country, never had the documents, had to leave them behind, or have lost them and cannot get duplicates. Many can't read English well enough to know the documents were important and discarded them; others can't read well enough to find these documents at home even when they *do* have them.

The Social Security Administration found that thousands of poor, elderly, blind, and disabled people were having their benefits cut off improperly, many for simply failing to provide proof of disability to the Social Security Administration.

State and local municipalities often take weeks or months to issue business licenses. In the meantime, many small business owners incur the costs of inventory, equipment, and bank loans while being unable to open their doors.

Several years ago, the Chicago city government decided to cut funds to the city's thousands of homeless, and then later decided to spend $100,000 for ornamental holiday lights on the city's bridges and for a New Year's Eve fireworks display. Other municipalities report similar incidents.

Banks are typical of businesses in regulated industries: they are conservative, traditional and are not risk takers. Banks have traditionally offered checking and savings accounts, safe deposits, loans, and, more recently, credit cards. They require customers to come to them. Loan officers are traditionally rewarded for not taking risks; that is, for approving loans for individuals most likely to pay them back or for businesses most likely to succeed. A bank's major competition has traditionally been other banks who offer similar services.

Hospitals, too, have traditionally required patients to come to them, ambulance service notwithstanding. The admissions process is an endless barrage of impersonal questions followed by your having to prove several times over that you can pay for treatment before anyone will even look at you. The message is often, "We're more concerned about getting paid and not being sued than we are about treating you." Then follows long periods of waiting: for doctors, for x-rays, for meals, for test results. Patients are often treated like numbers by technically competent, but insensitive, nurses, technicians, and doctors. The food is boring; rooms are usually sterile and unfriendly.

A commentary on the service provided in public schools is found in the fact that public school teachers are twice as likely to send their children to private schools as are parents who do not teach public school. Since teachers are often in the income bracket that can least afford private schools, what does their sacrifice to send their children to such schools tell us about the quality of the service they themselves—and the public schools overall—are providing?

The point of providing all these examples is that even industries and agencies with "captive customers" should be concerned with the level of service they provide. However, most are not.

Service is often perceived as being worse in the public sector than it is in the private sector. In 1979, the U.S. Office of Consumer Affairs (USOCA) published the results of studies of complaint-handling practices in 29 federal agencies, including the Postal Service, Veterans Administration, Federal Communications Commission, Securities and Exchange Commission, and the Departments of Interior, Justice, Labor, Transportation, and many more. At the same time, USOCA also studied consumer-complaint-handling practices in state and local governments and private volunteer agencies (referred to collectively as SLVs). Part of the study involved comparing complaint-handling practices in SLVs with those in businesses. TARP surveyed 643 private businesses representing a wide range of business sizes, product or service offerings, and price categories. The initial studies of government agencies and SLVs were repeated in 1986.

The studies revealed the following:

☐ Many consumers have difficulty gaining access to various agencies. Very few agencies have toll-free numbers, and complaint-handling is frequently handled by many different units within an agency. Consumers often don't know whether to contact a local office, a regional office, or a national office to voice their complaints. They're also unsure which government agency to contact for a specific problem. Therefore, consumers often get referred to several other agencies, which causes confusion and delays.

☐ The people least likely to complain are low-income, minority, handicapped, and elderly consumers. Especially in critical service areas (welfare, health, and utilities), fear of retribution discourages consumers in these groups from reporting the problems they encounter.

☐ Complaint-handling procedures, methods, and systems are frequently not coordinated within agencies. Basically, there is no overall system, efforts are often duplicated, and data is not shared among units. There is often little consistency in procedures for logging and classifying data within agencies. For example, in some agencies, people handling complaints in local offices have no means for communicating with their counterparts at headquarters. In effect, the left hand often doesn't know what the right hand is doing.

☐ Information gathered from consumers rarely finds its way to policymakers except on an informal, ad hoc basis.

☐ Very few agencies use surveys, audits, or other methods to gauge consumer satisfaction or identify areas needing improvement.

☐ Training for employees who handle consumer complaints is generally limited to written and/or oral communication skills. Only 53 percent of SLVs offer communications skills training to employees who handle customer complaints, as compared to 70 percent of private sector businesses.

☐ Only 39 percent of SLVs and 40 percent of private sector businesses report offering incentives to employees for providing good service to customers.

☐ Budgets for complaint-handling in SLVs are significantly lower than for complaint-handling in business.

☐ SLVs have fewer full-time people handling customer complaints than businesses do.

☐ Many SLVs handle more customer calls than businesses generally handle.

So the picture in many government and private agencies compared to that in the private sector is that public sector organizations handle the same number or a greater number of complaints, often with fewer people who are generally paid less. There are fewer toll-free numbers and less training. Some incentives for providing good service are offered in both the public and private sectors.

The image of public sector organizations—and most of their employees—is largely one of slow-moving indifference. Many give the impression that "We're already too busy with everybody else's problems to deal with yours right away" or "We'll have to study it and get approval from sixteen levels of people before we can give you an answer." Whether or not this picture is an accurate one isn't the issue. The issue is that many people *perceive* the public sector in this way. They *expect* slow, indifferent, incompetent service. That's the bad news. The good news is that, when service is seen as this bad, it doesn't take very much to exceed people's expectations and to provide what they perceive as above-average service.

SIMILARITIES BETWEEN PRIVATE AND PUBLIC SECTORS

Many of the problems and practices in the public sector are similar to those in the private sector. A few examples are included in this section.

The Atlanta metropolitan area includes six different counties. Due to local referendums, each county has a different sales tax. Some counties charge 4 percent, some 5 percent, some 6 percent. I needed to verify the sales tax for the county I live in, so I called the Dekalb County tax commissioner's office. The person who answered said, "I can't answer that. You'll have to call the sales tax number." She gave me the phone number.

I called the number. A woman answered, and I asked "Do you know what the sales tax is in this county?" She said, "I won't answer that. It's a conflict of interest. You'll have to call the sales tax division." Puzzled by her choice of words, I said, "Did you say you 'can't' or 'won't' answer my question?" She replied, "It's a conflict of interest."

A conflict of interest? Whose interest? I'm a taxpayer and I'm interested in learning what the sales tax is in my county. It's a matter of public record. What's the conflict?

I called the sales tax division. The line was busy for over 2 hours. When I did get through, it rang at least 15 times before anyone answered. Finally, a woman answered, and I asked how much the sales tax was in Dekalb County. She said, "I can't answer that. I'll have to connect you with an information officer." The information officer, at last, was able to answer my question.

Most of what happened in this situation is similar to what happens frequently in the private sector. The following factors account for the poor service:

1 The organization is highly departmentalized. Everyone has a specific job to do. Nobody's job seems to be helping customers (taxpayers) with questions.

2 The organization is so large (or complex) that even employees don't know who does what. The result is that customers have to make several phone calls to different departments just to find out whom to talk to about a certain issue.

3 Employees can only go by the book and cite the rules to customers. They are not trained or encouraged to think for themselves or bend the rules to help customers.

4 Employees are insensitive to customer needs and requests.

Here's another example:

Several years ago we were doing a lot of promotional mailings, so we bought a bulk-mail permit which entails an annual $60 fee. We also had thousands of envelopes printed with our bulk-mail number on them.

Our business took a different direction for a while, and we didn't do any bulk mailing for over a year. But we still paid the fee to keep our permit number current.

We received the renewal notice shown when it came time to pay our annual fee. Note the exceptionally poor quality of the notice—and the fact that it was not even straight on the page!

Eight days after we paid the fee, we received a notice telling us our permit number had been revoked because we hadn't used it for a year! It took 5 months, four letters, and over a dozen phone calls to get our $60 back.

The bulk mail center in Atlanta is 15 miles south of downtown, near the airport. The majority of private and public businesses in Atlanta are downtown or north of town, 30 to 40 miles from the airport. To start (or reopen) a bulk-mail account, customers must go to the bulk-mail center because it cannot be done at a regular post office or through the mail. (Isn't that ironic: You can't use the mail to open an account with the Postal Service!)

When using bulk mail, all letters must be sorted, bundled, bagged, and then delivered, along with the required form, to the bulk-mail center. The letters cannot be delivered to one of the local post offices, which would certainly be more convenient.

Our office manager, Brenda, went to the bulk-mail center to reopen our account. She

RENEWAL NOTICE FOR ANNUAL FEES

TYPE OF SERVICE	PERMIT NUMBER(S)	FEE AMOUNT	FEES PAID CURRENT YEAR	FEES DUE FOR UPCOMING YEAR
Business Reply Permit Fee(s)				
☞ Business Reply Accounting Fee(s)				
First-Class Presort Fee(s)		$60.00		
Third-Class Bulk Mailing Fee(s)		$50.00		*1989*
Special Fourth-Class Presort Fee(s)				
Merchandise Return Permit Fee(s)				

TOTAL AMOUNT ENCLOSED

Telephone Number where we can contact you if necessary

PERMIT # *3547*

Please indicate in the last column the services you will use next year. Total the fees and return this notice, with your check in the total amount, to the Postmaster (address shown on the reverse side of this notice). Make check payable to "U.S. Postal Service" or Postmaster.

Thank you for your business this past year, I look forward to meeting your postal needs as we move into the upcoming year.

(MAIL CHECK TO:)
FINANCE WINDOW M.P.O.
3900 CROWN ROAD
ATLANTA, GA 30304-9998

☞ Mailers who receive more than 1000 BRM pieces will achieve cost savings by paying the (optional) BRM Accounting Fee. The savings are 16 cents per piece.

Postmaster

PS Form 3621-A, Dec. 1987

learned that we could not keep our old permit number; we were assigned a new one. That meant we had to junk thousands of envelopes with our old number on them. Brenda explained this, but the clerk said those were the rules.

While she was at the bulk-mail center, Brenda talked to the clerk there about the procedures for sending out newsletters via bulk mail. (Up until then we had printed our old permit number on the newsletters. Since we had a new permit number, we were going to have to reprint our masthead.)

A few days later, Brenda noticed we were receiving mail with bulk-mail stamps instead of permit numbers. She called our local post office branch and learned she could buy the stamps there. The next day, she bought several hundred for a newsletter mailing we were doing. The clerk who sold them to her never asked about a permit number.

Our staff put bulk-mail stamps on over 300 newsletters and prepared them for delivery to the bulk-mail center. For mailings using bulk-mail stamps, the required form must be filled out differently than for mailings using permit numbers. Brenda called the bulk-mail center to find out how to do this, and the person who answered told her she needed a *different* permit number in order to use bulk-mail stamps!

We had already stamped all the newsletters, but the post office wouldn't accept them without the proper permit number. And you can only get these permits at the bulk mail center—in person. It took another 78-mile trip and another 3 hours to get the second permit.

This is an example of a service agency that appears to be located for the agency's convenience, not the customer's. And it is very difficult to do business with this agency. Customers must come to the agency, and it's time-consuming to go there. Everything must be done in person. Clerks provide incomplete information (in this example, only what was asked, instead of anything that could help the customer do more business). Bulk-mail procedures are complicated, and we often have questions about what to do and how to do it. Getting information or assistance is like pulling teeth. Every time Brenda deals with those people at the bulk-mail center, she says, "I hate dealing with them. They make me feel like such an idiot."

And another example:

A few years ago, Kay and I made a contribution to a local public television station during one of its subscription drives. According to the announcements, we were to receive a monthly program listing all the programs to be aired; however, we never received anything, not even a letter welcoming us as new subscribers or thanking us for subscribing. The first piece of mail we received from the station came 9 months later; it was a letter asking for more money. We have still never received a "thank you," and no one has ever asked us how we liked their programs. We stopped contributing to that station.

The sad part is that this station spent a lot of time and effort during its membership drive to get us as contributors, and then it did nothing to keep us. It really does cost much more to get new customers (or contributors) than it does to keep the ones you have.

WHY SERVICE IS SO POOR IN THE PUBLIC SECTOR

The reasons I hear most often concerning why service is so poor in the public sector are as follows:

1 Lack of competition and profit motive
2 Few rewards for risk-taking or successes; negative consequences for failures
3 Excessive size and bureaucracy
4 Rigid adherence to rules and regulations
5 Inability to hire and fire; low pay scales

Each of these reasons is expanded on below.

1. Lack of competition and profit motive

The argument here is that there's no reason for most public sector employees to provide good service, because there's no profit incentive and often no threat of competition. If you get poor service from the post office or the Motor Vehicles Department of the Veterans Administration, where else can you go for the services they offer?

Without the fear of bankruptcy, damaged reputation, competition, loss of market share, or other factors to threaten their continued existence, there's very little to influence the level of service provided in most agencies—or so the argument goes.

2. Too few rewards for risk-taking or successes, and too much punishment for errors or failures

The norm appears to be: "Do only what's expected, whatever is the minimum required." There's no incentive or reason to do more than what's expected or to do things differently. Doing so often results in negative consequences. Changing things or being noticed are often not part of the culture. Improving productivity or cutting costs doesn't mean much at salary reviews if people are locked into civil service raises. Bright-eyed, energetic, idealistic newcomers quickly learn the culture and conform to the norm. Of course, there are a few champions, but most employees realize it's easier and better for their careers if they go along with the norm rather than rock the boat.

Taking more risks implies more failures. Many public sector organizations and employees believe that their public trust prevents them from trying anything new or different because it might not work out. And many employees are more concerned with covering their rears if things go wrong than with trying anything new.

3. Excessive size and bureaucracy

The larger and more complex the organization, the worse the service. As in the private sector, the more levels between the "customer" and the executives, the slower and more impersonal the service, and the more room for errors. Government agencies are notorious for their size and their bureaucratic procedures. Because of politics, turf-guarding, multilevel reviews, numerous revisions, and complicated approval processes, decisions take longer. Most things must be done in triplicate and require multiple signatures.

And change comes slowly in large organizations. For example, in the highly regulated, conservative telephone industry, there have been a lot of changes in the past several years. A Southern Bell executive explained that, in the past, employees were much stricter about following the procedures book. For example, if a customer asked a craftsperson to drill a hole in a wall or pillar during an installation or repair call, procedures wouldn't allow it. However, now that the company emphasizes customer satisfacion, employees are able to honor such a request if it isn't dangerous or illegal. Southern Bell managers say employees initially resisted this more service-oriented approach because they were afraid they might get poor ratings from quality inspectors. After management repeatedly explained the importance of customer satisfaction, employees eventually began to see that taking risks wouldn't hurt their ratings.

In the past, Southern Bell procedures also called for service trucks to be returned to the service centers every evening. Now service people take their trucks home at night, and instead of going to the service center in the morning, they go directly to their first call. As a result, service people are able to complete more service calls per person, and the company closed several service centers. Interestingly, supervisors resisted this plan at first because they felt they wouldn't have training or motivation time with their employees. Since supervisors must now visit their employees at jobsites, they actually spend *more* time with them than they had in the past.

4. Rigid adherence to rules and regulations

The more employees are required to follow written policies, rules, and regulations, the less people are required to think for themselves. Government and regulated businesses tend to have more rules and policy manuals than other organizations have.

Overreliance on rules and policy manuals is a by-product of bigness. It communicates, "We're so big (or things are so complicated) that we can't be everywhere at once to be sure things are being done right. And we can't trust that employees will make intelligent, informed decisions in the best interests of the customer and the organization, so we don't want them to try. We just want them to follow the rules. And if you're ever in doubt, don't think—ask your supervisor."

In *Human Resource Executive*, Sal Vittolino wrote about Constance Horner, former director of the U.S. Office of Personnel Management (OPM). OPM is the agency responsible for over 2 million federal employees. Horner repeatedly called for "a major reform of the overly rigid system of rules and regulations that governs federal personnel, so that public employees can see a job that needs to be done and do it—without the delays and frustration and excessive regulation of their activity."

Horner regularly criticized supervisors for their lack of ability to think for themselves. For example, federal managers were asked to provide "a reasonable amount of leave for employees who arrive late" during snowstorms. One senior-level manager called Horner to ask for a definition of "reasonable amount." The executive wanted to know if that meant 10:00, 11:00, noon, or some other time. When Horner told him to use his own judgment on what constituted "reasonable amount," the manager became upset and demanded that Horner publish official guidelines on "reasonable amounts." Horner says that another manager recommended that the OPM establish criteria for evaluating snowstorms.

5. Inability to hire and fire; low pay scales

Federal and state government agencies are often required to accept civil service employees and can only pay them according to their pay grades. The agencies have difficulty firing such employees. Both government and nonprofit organizations typically pay less than do organizations in the private sector. Many critics say that they can't get good people for the money they pay and that they're often stuck with people they'd like to get rid of.

All of this combines to create a culture in which employees, especially those who have most frequent contact with "customers," are low-paid, poorly trained, and rule-bound. They are encouraged not to rock the boat or try new things, are rarely rewarded for exceptional service, see little chance for rapid advancement or money, and are frequently frustrated by excessive delays and approval cycles. They often feel like cogs in a massive machine—unnoticed, unappreciated, and unchallenged.

Since customer relations mirrors employee relations, it's no wonder many public sector organizations provide such poor service. And both customers and employees have come to expect it. In the private sector, many service-oriented oranizations help shape customers' expectations of good service. Companies like IBM, Federal Express, Maytag, 3M, and others do this by continuously telling customers and potential customers what they can expect and how good their service is. They also deliver what they promise.

Most government agencies, utilities, and nonprofit organizations don't do this. They do nothing to remind customers about their service or to change customers' expectations about service. They often fail to deliver what they promise. As a result, customers don't think about what these organizations do well; they only think about what they *don't* do—or how they mess things up. Customers come to expect slow, inept, uncaring service. The expression "Close enough for government work" captures these feelings.

One exception that comes to mind is United Way. The agency's advertising slogan, "Thanks to you, it works for all of us," continually reminds us how United Way helps people. United Way shows success stories of children, senior citizens, disabled persons, flood victims, and others who have benefited from donations.

HOW TO IMPROVE SERVICE IN THE PUBLIC SECTOR

Tom Peters was once asked how to motivate government employees. His reply was this:

> There are at least as many excellent public-sector organizations as private-sector operations. . . . The key is talking about "people," not "government employees." Almost anybody will rise to the occasion if given exciting and visionary goals, fair performance measures (developed in part by employees themselves), and well delineated responsibilities that can be tied to the "customer's" satisfaction. "Ownership" and self-esteem are the heart of the matter. As well, the most enlightened public-sector agencies are beginning to use incentive pay and rely almost exclusively on merit rather than [across-the-board pay increases]."

In *At America's Service*, Karl Albrecht said the first step to government organizations becoming more service-oriented is for someone in charge to care. Beyond that, if you work in a government organization and you want your organization to change, you must make a commitment and be willing to stick your neck out. To make a difference, you must be willing to buck decades of entrenched bureaucracy and the established culture. You must be willing to be unpopular in the eyes of many government employees who are threatened by changes in the organization.

Such change will require 10 times the skills, tenacity, vision, and commitment required of senior managers in the private sector, because you will not only be trying to *stop* the flow but also to *reverse* it. I liken it to standing in the middle of a railroad track with a slow-moving freight train coming at you. Your mission is to single-handedly stop the train and then push it backward—to change its direction *and* get it moving in the opposite direction faster than it was going to start with. As one state government manager said, "It's not a task for the faint-hearted!"

I agree. It's quite a challenge. And it's a task not likely to be completed during an individual's tenure. No wonder so few are willing to tackle it. But don't be discouraged by the size of the task. It *can* be done. So how does one person stop, and then reverse the direction, of a train? Certainly not empty-handed or alone. You'll need tools, equipment, resources, leverage, and other people. And the best way is to put *another* train on the track, going in the opposite direction!

The next several pages give suggestions for some specific things that can be done to improve service in public sector organizations. You'll notice that many of them are similar to the ideas presented in Part Four for private sector organizations.

Create a shift in people's perceptions and beliefs

Nothing will happen without this shift. You must begin the never-ending process of changing what employees think about. As long as people think "Why bother?" or "I'm just a cog in this huge machine," or "We can't do anything about it—*they're* the problem," or "So what, where else can they go, anyway?" nothing will change. When employees begin to believe, "I can make a difference," and "I *can* do something about it," and "They have to deal with us, so I'm going to do the best I can," service will improve.

Employees must believe, "I'm it. I'm responsible for the service, quality, and response time this organization provides. Sure there are other people here, but I'm personally responsible for making sure our customers get the best possible service I can provide." This thinking must start with top-level managers. If they don't believe it, say it, and prove it, no one else will either.

Employees must shift their focus from just doing their jobs to satisfying their customers. They must see that they *do* have customers—people (or other departments) who pay for their services. Especially in government agencies, employees must begin to think about taxpayers, homeowners, ambulance users, road users, school users, motor vehicle owners, and park users as their customers. These "customers" pay for these services (and agency employees' salaries). Shifting employee focus means shifting employee beliefs, language, and activities from thinking about "our" streets, parks, and ambulances to thinking about "your" streets, parks, and ambulances. In other organizations, it means thinking about who pays for all the facilities, supplies, and services—that is, the customers.

Establish a service vision

Just as in the private sector, public sector employees need to know what's possible, what exceptional service should look like, and what's expected. They need a unifying concept of service as a frame of reference. Without this vision, they're likely to see the purpose of their jobs as doing some work, following some rules, or doing some "things," instead of meeting needs.

Set standards

Establish, or redefine, your standards for providing your services. Set them high. Seek and use employee input concerning service standards such as response time, waiting time, routing telephone calls, and other key areas. Once standards have been set, expect people to meet them.

Run the organization like a business

The most successful, productive, and profitable public sector agencies, especially in government, recognize that they have products, customers, and costs. They realize that they *do* have competition and that they must make a profit.

Make no mistake—there *is* competition in the public sector. It just depends on how you define competition. People in government agencies, nonprofits, and similar organizations must begin to look at competition differently.

Every organization competes. Public sector organizations compete with the private sector *and* other public sector organizations for talented, competent employees. Every organization competes for money, facilities, and other resources. Every organization competes for technology. Even within the state and federal government, agencies compete for budget dollars, people, the governor's attention, favorable votes on relevant legislation, public opinion, and so on.

Many state and federal agencies also compete directly with private enterprise. For example:

- [ ] In several states, the state is in the alcoholic beverage business, competing with private distributors and retailers.
- [ ] In Utah, the state prison system makes and sells office furniture. The prison sold $6.5 million of furniture in 1987, competing with private enterprise.
- [ ] In many states, prison labor also competes with private enterprise by making license plates and traffic signs and providing printing services.

One of the biggest mistakes government agencies make is thinking they have no competition—that customers can't go elsewhere. When customers (citizens) no longer get the services they expect for the price they're paying, they *will* go elsewhere, if at all possible:

☐ Trash collection and sanitation has been a municipal service for years in many communities. It has also provided revenues. Many communities have voted the municipalities out of this service and now pay for private companies to handle it.

☐ Some municipal transit authorities contract out maintenance, landscaping, and other functions previously performed only by city or county employees.

☐ At one time, prison management was exclusively the purview of state and federal governments. Several states now hire prison-management firms.

☐ The U.S. Postal Service now competes with a host of overnight delivery companies, crosstown couriers, and fax machines to get letters and packages to their destinations faster.

☐ Many municipalities are no longer in the electric, gas, or water business. Private concerns now provide these services. In many communities, citizens have formed their own companies to provide electric power, thereby taking revenues from unresponsive utility companies.

☐ Many nonprofit organizations, associations, and fraternal organizations pay private firms to send dues notices, maintain mailing lists, print and mail their magazines or newsletters, and handle fund raising.

No one is immune. Everyone has competition. Even if you don't today, you will in the future. For example:

☐ Years ago, IBM had very little competition for its desktop personal computers. Then Apple developed a new technology to compete, and Compaq (and a host of others) created IBM clones.

☐ Twenty-five years ago, American car manufacturers had little foreign competition. Today, the Japanese and Germans dominate the industry, and practically every civilized nation in the world produces cars.

☐ Banks always thought they were the only source for financial services. Since insurance companies, investment companies, venture capitalists, Sears, American Express, and others have entered the financial services field, many banks have closed their doors, and others are scrambling to save assets.

☐ Once a virtual monopoly, AT&T now has only 70 percent of the long-distance market. Even before the divestiture, Ma Bell had competition from MCI, GTE, Contel, ITT, United, and other companies.

☐ Many government agencies or departments exist primarily to serve other agencies. Other departments or agencies are their only customers. Others have both internal and external customers. They think they have no competition, but their "customers" can and do go outside to purchase equipment, products, and services.

☐ On a lighter note: Several years ago, I was discussing recession-proof businesses with some associates. I jokingly suggested the toilet paper business. No matter what happened to the economy, I argued, people would still eat and would therefore always need toilet paper. That's not true anymore. A Japanese company now makes an electric toilet that "wipes" users with warm water, blows them dry, and then perfumes them. No toilet paper!

In addition to competition, there is also a profit motive in the public sector. Government agencies and nonprofits incur costs to provide their products or services to customers or to other departments or agencies, but many have just never looked at the situation in that way. There are costs involved in collecting taxes, issuing driver's licenses, delivering mail, administering parks, and maintaining streets. Taxpayers, consumer groups, and regulatory bodies are more and more conscious of where tax dollars go and are less tolerant of waste and mismanagement.

Government agencies that continually lose money may be reorganized or eliminated. There's always the threat of elimination. No person or department is indispensable. The more you can *demonstrate* your contribution to the organization, the more likely you are to keep you job. This requires thinking like a businessperson.

In nonprofit organizations, customers, subscribers, and dues-paying members are increasingly more concerned about where their money goes, and they want to know what they're getting for their money. In many cases, they *do* have choices. They can choose not to renew their membership, and they can halt or reduce the amount of their financial support.

Here are some things to consider if you wish to run your public sector organization more like a business:

- ☐ Identify your customers: Whom do you serve?
- ☐ Learn what your customers expect: What do they want?
- ☐ Define your products: What do you provide?
- ☐ What benefits do customers get from you?
- ☐ What does it cost you to provide your products or services?
- ☐ What's your profit margin? Do you at least break even? Do you (or can you) improve your profits?
- ☐ Define your competition: Who else can or does provide what you do? What do they do better and worse than you? Why should customers do business with you? What alternatives do they have?
- ☐ How are you held accountable? Whom must you answer to?
- ☐ How will your service be measured?
- ☐ Define your service cycles: How do internal or external customers interact with your organization? What are the steps in your service cycle?
- ☐ What are the possible—or actual—problems at each step in the cycle? How can these be improved?

☐ Survey your customers: What do they expect? How well do they think you're providing what they expect? What can you improve?

☐ Recognize your moments of truth: Recognize that every contact with any aspect of your agency communicates something to your customers and helps shape their impressions of you, your agency, and the service you provide. Every contact people have with road crews, motor vehicle clerks, water department clerks, trash collectors, housing officials, hospital workers, or food stamp employees is a moment of truth. So is correspondence.

Require government agencies to be competitive

All government agencies who get services from other agencies should be required to seek the best providers in terms of price *and* service. Agency funding should be cut and agencies should be required to "buy" services from the best suppliers, based on both price and service. If an agency can get better quality, delivery time, support, or other service from the private sector, it should be required to do so. The government agency or department providing that service should lose the budget funds it was "earning" for providing that service. If that agency or department must close down because its services are no longer needed, or if it's not profitable because private organizations are providing the service better, faster, or cheaper, then so be it.

Put the right people in key positions, especially in customer-contact positions

Place people according to their skills and ability to deal with the public rather than according to longevity or seniority.

Give people the responsibility for providing good service

Believe in employees as a source of ideas: Ask them to become involved in finding better ways to do things, eliminating bureaucracy, and eliminating needless rules.

Make people responsible for their business. Hold them accountable for the bottom line, for quality, for on-time delivery, for responsiveness, and for timelines of their project, area, or operation—no matter how large or small. Build ownership in what they do. Eliminate scapegoating: do not allow employees to blame other people, departments, the system, the computer, or anything else for not providing service, for delays, or for other problems.

Give people the freedom to do their jobs

Reduce or eliminate policies, regulations, rules, and practices that get in the way of accomplishing the organization's mission. Establish a simple, fast way to eliminate needless policies or practices.

Create quality-service teams and task forces to generate ways to improve service, identify obstacles to doing jobs, and improve operations. Encourage teams, task forces, and individual employees to tear down departmental barriers and look at what needs to be done rather than who does it.

Reduce the number of administrative levels. Eliminate or reduce the size of agencies or departments. Eliminate duplicate functions. Break down departmental barriers. Streamline.

Simplify forms and procedures for customers and provide alternatives for people who have difficulty filling out the forms. Use students, retired or disabled people, or housewives to work part-time as readers or writers to assist people who cannot read or fill out forms.

Encourage people to think for themselves

Encourage people to figure things out and make decisions. Reduce or eliminate manuals. Reduce the number of rules and other practices that eliminate the need for people to think.

Change the role of the supervisors

Shift the focus of supervisors from policing to empowering. Encourage supervisors to get out of their offices and practice "MBWA" (Management by Walking Around). Encourage managers to "get their hands dirty" by working on the front lines and talking to customers.

Provide training, especially for managers

Give them business skills to help them think more like private sector managers. Teach them how to cut costs and build profits without sacrificing quality or service. Provide skills in teamwork and communications. Teach decision making, problem solving, and conflict resolution. Help managers become better risk-takers by building self-esteem and confidence.

Encourage and reward risk taking

Reward new ideas, initiative, and good efforts, even if they don't always work out. This will send the message that it's OK to try new things. Celebrate all wins and successes. Recognize and reward even small accomplishments. Look for milestones along the way to larger objectives. Celebrate these as they are reached. (This encouragement is not a license for incompetence or irresponsible ideas or actions but rather a way to encourage creativity and innovation.)

Change the reward system

If service is really an important component for government agencies, define it and hold managers and individuals accountable for it. Reward service, not just productivity. Make service part of performance review process.

Tie customer service ratings to departmental reviews and to individual performance ratings. Regularly survey customers—internal and external—for service ratings. Rank customer satisfaction and service levels for each unit or department on a scale of 0–100.

Make customer satisfaction part of the budget process. Decide what percent of budget allocations are determined by service ratings. For example, if service ratings account for 50 percent of a budget allocation and a department's ratings for the current year only ranked 50 on a 0–100 scale, the department's budget could be cut 25 percent for the next year (50 percent of 50 percent). This could mean some departments might have to cut back on employees, equipment, travel, or other items, and it wouldn't take long for the message to get around that *service matters*. People are much more likely to become interested in what their department can do to provide better service if their budgets are at stake.

Of course, you may have to temper this approach somewhat to avoid cutting back critical resources so far that service to the customer suffers. You can decide how much weight you want to give customer satisfaction and service levels in the budgeting process. You can also start doing all the other things private sector organizations do: customer surveys to determine needs, report cards, service circles, flattening the pyramid, and so on.

Individual employee performance rating and annual pay should also be largely determined by service. Make customer satisfaction a sizable portion of the employee performance review process. Eliminate across-the-board pay increases. Pay for performance instead, and define "service" performance as "customer satisfaction." Determine who the internal and external customers of each employee are and determine what's important to these customers. Survey customers prior to each employee's performance review.

Reward the behavior you want. Provide incentives and other rewards to people who reduce errors, reduce costs, increase productivity, and otherwise provide excellent service.

In addition to compensation, use other means of reward and recognition. Pins, plaques, group meetings, certificates, contest, awards presentations, and other methods described in Part Four are relatively inexpensive and quite effective.

Change the culture

Talk about customers and service. Retell stories of people who went out of their way for customers. Indoctrinate new hires with a service attitude. Tell customers what they can expect from you. Deliver on your promises. Eliminate negatives: Shift from "No, we can't," "It's against our policy," and "There's nothing I can do," to "No problem," "What we *can* do is this," "Here's what I *can* do."

Show employees you care about them

As I have stressed throughout this book, customer relations mirror employee relations. Employees are not likely to show customers they care unless they feel their organization cares about them. Keep employees informed. Give them both the good news and the bad news about budgets, new projects, layoffs, productivity, and anything else *they* think they need to know to accomplish their mission.

Show customers you care about them

Personalize service. Include the name of a responsible person on all documents, correspondence, and forms so customers know whom to contact. Reduce waiting times. Honor commitments, deadlines, and appointments. Identify employees who speak second languages and position them to help second-language customers.

Change customer expectations

Toot your own horn. Remind customers what you've done for them lately, how efficient you are, how much you appreciate them. Share wins, success stories, and accomplishments with them. If your association successfully lobbied for a bill that saves members money, let them know. If you cut spending by 26 percent without hurting productivity or reducing your services, let them know. Tell customers if you have special services for elderly, disabled, or second-language customers.

EXAMPLES OF WHAT IS BEING DONE

Below are some examples of things being done by government agencies, regulated business, nonprofits, municipalities, and schools to become more customer-conscious and improve their services.

The Postal Service

Most postal services are available only if you go to the post office. In an effort to be more service-oriented and to compete with delivery services that pick up and deliver to customer locations, the Charlotte, North Carolina, Postal Service developed a mobile cart that goes to office buildings. Customers can buy stamps, weigh packages, set postage meters, and drop off outgoing mail.

The Internal Revenue Service

Even the much-maligned IRS is beginning to shift its focus. The IRS is attempting to change its approach from collecting revenues to serving customers. The current thinking is that citizens deserve the same kind of service from the public sector that they expect from the private sector. And the IRS now believes that it is more cost-effective to help taxpayers comply with tax regulations and procedures than it is to pursue offenders. As a result, less of the IRS budget now goes for enforcement and more goes into taxpayer services. Training has been expanded and improved. Quality-improvement teams abound. A quality newsletter, congratulatory letters, and service certificates all help call attention to improved service.

Banking

First Union Bank in Atlanta, Georgia, offers a service guarantee. If customers aren't satisfied with the way they're treated, First Union refunds the service charges. First Union also uses mystery shoppers to evaluate employee service. Employees and branches with the highest scores are rewarded with cash and special events.

Hibernia Bank in San Francisco spends twice the industry average to train its new and existing employees. The training emphasizes basic things like greeting all customers by name, answering phones by the third ring, not keeping customers on hold for more than 20 seconds, and finding ways to say "yes" instead of "no." Tellers are also urged to pay close attention to customer comments and situations in order to sell other, bank services. Hibernia generates $100,000 more in revenue per employee each year than the industry average.

Traditional banks require that you bank in person or by mail. But many elderly people can't get to the bank or can't use the mail services for depositing cash or cashing checks. Southern Federal Savings and Loan in Atlanta, Georgia, has equipped three special vans to be mobile banks. The vans go to retirement communities so senior citizens can do their routine banking transactions within walking distance of their homes. The mobile bank service has also gained many new customers for the bank and has improved the bank's assets.

University National Bank in Palo Alto, California, breaks all the rules for providing service. Tellers know most customers by name. The bank has vans that pick up deposits from customers at no charge. There are rarely lines, and if there are more than a few people in line, an executive will come over to help the tellers. University National also provides an office and adding machines for customers to use, postage stamps at cost, free parking, free shoeshines, and balloons for kids. If there's an overdraft, employees assume it was an inadvertent error and go out of their way to notify the customer and *not* charge a fee. The bank will open any time a customer needs it, even late at night and on short notice. And all customers get their statements by the first of the month. University National's return on assets is about 75 percent higher than the California average.

Municipal government

The municipal government of Montgomery County, Ohio, has shifted its focus to become a more service-oriented government. It began by realizing that, although its citizens had nowhere else to go for many services, they were still entitled to quality service. Employees of Montgomery County committed themselves to providing the best service possible and to changing citizen's perceptions of county government services and employees.

County agencies began by defining their "customers" as voters, residents, patients, employers, etc. They also surveyed customer groups to learn how customers felt about the services they were getting. As a result, excessive waiting time in social service agencies was reduced; all county employees readily tell customers their names in interviews and telephone conversations; human services staffers are now responsible for all aspects of a client's needs; and if a client needs information from another agency, didn't receive a check, or is missing paperwork, the caseworker is responsible for taking care of the problem. In all agencies, customer satisfaction is now as important as the number of cases handled or orders processed. Customer satisfaction is measured regularly. Employee groups meet regularly to find ways to make their system more "user-friendly."

Hospitals

Piedmont Hospital in Atlanta, Georgia, is bringing the hospital to its patients with several walk-in clinics. One is downtown in the heart of the business district. The clinic handles minor emergencies and simple outpatient surgical procedures. It opens early and stays open late so office workers can stop in before or after work. And it will even send a taxi to pick people up.

At some hospitals, patients are first taken to their rooms and made comfortable. Then an admissions staffer comes to the room to get the necessary information. Boston's Beth Israel Hospital (and others) offers patients attractive, well-decorated rooms and visiting areas, and choices in amenities and food service. More important, it offers concern for patients as people. Nurses, staffers, and other employees have shifted their focus from treating heart attacks, burn cases, and pregnancies to treating *people* who have certain medical needs.

Public schools

And at least one public school official has started to preach a message to school students about accepting responsibility for improving conditions in the schools. Prompted by the killing of a high school girl on the way home from a school dance, a group of parents, students, and teachers met with Atlanta's former school superintendent, J. Jerome Harris, to ask what he was going to do about the troublemakers, weapons, violence, drugs, outdated textbooks, lack of guidance counselors, and related issues in Atlanta's schools.

Harris told the group: "You're asking me what *I'm* going to do about it, but you're the ones who know which students have weapons and drugs at school. So I should be asking you, what are *you* going to do about it?" He went on to say that students are usually the first to know when other students bring a gun to school, and they should tell school officials so no one gets hurt. He urged students to confront their principals about outdated textbooks, too-strict dress codes, and other issues that bother them. He also told students to take the initiative to ensure they know which classes they need in order to graduate, to learn about financial assistance, and to seek out adults who can help them with personal problems.

At another time, speaking about what he envisions for Atlanta's schools, Harris seemed to capture the idea that, even in public schools that cater largely to inner-city minorities, the trick is to find out what your "customers" want or need and give it to them, rather than making them adapt to what you provide. Harris talked about kids who have trouble learning in schools:

> [T]his is the only place they seem to have problems learning. They certainly learn the rap songs, which means they can memorize. So you tell me why they can't learn the Constitution. They learn how to shoot pool, which is a math kind of thing. They learn to shoot dice, which is a math kind of thing. You tell me why they can't learn.
> What I'm saying is, his style of learning is different from the style of teaching we have. We have an obligation to modify our style, since the kid is not going to modify his. . . . The kids know how to learn in more ways than we know how to teach.

Nonprofit organizations

Kay and I support several charitable organizations. Some send us a preprinted postcard acknowledging our contributions. Others send personalized, appreciative letters acknowledging every contribution, regardless of the amount. We get personal, effusive letters from the Humane Society, individually signed by the executive director. We also get personalized letters from the head of the Liberal Arts fund at Penn State University, as well as periodic reports telling us how the money in the fund is being used.

The court system

A judge in Milwaukee's county court system listened to what jurors had been telling him for over 30 years on the bench and changed his courtroom procedures as a result. Judge Robert Landry learned that jurors frequently have questions they'd like to ask witnesses—for example, issues not covered during the trial or things the jurors are unclear about. Judge Landry developed and uses a procedure for allowing jurors to get the information they need.

I had personal experience with the court system when I was called for jury duty not long ago. Because the law requires prospective jurors to appear when summoned, the courts could easily take the approach that people *have* to be here, so they don't have to go out of their way to accommodate the jurors. I suppose it's like that in some courts, but it wasn't like that in Dekalb County, Georgia.

I expected a cold, formal, mechanical process. Other prospective jurors I spoke with that day expected the same thing and told me they were also unfamiliar with the court system, apprehensive about what would happen during the process, nervous about the kinds of questions they'd be asked by attorneys, uncertain as to how long they'd be away from home or work, and anxious about actually serving on a jury.

From the outset, the chief clerk, Whit Smith, tried to put the approximately 100 people assembled at ease. He showed a recently produced videotape that explained how the court system works and introduced the judges; then he explained what we could expect, where we'd be going, and what we'd be doing. Unlike many government (and other) employees who do the same thing every day, Whit Smith did his job with humor, concern, and sincerity.

The jury panel I was with went to Judge Mathew Robins' courtroom. Throughout the day, Judge Robins explained to the plaintiff, defendant, and jurors what would occur and repeatedly asked if we had any questions. [He was interested in our reaction to the new videotape and asked for our suggestions to improve it.] While the attorneys were selecting the jury, Judge Robins again solicited our questions and suggestions about the court system.

After the jury had been selected and seated, Judge Robins sincerely thanked us and emphasized how important it was that we were willing to take part in the process. Several days later, each prospective juror received a personal letter from Judge Robins. The Judge thanked us again for our time and once more asked for suggestions about how to improve the system or make the process more pleasant for future jurors.

Now that you have read about improving service in government agencies, regulated industries, and nonprofit organizations, be sure to go back to the "Putting Ideas into Action" section of Part Four to incorporate any new ideas you have discovered into your Action Plan—or to draw up your Action Plan, if you haven't started it yet.

PART SEVEN

PROVIDING SERVICE DURING AND AFTER A REORGANIZATION

Mergers, acquisitions, takeovers, reorganizations, and downsizings are becoming a common part of business life. By their very nature, these reorganizations are fraught with changes. In fact, they're *supposed* to create changes. Company names, job titles, locations, products, procedures, staffing, management styles, financing, and many other aspects can change.

This part of the book is not about how to deal with business reorganizations. Others have written on this subject. However, the effect of these reorganizations on service deserves more attention than it gets, and that is our subject here.

Bob Hassmiller is the director of education for the Club Managers Association of America (CMAA). One of his responsibilities is to plan and manage educational sessions at his association's annual conference and at various national and state meetings. As corporate and association meeting planners know, planning a major meeting or convention requires extensive and ongoing contact between the meeting planner (and staff) and the hotel to coordinate sleeping-room assignments, meeting-room setup, meals, audiovisual requirements, registration, budgeting, and a thousand other details.

Bob told us about a hotel CMAA had booked for a conference. After the meeting had been booked, there were details to work out and questions to be answered. Bob says his staff was unable to reach anyone from the hotel for months. The people they needed to reach—sales managers, banquet managers, catering managers—were never there and never returned phone calls. Bob says he finally called the hotel personally and demanded to speak to the general manager. When given the runaround again, he explained that his group had a major meeting planned there and if he didn't get to speak to the general manager immediately he was going to move the meeting to another hotel.

Only then did Bob learn that the hotel had been bought and had all new management. All the people the CMAA staff had been dealing with were gone. The new managers didn't know Bob and had incomplete records on the details of their meeting. The result was that the CMAA staff practically had to start from scratch to plan the meeting—again—with the hotel. During the buyout, the customer fell between the cracks.

Similar situations happen in practically every industry. A recent *Fortune* magazine article examined "What Ails Retailing." Author Susan Caminiti observes, "Mergers and buyouts are widening the gulf between merchant and customer. Financiers are now in charge at many of the huge retailing empires, and they are running their stores to generate the maximum cash flow to service the mountainous debts these deals leave behind." Caminiti also describes the effect on customers: "As a result of megamergers, decision-making often gets pushed up the hierarchy, and the people closest to the customer no longer have the authority to do the buying." She quotes a national sales manager for a major manufacturer of jeans: "The shots are being called by someone who is much more removed from the customer." And Ira Quint, CEO of Lane Bryant, a division of The Limited, notes that managers in some stores today "know how to read computer printouts but not how to walk on the floor and see what's going on."

Although many of the changes that occur during a major reorganization are *internal*, they also affect customers. Customers and employees must deal with the new name or location; learn new names, phone numbers, policies, and procedures; and fill out new forms. There may be clashes in cultures of the merged organizations; loss of friends if people were transferred or let go; new bosses; and new internal policies, procedures, forms, people, and management styles. Customers are rarely informed about these changes or even realize they're occurring.

Many organizations use these changes as excuses for lack of service during a reorganization: "We couldn't get your order out on time because of the merger. They're trying to keep our inventory levels down until all this is finalized"; or "I tried to get it to you, but the managers they brought over from the other company don't know what they're doing."

Enormous amounts of additional physical, intellectual, and emotional energy are required to deal with any major change (merger, acquisition, buyout, reorganization, downsizing) in an organization. People are frequently on overload for weeks or months. When so much energy is directed to internal changes, processes, and procedures, there's very little left over for customers.

However, customers may actually need even more nurturing during these changes. They may be wondering, "Will this company still take care of me the way it used to? How will things be different?" Your competition may be spreading misinformation about your ability to meet your customers' needs. Other organizations—suppliers, shopping malls, retailers, banks, community organizations your organization supported, and others who depend on income from your organization or your employees—may also be concerned about their future.

It's important during these hectic, uncertain times to pay special attention to customers. Even during a reorganization, customer relations mirror employee relations. If employees feel they're being kept in the dark, are worried about the future of their organization or their jobs, or feel they're being ripped off, customers will suffer.

Below are some suggestions for handling both customers and employees during and after a major reorganization.

1 Look at what will be required of your customer-contact people during and after the reorganization. Quickly determine what skills, background, knowledge, experience, temperament, or other characteristics are most needed now and after the merger. You may need different people with different

skills to handle customers during times of rapid change, compared to the people and skills you'll need later when the dust settles.

2 Make fair and compassionate asessments of all your employees. In a merger situation, seek ways to identify the employees in both companies who have the skills and background you're seeking. Strive to mix and balance people from both companies in customer-contact positions. Remember, they're going to be talking to customers and prospects of *both* companies.

3 Keep employees informed. Overcommunicate. When you're sure you've done enough to keep people informed of changes in products, personnel, policies, or anything else, do more—especially for people in constant contact with your customers. Customer-contact people need to feel they know what's going on so they can talk intelligently about your organization and its ability to meet customer needs. There's nothing worse than frontline people getting news about your organization from your customers instead of from you.

4 Reassure people frequently. Major changes and reorganizations create high levels of uncertainty, stress, and anxiety. People need high touch and lots of attention. Letters, memos, and newsletters are important, but don't rely too heavily on them. Employees and customers want to see and hear firsthand what's happening. Get executives out of their offices and executive meetings to talk with employees and answer their questions. Have them talk with major customers, too. Hold frequent meetings at all levels and at all locations to keep people informed, answer questions, and gauge reactions.

5 Be honest. Even if it's painful, it's better to tell employees and customers what to expect than try to paint a rosy picture that is misleading. Don't make promises you can't keep.

6 Keep customers and suppliers informed. Give them as much notice as possible about changes in management, location, mailing address, procedures, ordering processes, delivery dates, payment terms, and anything else that affects them. Create a way for them to ask questions, perhaps by setting up a special toll-free answer line.

7 In times of major change, it's easy for rumors to get started and spread quickly. Your frontline people can be a major factor in keeping these in check and correcting misinformation. When customers say, "I've heard you're going to be relocating to Kansas," or "Now that you've merged with XYZ Corporation, are you going to be. . . ," your employees can provide accurate information. But that means you have to be sure employees get it from you.

8 Recognize that adjusting to change is a slow process. Don't let up after a few weeks or months. It often takes a year or more *after* a major change or reorganization to finalize new policies, procedures, systems, and so on. And it may take even longer for some customers and employees to accept the changes, adopt them, and develop new comfort zones. Stress and anxiety can remain high. There are usually many questions to answer. In an effort to get along and be team players, many people keep their anxiety, concerns, and questions to themselves. As time goes on, just because change-related stress is not as obvious as it was before doesn't mean it's not there.

9 Handle outplacements fairly and compassionately. Customer treatment mirrors employee treatment. Granted there are often tough decisions involved in mergers, acquisitions, and downsizings. Some employees never do make the transition to the new culture or way of doing things. The way you treat the people who leave affects those who stay.

10 To the extent possible, keep terminations, transfers, or demotions upbeat. Provide people with alternatives. Provide career counseling. Provide ample notice and fair severance packages.

11 Be careful with incentives for voluntary termination or retirement. Some organizations make the offers to leave so attractive that many of their brightest and most experienced people leave. As a result, they lose experienced managers, role models, and people who "know the ropes." In these cases, organizations are often forced into promoting less experienced people too quickly. In other organizations, many young, innovative people leave. This kind of exodus leaves the organization with an abundance of older, more conservative, cautious employees and managers. Either situation can have a negative effect on your organization.

If you are undergoing a reorganization, be sure to add any new ideas you got from this section to the Action Plan detailed at the end of Part Four.

APPENDIX A

AN ORGANIZATIONAL SELF-ASSESSMENT

BIBLIOGRAPHY

Albrecht, Karl. *At America's Service.* Homewood, Ill.: Dow Jones-Irwin, 1988.

Albrecht, Karl, and Ron Zemke. *Service America!* Homewood, Ill.: Dow Jones-Irwin, 1985.

Allison, David. "MSA's Razzle-Dazzle Intro Designed to Raise Spirits." *Atlanta Business Chronicle,* November 2, 1988, p. 4A.

"At Sonesta, Service Is a Serious Game." *Sales & Marketing Management,* October 1987, p. 31.

"Attorney General Urges His Workers to Prove They Have High Standards." *The Atlanta Journal & Constitution,* October 8, 1988, p. A-6.

Axel, Helen. "Playing Catch-Up: Working Women's Progress at a Glance," *Across the Board,* July/August 1988, p. 30.

Beinetti, Peter G. "Through The Customer's Eyes." *Sky,* November 1987, p. 147

Berger, David. "Is Your Training Scorching on the Back Burner?" *Telemarketing,* June 1989, p. 22.

Bessonette, Colin. "It's Not Cheap, but You'll Get the Royal Treatment on Cunard Sea Goddess Ships." *The Atlanta Journal & Constitution,* October 16, 1988, p. J-1.

Birnbach, Lisa. "How to Work for Somebody Else, and Still Be Yourself." *Parade Magazine,* October 1988, p. 14.

Block, Peter. "Empowering Employees to Claim Their Autonomy." Presentation delivered to American Society for Training and Development, May 23, 1988, Dallas Convention Center.

Bowes, Lee. *No One Need Apply.* Boston: Harvard Business School Press, 1988.

Broderson, Linda C. "Wellness Programs: The Investment in Good Health for Employees Should Pay Off Handily at the Bottom Line." "The Magazine" *Atlanta Business Chronicle,* July 11, 1988, pp. 10–12.

Bruce, Grady, and Eric Johnson. "The Quality Service Paradox and How to Beat the Problem." *Atlanta Business Chronicle,* January 5, 1987, p. 5A.

Buritt, Chris. "Rich's Refocuses on Customer Service As Cornerstone of New Business Plan." *The Atlanta Journal & Constitution,* October 16, 1988, p. E-1.

Caminiti, Susan. "What Ails Retailing?" *Fortune,* January 30, 1989, p. 64.

Carlzon, Jan. *Moments of Truth.* Cambridge, Mass.: Ballinger Publishing Company, 1987.

"Charlotte Postal Service—No Oxymoron," in *On Achieving Excellence,* Jayne A. Pearl, editor. October 1987, p. 8.

Clarke, Ronald H., and James R. Morris. "Workers' Attitudes Toward Productivity: A New Survey." Washington, D.C.: Chamber of Commerce of the United States, 1980.

Clifford, Donald K., and Richard E. Cavanagh. *The Winning Performance.* New York: Bantam Books, 1985.

Cline, Kenneth. "Southern Federal Tries Mobile Banking." *Atlanta Business Chronicle,* June 27, 1988, p. 13A.

"Consumer Complaint Handling in America: An Update Study, Part I. A How-To-Do-It Manual for Implementing Cost-Effective Consumer Complaint Handling Procedures (Revised)." A research project undertaken by Technical Assistance Research Programs Institute (TARP) at the request of the United States Office of Consumer Affairs. September 30, 1985.

"Consumer Complaint Handling in America: An Update Study, Part II. Complaint Handling Practices of Business, State/Local Government, and Private Voluntary Agencies; and A Review of Recent Studies." A research project undertaken by Technical Assistance Research Programs Institute (TARP) at the request of the United States Office of Consumer Affairs. March 31, 1986.

"Consumer Complaint Handling in America: An Update Study, Part III. The Assessment of Complaint Handling Practices in the Federal Establishment." A research project undertaken by Technical Assistance Research Programs Institute (TARP) at the request of the United States Office of Consumer Affairs. February 26, 1986.

Cushing, Nancy, Carol Laughlin, and Roland Dumas. "Service Quality: The Future of Competitive Advantage." A report on service quality written by Zenger-Miller. Mimeographed. January 27, 1987.

"Customer Focus Research: Executive Briefing." The Forum Corporation. April 1988. Presented at American Society for Training and Development National Convention in Dallas, Texas, May 28, 1988. Mimeographed.

DeLapa, Gina. "Employee Orientation." *Telemarketing*, January 1989, p. 58.

Desatnick, Robert L. *Managing to Keep the Customer*. San Francisco: Jossey-Bass Inc., 1987.

"Does Your Doctor Really Care?" Segment aired on ABC's "20/20" in January and August of 1988. Portions of transcript from ABC News "20/20" reprinted by permission. Copyright 1988 American Broadcasting Companies, Inc. All rights reserved.

Drucker, Peter F. "Timeless Truths About Performing at Your Best." *Working Smart '87*. Stamford, Conn.: Learning International, 1987, pp. 8–9.

"Errors Cut Welfare Aid to Ill, Aged." The Associated Press. *The Atlanta Journal & Constitution*, December 9, 1989, p. A-4.

Fishner, Steven L. "Earning Organizational Commitment at Panasonic." *Forum Issues 8*, The Forum Corporation, Boston, Fall 1987, p. 1. Copyright © 1987 by the Forum Corporation. Portions reprinted with permission.

Friedland, Lois. "Learning the Slopes." *Sky*, August 1988, p. 49.

Gabarro, John J. *The Dynamics of Taking Charge*. Cambridge, Mass.: Harvard Business School Press, 1987.

"Gaining the Competitive Edge." The American Society for Training and Development, 1988.

Garfield, Charles. *Peak Performance*. New York: William Morrow, 1986.

Garvin, David A. "Quality on the Line." *Harvard Business Review*. September/October 1983, pp. 65–73.

"General Motors' Bay City, Michigan Plant," in *On Achieving Excellence*, Jayne A. Pearl, editor. April 1988, p. 3.

Glackin, Robin R. "Breaking the Rules and Winning." *The Journal of Services Marketing*, Summer 1987, p. 53.

Gore, W. L. "Freedom Versus Structure: The Lattice Organization," *Handbook For Creative & Innovative Managers*, Robert L. Kuhn, editor. New York: McGraw-Hill, 1988.

Gray, Barbara Jean. "Ryder's Quest for Quality." *Human Resource Executive*, June 1988, pp. 36–38.

Harrington, H. James. *The Improvement Process: How America's Leading Companies Improve Quality*. New York: McGraw-Hill, 1988.

Hart, Christopher W. L. "The Power of Unconditional Service Guarantees." *Harvard Business Review*, July-August 1988, pp. 54–62.

Haupt, William F. "General Motors: Repositioning with the Help of Training." *Forum Issues 6*, Summer-Fall 1986, pp. 1–3. Copyright © 1986 by the Forum Corporation. Portions reprinted with permission.

Heath, Marcia N. "Vision Gap." Newsletter of Learning International, No. 31. Mimeographed.

Henry, Sherrye. "What Is Your Dream?" *Parade Magazine*, July 31, 1988, p. 10.

Herzberg, Frederick. "One More Time: How Do You Motivate Employees?" *Harvard Business Review* issue called "People: Managing Your Most Important Asset," 1987, pp. 26–35.

"Hibernia Bank's Tellers Are Sellers," in *On Achieving Excellence*, Jayne A. Pearl, editor. October 1987, p. 8.

Hillkirk, John. "The Man Japanese Firms Follow." *USA Today*, May 23, 1988, p. 7B.

Imai, Masaski. *Kaizen: The Key to Japan's Competitiveness*. New York: Random House, 1986.

"Increasing Customer Satisfaction Through Effective Corporate Complaint Handling." United States Office of Consumer Affairs, 1985.

"Indexing Bonus to Customer Satisfaction." *Sales & Marketing Management*, October 1988, p. 37.

Jackson, Jane Carroll. "How to Implement Customer Focus." *Forum Issues 8*, The Forum Corporation, Boston, Fall 1987, p. 4.

Kelly, Bill. "Selling Behind Bars." *Sales & Marketing Management*, March 1989, p. 29.

Kraar, Louis. "Japan's Gung-Ho U.S. Car Plants." *Fortune*, January 30, 1989, p. 98.

Lawrence, Paul R. "How to Deal with Resistance to Change." *Harvard Business Review* issue called "People: Managing Your Most Important Asset," 1987, pp. 36–44.

LeBoeuf, Michael. *How to Win Customers and Keep Them for Life*. New York: G.P. Putnam's Sons, 1988.

Lele, Milind M., with Jagdish N. Sheth. *The Customer Is Key*. New York: John Wiley & Sons, 1987.

Levering, Robert, Milton Moskowitz, and Michael Katz. *The 100 Best Companies to Work for in America*. Reading, Mass.: Addison-Wesley, 1984.

Levitt, Theodore. *The Marketing Imagination*. New York: The Free Press, 1986.

Mackle, Elliot. "Putting on the Show—Ritz-Style." *The Atlanta Journal & Constitution*, May 8, 1988, p. 1G.

Manske, Fred, Jr. *Secrets of Effective Leadership: A Practical Guide for Success*. Germantown, Tenn.: Leadership Education and Development, 1987.

Markiewicz, David A. "Paid in Full: Hero Won't Be Docked." *Detroit News*, August 27, 1989, p. 1.

Martin, William B. *Quality Customer Service*. Los Altos, California: Crisp Publications, Inc., 1987.

Miller, Andy, "Harris: To Reach Out to Students, City Will Focus on Inspired Teaching." *The Atlanta Journal & Constitution*, August 3, 1989, p. A-9.

Mills, D. Quinn. "Advice on Getting Ahead in the Competitive '80s." *Working Smart '87*. Stamford, Conn.: Learning International, 1987, pp. 26–27.

Mills, D. Quinn. "Not Like Our Parents." Presentation given to American Society for Training and Development, May 25, 1987, Dallas Convention Center.

"Merchant Prince: Stanley Marcus." *Inc.*, June 1987, pp. 41–48.

Monaghan, Tom. *Pizza Tiger*. New York: Random House, 1986.

Moskal, Brian S. "Glasnost in Dearborn." *Industry Week*, September 21, 1987, p. 53.

Mountcastle, Amy. "Life in the Fast [Food] Lane." *Human Resource Executive*, September 1988, p. 26.

Naisbitt Group Staff and John Naisbitt. *The Year Ahead: 1985*. New York: Warner Books, 1984.

Nemeroff, Dinah. "Service Delivery Practices and Issues in Leading Consumer Service Businesses: A Report to Participating Companies." New York: Citibank, April 1980. Mimeograph.

Newman, Kay. "Corporate Values." *Atlanta Small Business Monthly*, April 1989, p. 6.

Oliver, Thomas. "The Sorry State of Service," *The Atlanta Journal & Constitution*, March 1, 1987, p. 1E.

Parasuraman, A., V. A. Zeithaml, and L. L. Berry. "A Conceptual Model of Service Quality and Its Implications for Future Research." Report 84-106, 1984, Marketing Sciences Institute, Cambridge, Mass.

Peters, Tom. "The Changing Role of First-Line Supervisors," in *On Achieving Excellence*, Jayne A. Pearl, editor. April 1988, p. 1.

Peters, Tom. "Questions from Our Readers," in *On Achieving Excellence*, Jayne A. Pearl, editor. June 1988, p. 7.

Peters, Thomas J., and Robert H. Waterman, Jr. *In Search of Excellence: Lessons from America's Best-Run Companies*. New York: Harper and Row, 1982.

Peterson, Donald E. Remarks delivered after accepting the corporate award for Excellence in Human Relations from the American Society for Training and Development at the 1987 national conference in Dallas, May 26, 1987.

"Police Say He's a Hero, but His Boss Disagrees." The Associated Press. *The Atlanta Journal & Constitution*, June 17, 1988.

"P.T.S.D." Segment aired on CBS program "60 Minutes" on June 5, 1989.

Rodgers, Buck. *The IBM Way: Insights into the World's Most Successful Marketing Company*. New York: Harper & Row, 1986.

Ryan, Michael. "When a Jury Won't Sit Still." *Parade Magazine*, August 27, 1989, p. 8.

Rydz, John. *Managing Innovation*. Cambridge, Mass.: Ballinger Publishing Company, 1986.

Schiffman, Lewis F. "Managers Often to Blame for Employee's Job Stress." *The Atlanta Business Chronicle*, August 29, 1988, p. B8.

Schlesinger, Leonard A., Davis Dyer, Thomas N. Clough, and Diane Landau. *Chronicles of Corporate Change: Management Lessons from AT&T and Its Offspring*. Lexington, Mass.: Lexington Books, 1987.

Schneider, Benjamin, and David E. Bowen. "Employee and Customer Perceptions of Service in Banks: Replication and Extension." *Journal of Applied Psychology*, May 1985, p. 423.

Scott, Cynthia D., and Dennis T. Jaffee. "Survive and Thrive in Times of Change." *Training and Development Journal*, April 1988, p. 26.

Service Journal." *The Service Edge*, Ron Zemke, editor. Minneapolis, Minn.: Lakewood Publications, February 1989, p. 5.

Shames, Laurence. *The Big Time: The Harvard Business School's Most Successful Class and How It Shaped America*. New York: Harper & Row, 1986.

Sherman, V. Clayton. *From Losers to Winners: How to Manage Problem Employees and What to Do If You Can't*. New York: AMACOM, 1988.

"Should You Look for Alternatives to Firing Some Employees?" "Best Advice" column of *Sales & Marketing Management*, January 1989, p. 21.

"Shrewd New Management Made the Walt Disney Company an Investor's Dream." *The Atlanta Journal & Constitution*, August 20, 1989, p. B6.

"Southern Bell Puts More Responsibility on the Line," in *On Achieving Excellence*, Jayne A. Pearl, editor. November 1987, p. 4.

Stevenson, Richard W. "Watch Out Macy's, Here Comes Nordstrom." *The New York Times Magazine*, August 27, 1989, p. 34.

"Strange Marriage—Marketing and Personnel," in *On Achieving Excellence*, Jayne A. Pearl, editor. April 1988, p. 8.

Strazewski, Len. "The Anatomy of a Merger." *Human Resource Executive*, November/December 1987, pp. 25–27.

Szabo, Joan C. "Service = Survival." *Nation's Business*, March 1989, p. 16.

Thomas, Emory, Jr. "Consumers: Bank Service Doesn't Measure Up." *Atlanta Business Chronicle*, August 8, 1988, p. 6B.

Thompson, Alicia. "Customer Contact Personnel: Using Interviewing Techniques to Select for Adaptability." *The Journal of Services Marketing*, Winter 1989, p. 57.

"Total Commitment to Quality is New Focus at Adel Plant." Article in "Composites Bulletin." Weyerhaeuser Company, Atlanta, Ga., May-June 1988, p. 3.

Tucci, Rick. "On Becoming Customer Driven." *Forum Issues 6*, The Forum Corporation, Boston, Summer-Fall 1986, p. 4. Copyright © 1986 by the Forum Corporation. Reprinted with permission.

Tunstall, Stuart. "How to Switch on to Customer Care." *The London Times*. September 11, 1988, p. E1.

"Turnabout: Put Yourself in the Customer's Shoes." A training program by the Dartnell Corporation; Chicago, 1988.

Vines, Linda Stockman. "Herman Miller Nails Down the Problem." *Human Resource Executive*, June 1988, pp. 39–41.

Vines, Linda Stockman. "Reevaluating Assessment Methods." *Human Resource Executive*, April 1988, p. 50.

Vittolino, Sal. "The Biggest Boss in America." *Human Resource Executive*, June 1988, p. 21.

Vittolino, Sal. "Rubbermaid's Unbending Attention to Detail." *Human Resource Executive*, April 1988, p. 28.

Vittolino, Sal. "Squibb's Prescription for Success." *Human Resource Executive*, April 1988, p. 30.

Walton, William B. *The New Bottom Line: People and Loyalty in Business.* New York: Harper & Row, 1986.

Webster, Frederick E., Jr. "Rediscovering the Marketing Concept." *Marketing Science Institute Review*, Cambridge, Mass.: Spring 1988, p. 1.

"What Managers Know About Employee Relations." American Productivity & Quality Center *Letter*, September 1988, p. 8.

Whilely, Richard C. "Customer Focus Research Results." Presentation given at the Dallas Hyatt Regency Hotel, Dallas, May 26, 1988, during a seminar on "Rediscovering the Customer."

White, Betsy. "Superintendent Urges Students to Show Initiative in Class, Life." *The Atlanta Journal & Constitution*, October 2, 1988, p. 1C.

Wild, Ray, ed. *How to Manage: By More Than 100 of the World's Leading Business Experts.* New York: Facts On File Publications, 1985.

Wright, Alice Murray. "Driving Force." *The Atlanta Journal & Constitution*, November 11, 1988, p. S-1.

Wriston, Walter B. "An Interview with Walter Wriston." *Forum Issues 8*, The Forum Corporation, Boston, Fall 1987, pp. 11–13. Copyright © 1987 by the Forum Corporation. Reprinted with permission.

Zemke, Ron. "Contact! Training Employees to Meet the Public." *Training*, August 1988, p. 41.

Zemke, Ron, with Dick Schaaf. *The Service Edge.* New York: New American Library, 1988.

INDEX

Action Plan

A Desired Result	B Priority	C Actions Needed	D Sequence	E Start Date	F Resources Needed	G End Date

Action Plan

A Desired Result	B Priority	C Actions Needed	D Sequence	E Start Date	F Resources Needed	G End Date

Action Plan

A	B	C	D	E	F	G
Desired Result	Priority	Actions Needed	Sequence	Start Date	Resources Needed	End Date